마이갓 5 Step 모의고사 공부법

1 ● **Vocabulary 필수 단어 암기 & Test**
① 단원별 필수 단어 암기 ② 영어 → 한글 Test ③ 한글 → 영어 Test

2 ● **Text 지문과 해설**
① 전체 지문 해석 ② 페이지별 필기 공간 확보 ③ N회독을 통한 지문 습득

3 ● **Practice 1 빈칸 시험 (w/ 문법 힌트)**
① 해석 없는 반복 빈칸 시험 ② 문법 힌트를 통한 어법 숙지
③ 주요 문법과 암기 내용 최종 확인

4 ● **Practice 2 빈칸 시험 (w/ 해석)**
① 주요 내용/어법/어휘 빈칸 ② 한글을 통한 내용 숙지
③ 반복 시험을 통한 빈칸 암기

5 ● **Quiz 객관식 예상문제를 콕콕!**
① 수능형 객관식 변형문제 ② 100% 자체 제작 변형문제 ③ 빈출 내신 문제 유형 연습

영어 내신의 끝
마이갓 모의고사 고1,2

1 등급을 위한 5단계 노하우
2 모의고사 연도 및 시행월 별 완전정복
3 내신변형 완전정복

영어 내신의 끝
마이갓 교과서 고1,2

1 등급을 위한 10단계 노하우
2 교과서 레슨별 완전정복
3 영어 영역 마스터를 위한 지름길

마이갓 교재
보듬책방 온라인 스토어 (https://smartstore.naver.com/bdbooks)

마이갓 10 Step 영어 내신 공부법

Vocabulary
필수 단어 암기 & Test
① 단원별 필수 단어 암기
② 영어 → 한글 Test
③ 한글 → 영어 Test

Grammar
단원별 중요 문법과 연습 문제
① 기초 문법 설명
② 교과서 적용 예시 소개
③ 기초/ Advanced Test

Text
지문과 해설
① 전체 지문 해석
② 페이지별 필기 공간 확보
③ N회독을 통한 지문 습득

Practice 3
빈칸 시험 (w/ 해석)
① 주요 내용/어법/어휘 빈칸
② 한글을 통한 내용 숙지
③ 반복 시험을 통한 빈칸 암기

Practice 2
빈칸 시험 (w/ 해석)
① 주요 내용/어법/어휘 빈칸
② 한글을 통한 내용 숙지
③ 반복 시험을 통한 빈칸 암기

Practice 1
어휘 & 어법 선택 시험
① 시험에 나오는 어법 어휘 공략
② 중요 어법/어휘 선택형 시험
③ 반복 시험을 통한 포인트 숙지

Quiz
객관식 예상문제를 콕콕!
① 수능형 객관식 변형문제
② 100% 자체 제작 변형문제
③ 빈출 내신 문제 유형 연습

Final Test
주관식 서술형 예상문제
① 어순/영작/어법 등
  주관식 서술형 문제 대비!
② 100% 자체 제작 변형문제

전체 영작 연습
직접 영작 해보기
① 주어진 단어를 활용한
  전체 서술형 영작 훈련
② 쓰기를 통한 내용 암기

학교 기출 문제
지문과 해설
① 단원별 실제 학교 기출
  문제 모음
② 객관식부터 서술형까지
  완벽 커버!

24년 고2
3월 모의고사

마이갓

연습과 실전 모두 잡는 내신대비 완벽
| workbook |

보듬영어

2024 고2

3월

WORK BOOK

———

2024년 고2 3월 모의고사 내신대비용 WorkBook & 변형문제

CONTENTS

2024 고2 3월 WORK BOOK

—

 보듬영어

Voca

18	annual	연례의		mere	단순한
	craft	공예품		patience	인내심
	fair	박람회		fall prey to	~의 먹잇감이 되다
	registration form	신청서		impatience	조바심
	rental	대여; 대여의	21	self-driving	자율 주행; 자율 주행의
	fee	요금		accelerator	가속 페달
	support	지원하다		vehicle	자동차, 교통수단
	upcoming	예정된		on one's own	스스로
	throughout the year	연중		barrier	장애물
19	confidence	자신감		obviously	분명히
	judgment	심사		entire	전체의
	judge	심사위원		pursue	추구하다
	announce	발표하다		possess	가지고 있다
	one by one	한명씩		tape	테이프로 묶다
	uniqueness	독창성		approach	접근하다
	confirm	확인해 주다		bring ~ to bear	~을 도입하다
	identity	정체성		appropriate	적절한
20	generation	세대		advance	증진하다
	overnight	하룻밤 사이에		unique	고유한
	discourage ~ from ...ing	~이 ...하는 것을 방해하다		refined	정제된
	high tech	첨단 기술	22	overrate	과대평가하다
	comfort	편안함		impact	영향
	convenience	편리함		in part	부분적으로
	be tempted to	~하게끔 유혹을 받다		absorb	흡수하다
	require	필요로 하다		so as to	~할 만큼

| ❶ voca | ❷ text | ❸ [/] | ❹ _____ | ❺ quiz 1 | ❻ quiz 2 | ❼ quiz 3 | ❽ quiz 4 | ❾ quiz 5 |

	invisible	눈에 보이지 않는		obligation	의무
	implement	도구		relate	공감하다
	transform	바꾸다		pressure	압박
	fundamental	근본적인		ins and outs	세부적인 것들
	classic	전형적인		interaction	상호작용
	exercise	발휘하다		induce	유발하다
	function	기능을 하다		aggressive	공격적인
	bottle feeding	젖병 수유	25	protein	단백질
	substitute for	~을 대신하다		consumption	섭취
	potentially	잠재적으로		average	평균
	implication	영향		category	범주
	entirely	완전히		respectively	각각
	overlook	간과하다		least	가장 적은
23	cognitive	인지적인		rank	(순위를) 차지하다
	perspective	관점	26	mind	지성인
	negotiate	협상하다		talent	재능
	affective	정서적인		doctoral degree	박사 학위
	concern	관심		director	소장
	consultant	자문 위원	27	present	표현하다
	foster	기르다		steam	데우다
	the blind	시각 장애인		pour	따르다
	the deaf	청각 장애인		registration	등록
	the color-blind	색맹		ingredient	재료
24	prevalent	일반적인		dairy alternative	대체 유제품
	accessible	연락될 수 있는, 연락 가능한		available	사용할 수 있는

Voca

❶ voca	❷ text	❸ [/]	❹ ____	❺ quiz 1	❻ quiz 2	❼ quiz 3	❽ quiz 4	❾ quiz 5

28	bonding	유대		agent	주체, 행위자
	preserve	보호 구역		likelihood	가능성
	guideline	지침		comparable	비슷한
	be accompanied by	~을 동반하다		practice	(습관적) 행동
	legal guardian	법적 보호자		whereas	반면에
	instruction	지시		soothing	위로
	first aid kit	구급상자		directive	지시적인
29	psychologist	심리학자		beneficial	도움이 되는
	personality	성격		autonomy	자율성
	target	대상으로 하다		striving	추구
	addiction	중독		turn toward	~에 의지하다
	combined with	~과 결합된		adjust	조정하다
	suggestion	암시		suitable	적합한
	alongside	~과 함께		awareness	인식
	modification	수정		nonjudgmental	무비판적인
	tactic	기법	31	capability	능력, 역량
	cope	대응하다		misguided	잘못 이해한
	strategy	전략		accomplish	달성하다
	reinforce	강화하다		repetitive	반복적인
30	socialization	사회화		vertical	수직의
	foundational	기초적인		rapid	빠른
	regulation	조절		impose	주다, 부여하다
	extrafamilial	가족 이외의		by nature	선천적으로
	adolescence	청소년기		efficiently	효율적으로
	primary	주된		minimize	최소화하다

❶ voca	❷ text	❸ [/]	❹ _____	❺ quiz 1	❻ quiz 2	❼ quiz 3	❽ quiz 4	❾ quiz 5

	potential	잠재적인		curiosity	호기심
	injury	부상		reward	보상
32	explore	탐구하다		phrase	(음악의) 구절
	production	제작		resulting	결과로 얻어지는
	consumption	소비		investigator	연구자
	imply	암시하다, 의미하다		composition	작곡
	ownership	소유권		reveal	보여 주다
	supposedly	소위	34	technologist	기술자
	considerable	상당한, 중요한		on the lookout for	~을 찾고 있는
	crossover	넘나듦, 교차		quantifiable	정량화할 수 있는
	composition	구성		measurable	측정 가능한
	theatrical	극장의		lifeblood	생명줄
	comprise	차지하다		identify	식별하다
	box office	(극장 흥행) 수익		concrete	구체적인
	phenomenon	현상		assess	평가하다
	correspond with	~과 일치하다		bias	편향, 편견
	embrace	수용		complicated	복잡한
	seemingly	겉으로는 ~처럼 보이는		imperfect	불완전한
	prejudice	편견		illusion	환영, 착각
	realm	영역		end	목적
	legitimate	제대로 된		genuine	진정한
	contemporary	현대의		count	중요하다, (수를) 세다
33	drive	욕구; 이끌다	35	season	양념을 하다
	novel	새로운		deliberately	의도적으로
	reflection	반영		alter	바꾸다

Voca

| ❶ voca | ❷ text | ❸ [/] | ❹ _____ | ❺ quiz 1 | ❻ quiz 2 | ❼ quiz 3 | ❽ quiz 4 | ❾ quiz 5 |

	flavor	맛; 맛을 내다		genetically	유전적으로
	spice	향신료		phase	단계
	evolutionary	진화적인		exhibit	보여 주다
	antibacterial	항균의		criteria	기준
	property	특성		favor	선호하다
	seasoning	조미료	37	everincreasing	계속 증가하는
	inhibit	억제하다		elderly	노인의
	coriander	고수		needy	빈곤한
	spoilage	부패		contribute	기여하다
	significant	많은		resolution	해결책
	availability	이용 가능성		perceive	인식하다
	ultimately	궁극적으로		a set of	일련의, 많은
	arise	생겨나다		as ~ as possible	가능한 한 ~하게
36	random	무작위의		specify	명시하다
	variation	변이		budget	예산
	stimulate	활성화하다, 자극하다		distribution	분배
	eliminate	제거하다		visible	잘 보이는
	sculpting	조각		perception	입장, 인식
	consequence	결과		controllable	통제 가능한
	variability	변이성		enquire	묻다
	largescale	전체의, 대규모의		rigid	엄격한
	serve to	~하는 역할을 하다		result in	~한 결과를 초래하다
	undergo	겪다		overloaded	너무 많은 부담을 진
	immune	면역의		demotivated	의욕을 잃은
	extension	확장	38	rare	드문

| ❶ voca | ❷ text | ❸ [/] | ❹ ____ | ❺ quiz 1 | ❻ quiz 2 | ❼ quiz 3 | ❽ quiz 4 | ❾ quiz 5 |

	occasion	경우		exceed	뛰어넘다, 초과하다
	dramatically	극적으로		tomb	무덤
	population	개체수		archive	(기록)저장소
	reorientate	방향을 다시 잡다		instinct	직관
	undoubtedly	의심할 여지 없이		extract	추출하다
	perish	죽다		typically	일반적으로
	infrequent	드문		domain	분야
	timescale	시간		manually	수동으로
	profound	중대한		procedure	방법, 절차
	migration	이동, 이주		systematic	체계적인
	wintering location	월동 장소	41-42	shift	전환하다; 전환
	frequency	빈도		sequentially	순차적으로
39	in accordance with	~에 따라		fraction	아주 조금, 파편
	internalized	내재된		switch	전환
	expertise	전문 지식		interrupt	중단시키다
	hardearned	힘들여 얻은		latest	최신의
	on one's feet	즉각적으로		simultaneously	동시에
	conviction	확신		automatic pilot	자동 조종
	crisis	(pl. crises) 위기		insurance	보험
	substance	실체		redesign	재설계하다
	inclined	성향이 있는	43-45	furry	털북숭이의
	rational	합리적인		receptionist	접수원
	sensible	분별 있는		symptom	증상
40	tremendous	엄청난		anxiously	초조하게
	numerous	수많은		vet	(=veterinarian) 수의사

examine	진찰하다							
medication	약물 치료, 약물							
administer	(약을) 투여하다							
spirit	활기							
infection	감염							
heartbreaking	가슴 아픈							

18	annual				mere			
	craft				patience			
	fair				fall prey to			
	registration form				impatience			
	rental			21	self-driving			
	fee				accelerator			
	support				vehicle			
	upcoming				on one's own			
	throughout the year				barrier			
19	confidence				obviously			
	judgment				entire			
	judge				pursue			
	announce				possess			
	one by one				tape			
	uniqueness				approach			
	confirm				bring ~ to bear			
	identity				appropriate			
20	generation				advance			
	overnight				unique			
	discourage ~ from ...ing				refined			
	high tech			22	overrate			
	comfort				impact			
	convenience				in part			
	be tempted to				absorb			
	require				so as to			

Voca

	invisible			obligation	
	implement			relate	
	transform			pressure	
	fundamental			ins and outs	
	classic			interaction	
	exercise			induce	
	function			aggressive	
	bottle feeding		25	protein	
	substitute for			consumption	
	potentially			average	
	implication			category	
	entirely			respectively	
	overlook			least	
23	cognitive			rank	
	perspective		26	mind	
	negotiate			talent	
	affective			doctoral degree	
	concern			director	
	consultant		27	present	
	foster			steam	
	the blind			pour	
	the deaf			registration	
	the color-blind			ingredient	
24	prevalent			dairy alternative	
	accessible			available	

Voca Test

영 > 한

| ❶ voca | ❷ text | ❸ [/] | ❹ ___ | ❺ quiz 1 | ❻ quiz 2 | ❼ quiz 3 | ❽ quiz 4 | ❾ quiz 5 |

28	bonding				agent			
	preserve				likelihood			
	guideline				comparable			
	be accompanied by				practice			
	legal guardian				whereas			
	instruction				soothing			
	first aid kit				directive			
29	psychologist				beneficial			
	personality				autonomy			
	target				striving			
	addiction				turn toward			
	combined with				adjust			
	suggestion				suitable			
	alongside				awareness			
	modification				nonjudgmental			
	tactic			31	capability			
	cope				misguided			
	strategy				accomplish			
	reinforce				repetitive			
30	socialization				vertical			
	foundational				rapid			
	regulation				impose			
	extrafamilial				by nature			
	adolescence				efficiently			
	primary				minimize			

Voca Test

❶ voca	❷ text	❸ [/]	❹ ___	❺ quiz 1	❻ quiz 2	❼ quiz 3	❽ quiz 4	❾ quiz 5
	potential				curiosity			
	injury				reward			
32	explore				phrase			
	production				resulting			
	consumption				investigator			
	imply				composition			
	ownership				reveal			
	supposedly			34	technologist			
	considerable				on the lookout for			
	crossover				quantifiable			
	composition				measurable			
	theatrical				lifeblood			
	comprise				identify			
	box office				concrete			
	phenomenon				assess			
	correspond with				bias			
	embrace				complicated			
	seemingly				imperfect			
	prejudice				illusion			
	realm				end			
	legitimate				genuine			
	contemporary				count			
33	drive			35	season			
	novel				deliberately			
	reflection				alter			

Voca Test

❶ voca	❷ text	❸ [/]	❹ ＿＿	❺ quiz 1	❻ quiz 2	❼ quiz 3	❽ quiz 4	❾ quiz 5
	flavor			genetically				
	spice			phase				
	evolutionary			exhibit				
	antibacterial			criteria				
	property			favor				
	seasoning		37	everincreasing				
	inhibit			elderly				
	coriander			needy				
	spoilage			contribute				
	significant			resolution				
	availability			perceive				
	ultimately			a set of				
	arise			as ~ as possible				
36	random			specify				
	variation			budget				
	stimulate			distribution				
	eliminate			visible				
	sculpting			perception				
	consequence			controllable				
	variability			enquire				
	largescale			rigid				
	serve to			result in				
	undergo			overloaded				
	immune			demotivated				
	extension		38	rare				

Voca Test

	❶ voca	❷ text	❸ [/]	❹ ___	❺ quiz 1	❻ quiz 2	❼ quiz 3	❽ quiz 4	❾ quiz 5
	occasion				exceed				
	dramatically				tomb				
	population				archive				
	reorientate				instinct				
	undoubtedly				extract				
	perish				typically				
	infrequent				domain				
	timescale				manually				
	profound				procedure				
	migration				systematic				
	wintering location		41-42		shift				
	frequency				sequentially				
39	in accordance with				fraction				
	internalized				switch				
	expertise				interrupt				
	hardearned				latest				
	on one's feet				simultaneously				
	conviction				automatic pilot				
	crisis				insurance				
	substance				redesign				
	inclined		43-45		furry				
	rational				receptionist				
	sensible				symptom				
40	tremendous				anxiously				
	numerous				vet				

Voca Tes

영) 한

❶ voca	❷ text	❸ [/]	❹ _____	❺ quiz 1	❻ quiz 2	❼ quiz 3	❽ quiz 4	❾ quiz 5
examine								
medication								
administer								
spirit								
infection								
heartbreaking								

Voca Test

❶ voca	❷ text	❸ [/]	❹ ____	❺ quiz 1	❻ quiz 2	❼ quiz 3	❽ quiz 4	❾ quiz 5
18		연례의					단순한	
		공예품					인내심	
		박람회					~의 먹잇감이 되다	
		신청서					조바심	
		대여; 대여의	21				자율 주행; 자율 주행의	
		요금					가속 페달	
		지원하다					자동차, 교통수단	
		예정된					스스로	
		연중					장애물	
19		자신감					분명히	
		심사					전체의	
		심사위원					추구하다	
		발표하다					가지고 있다	
		한명씩					테이프로 묶다	
		독창성					접근하다	
		확인해 주다					~을 도입하다	
		정체성					적절한	
20		세대					증진하다	
		하룻밤 사이에					고유한	
		~이 ...하는 것을 방해하다					정제된	
		첨단 기술	22				과대평가하다	
		편안함					영향	
		편리함					부분적으로	
		~하게끔 유혹을 받다					흡수하다	
		필요로 하다					~할 만큼	

Voca Test

영 ⟩ 한

❶ voca	❷ text	❸ [/]	❹ ____	❺ quiz 1	❻ quiz 2	❼ quiz 3	❽ quiz 4	❾ quiz 5

No.	뜻 (좌)	No.	뜻 (우)
	눈에 보이지 않는		의무
	도구		공감하다
	바꾸다		압박
	근본적인		세부적인 것들
	전형적인		상호작용
	발휘하다		유발하다
	기능을 하다		공격적인
	젖병 수유	25	단백질
	~을 대신하다		섭취
	잠재적으로		평균
	영향		범주
	완전히		각각
	간과하다		가장 적은
23	인지적인		(순위를) 차지하다
	관점	26	지성인
	협상하다		재능
	정서적인		박사 학위
	관심		소장
	자문 위원	27	표현하다
	기르다		데우다
	시각 장애인		따르다
	청각 장애인		등록
	색맹		재료
24	일반적인		대체 유제품
	연락될 수 있는, 연락 가능한		사용할 수 있는

Voca Test

28		유대		주체, 행위자
		보호 구역		가능성
		지침		비슷한
		~을 동반하다		(습관적) 행동
		법적 보호자		반면에
		지시		위로
		구급상자		지시적인
29		심리학자		도움이 되는
		성격		자율성
		대상으로 하다		추구
		중독		~에 의지하다
		~과 결합된		조정하다
		암시		적합한
		~과 함께		인식
		수정		무비판적인
		기법	31	능력, 역량
		대응하다		잘못 이해한
		전략		달성하다
		강화하다		반복적인
30		사회화		수직의
		기초적인		빠른
		조절		주다, 부여하다
		가족 이외의		선천적으로
		청소년기		효율적으로
		주된		최소화하다

Voca Test

영 ● 한

❶ voca	❷ text	❸ [/]	❹ ____	❺ quiz 1	❻ quiz 2	❼ quiz 3	❽ quiz 4	❾ quiz 5

32		잠재적인		호기심
		부상		보상
		탐구하다		(음악의) 구절
		제작		결과로 얻어지는
		소비		연구자
		암시하다, 의미하다		작곡
		소유권		보여 주다
		소위	**34**	기술자
		상당한, 중요한		~을 찾고 있는
		넘나듦, 교차		정량화할 수 있는
		구성		측정 가능한
		극장의		생명줄
		차지하다		식별하다
		(극장 흥행) 수익		구체적인
		현상		평가하다
		~과 일치하다		편향, 편견
		수용		복잡한
		겉으로는 ~처럼 보이는		불완전한
		편견		환영, 착각
		영역		목적
		제대로 된		진정한
		현대의		중요하다, (수를) 세다
33		욕구; 이끌다	**35**	양념을 하다
		새로운		의도적으로
		반영		바꾸다

Voca Test

영 ▶ 한

❶ voca	❷ text	❸ [/]	❹ _____	❺ quiz 1	❻ quiz 2	❼ quiz 3	❽ quiz 4	❾ quiz 5
		맛; 맛을 내다				유전적으로		
		향신료				단계		
		진화적인				보여 주다		
		항균의				기준		
		특성				선호하다		
		조미료	37			계속 증가하는		
		억제하다				노인의		
		고수				빈곤한		
		부패				기여하다		
		많은				해결책		
		이용 가능성				인식하다		
		궁극적으로				일련의, 많은		
		생겨나다				가능한 한 ~하게		
36		무작위의				명시하다		
		변이				예산		
		활성화하다, 자극하다				분배		
		제거하다				잘 보이는		
		조각				입장, 인식		
		결과				통제 가능한		
		변이성				묻다		
		전체의, 대규모의				엄격한		
		~하는 역할을 하다				~한 결과를 초래하다		
		겪다				너무 많은 부담을 진		
		면역의				의욕을 잃은		
		확장	38			드문		

Voca Test

❶ voca	❷ text	❸ [/]	❹ _____	❺ quiz 1	❻ quiz 2	❼ quiz 3	❽ quiz 4	❾ quiz 5
		경우				뛰어넘다, 초과하다		
		극적으로				무덤		
		개체수				(기록)저장소		
		방향을 다시 잡다				직관		
		의심할 여지 없이				추출하다		
		죽다				일반적으로		
		드문				분야		
		시간				수동으로		
		중대한				방법, 절차		
		이동, 이주				체계적인		
		월동 장소	41-42			전환하다; 전환		
		빈도				순차적으로		
39		~에 따라				아주 조금, 파편		
		내재된				전환		
		전문 지식				중단시키다		
		힘들여 얻은				최신의		
		즉각적으로				동시에		
		확신				자동 조종		
		(pl. crises) 위기				보험		
		실체				재설계하다		
		성향이 있는	43-45			털북숭이의		
		합리적인				접수원		
		분별 있는				증상		
40		엄청난				초조하게		
		수많은				(=veterinarian) 수의사		

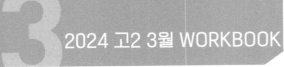
Voca Test

영 ○ 한

❶ voca	❷ text	❸ [/]	❹ ___	❺ quiz 1	❻ quiz 2	❼ quiz 3	❽ quiz 4	❾ quiz 5
		진찰하다						
		약물 치료, 약물						
		(약을) 투여하다						
		활기						
		감염						
		가슴 아픈						

2024 고2 3월 모의고사

❶ voca ❷ text ❸ [/] ❹ _____ ❺ quiz 1 ❻ quiz 2 ❼ quiz 3 ❽ quiz 4 ❾ quiz 5

18 목적

❶ Dear Art Crafts People of Greenville,

친애하는 Greenville의 공예가들에게

❷ For the annual Crafts Fair on May 25 from 1 p.m. to 6 p.m., the Greenville Community Center is providing booth spaces to rent as in previous years.

5월 25일 오후 1시부터 6시까지 열리는 연례 공예품 박람회를 위해서, Greenville 커뮤니티 센터에서는 지난 몇 년간처럼 대여 부스 공간을 제공합니다.

❸ To reserve your space, please visit our website and complete a registration form by April 20.
The rental fee is $50.

공간을 예약하려면 저희 웹사이트를 방문하여 4월 20일까지 신청서를 작성하시기 바랍니다.

❹ The rental fee is $50.

대여 요금은 50달러입니다.

❺ All the money we receive from rental fees goes to support upcoming activities throughout the year.

부스 대여료로 받은 모든 돈은 연중 예정된 활동을 지원하는 데 사용됩니다..

❻ We expect all available spaces to be fully booked soon, so don't get left out.

모든 이용할 수 있는 공간이 곧 모두 예약될 것으로 예상되니 놓치지 마세요.

❼ We hope to see you at the fair.

박람회에서 뵙기를 바랍니다.

19 심경

❶ Sarah, a young artist with a love for painting, entered a local art contest.

그림 그리기를 좋아하는 젊은 예술가 Sarah는 지역 미술 대회에 참가했다.

❷ As she looked at the amazing artworks made by others, her confidence dropped.

다른 사람들이 만든 놀라운 예술 작품들을 보면서 그녀의 자신감은 떨어졌다.

❸ She quietly thought, 'I might not win an award.'

그녀는 '내가 상을 받지 못할 수도 있겠네.'라고 조용히 생각했다.

❹ The moment of judgment arrived, and the judges began announcing winners one by one.

심사의 순간이 다가왔고, 심사위원들은 수상자를 한 명씩 발표하기 시작했다.

❺ It wasn't until the end that she heard her name.

그녀는 마지막에야 자신의 이름을 들었다.

❻ The head of the judges said, "Congratulations, Sarah Parker! You won first prize.

심사위원장이 "축하해요, Sarah Parker! 당신이 1등을 했습니다.

❼ We loved the uniqueness of your work."
당신 작품의 독창성이 정말 좋았습니다."라고 말했다.

❽ Sarah was overcome with joy, and she couldn't stop smiling.
Sarah는 기쁨에 휩싸였고 미소가 가시지 않았다.

❾ This experience meant more than just winning; it confirmed her identity as an artist.
이 경험은 단순한 우승 이상의 의미를 지녔고, 그녀에게 예술가로서의 정체성을 확인해 주었다.

20 요지

❶ Too many times people, especially in today's generation, expect things to just happen overnight.
너무나 많은 경우에, 사람들, 특히 오늘날의 세대는, 일이 하룻밤 사이에 일어나기를 기대한다.

❷ When we have these false expectations, it tends to discourage us from continuing to move forward.
우리가 이러한 잘못된 기대를 가질 때, 그것은 우리가 계속해서 앞으로 나아가는 것을 방해하는 경향이 있다.

❸ Because this is a high tech society, everything we want has to be within the parameters of our comfort and convenience.
지금은 첨단 기술 사회이기 때문에, 우리가 원하는 모든 것은 편안함과 편리함이라는 제한 내에 있어야 한다.

❹ If it doesn't happen fast enough, we're tempted to lose interest.
그 일이 충분히 빨리 일어나지 않으면, 우리는 흥미를 잃게끔 유혹을 받는다.

❺ So many people don't want to take the time it requires to be successful.
그래서 많은 사람들은 성공하는 데 필요한 시간을 들이는 것을 원하지 않는다.

❻ Success is not a matter of mere desire; you should develop patience in order to achieve it.
성공은 단순한 욕망의 문제가 아니다. 여러분은 그것(성공)을 이루기 위해 인내심을 길러야 한다.

❼ Have you fallen prey to impatience?
여러분은 조바심의 먹잇감이 되어 본 적이 있는가?

❽ Great things take time to build.
위대한 일이 이루어지는 데에는 시간이 걸린다.

21 주장

❶ If you had wanted to create a "selfdriving" car in the 1950s, your best option might have been to strap a brick to the accelerator.

만약 '자율 주행' 자동차를 1950년대에 만들고 싶었다면, 가장 좋은 선택은 가속 페달에 벽돌을 끈으로 묶는 것이었을 것이다.

❷ Yes, the vehicle would have been able to move forward on its own, but it could not slow down, stop, or turn to avoid barriers.

물론, 자동차가 스스로 앞으로 나아갈 수는 있었겠지만, 속도를 줄이거나 멈추거나 또는 장애물을 피하기 위해 방향을 전환할 수는 없었다.

❸ Obviously not ideal.

분명히, 이상적이지는 않다.

❹ But does that mean the entire concept of the self-driving car is not worth pursuing?

그러나 그것이 자율 주행 자동차라는 전체 개념이 추구할 만한 가치가 없다는 의미일까?

❺ No, it only means that at the time we did not yet have the tools we now possess to help enable vehicles to operate both autonomously and safely.

아니다, 그것은 단지 우리가 지금은 갖고 있는, 자동차를 자율적이고도 안전하게 작동할 수 있도록 해 주는 도구를, 그 당시에는 우리가 아직 갖고 있지 않았다는 것을 의미할 뿐이다.

❻ It is much the same story in medicine.

이는 의학에서도 마찬가지이다.

❼ Two decades ago, we were still taping bricks to accelerators.

20년 전에, 우리는 여전히 가속 페달에 벽돌을 테이프로 묶어 두고 있었다.

❽ Today, we are approaching the point where we can begin to bring some appropriate technology to bear in ways that advance our understanding of patients as unique individuals.

오늘날, 우리는 환자를 고유한 개인으로서 이해하는 것을 증진하는 방식에 맞는 적절한 기 술을 도입하기 시작하는 지점에 접근하고 있다.

❾ In fact, many patients are already wearing devices that monitor their conditions in real time, which allows doctors to talk to their patients in a specific, refined, and feedback-driven way that was not even possible a decade ago.

사실, 많은 환자들이 이미 자신의 상태를 실시간으로 관찰하는 장치를 착용하고 있는데, 이는 의사가 구체적이고도 정제되었으며 피드백을 기반으로 하는, 십 년 전에는 전혀 가능하지 않았던 방식으로 환자에게 말할 수 있도록 해주었다.

22 의미

❶ We tend to overrate the impact of new technologies in part because older technologies have become absorbed into the furniture of our lives, so as to be almost invisible.

우리는 새로운 기술의 영향을 과대평가하는 경향이 있는데, 부분적으로 그 이유는 기존 기술이 눈에 거의 보이지 않을 만큼 우리 삶의 일부로 흡수되었기 때문이다.

❷ Take the baby bottle.

젖병을 예로 들어 보자.

❸ Here is a simple implement that has transformed a fundamental human experience for vast numbers of infants and mothers, yet it finds no place in our histories of technology.

여기에 수많은 영유아와 엄마들의 인간으로서의 근본적인 경험을 바꿨으나, 기술의 역사에서 그 자리를 찾지 못한 단순한 도구가 있다.

❹ This technology might be thought of as a classic timeshifting device, as it enables mothers to exercise more control over the timing of feeding.

이 기술은 전형적으로 시간을 조절하는 장치라고 여겨지는데 이는 엄마가 수유 시간에 대해 더 많은 통제력을 발휘할 수 있게 하기 때문이다.

❺ It can also function to save time, as bottle feeding allows for someone else to substitute for the mother's time.

또한 젖병 수유는 시간을 절약하는 기능도 하는데, 이는 다른 사람이 엄마의 (수유) 시간을 대신하도록 허락하기 때문이다.

❻ Potentially, therefore, it has huge implications for the management of time in everyday life, yet it is entirely overlooked in discussions of high-speed society.

따라서, 잠재적으로 그것(젖병)은 일상 생활의 시간 관리에 큰 영향을 미치지만, 빠른 속도의 사회적 논의에서는 완전히 간과되고 있다.

23 주제

❶ Empathy is frequently listed as one of the most desired skills in an employer or employee, although without specifying exactly what is meant by empathy.

'공감'이 무엇을 의미하는지 정확히 밝히지는 않지만, 공감은 고용주나 직원에게 가장 바라는 기술 중 하나로 목록에 종종 오른다.

❷ Some businesses stress cognitive empathy, emphasizing the need for leaders to understand the perspective of employees and customers when negotiating deals and making decisions.

일부 기업은 인지적 공감을 강조하여 리더가 거래를 협상하고 결정을 내릴 때 직원과 고객의 관점을 이해할 필요성에 중점을 둔다.

❸ Others stress affective empathy and empathic concern, emphasizing the ability of leaders to gain trust from employees and customers by treating them with real concern and compassion.

다른 기업은 정서적 공감과 공감적 관심을 강조하여 진정한 관심과 동정심으로 직원과 고객을 대함으로써 그들의 신뢰를 얻는 리더의 능력에 중점을 둔다.

❹ When some consultants argue that successful companies foster empathy, what that translates to is that companies should conduct good market research.

일부 자문 위원이 성공하려는 기업은 공감 능력을 길러야 한다고 주장할 때, 그것이 의미하는 바는 기업이 시장 조사를 잘 수행해야 한다는 것이다.

❺ In other words, an "empathic" company understands the needs and wants of its customers and seeks to fulfill those needs and wants.

다시 말해, '공감적인' 기업은 고객의 필요와 요구를 이해하고, 그 필요와 요구를 충족시키기 위해 노력한다.

❻ When some people speak of design with empathy, what that translates to is that companies should take into account the specific needs of different populations — the blind, the deaf, the elderly, non-English speakers, the colorblind, and so on — when designing products.
일부 사람들이 공감을 담은 디자인을 말할 때, 그것이 의미하는 바는 회사가 제품을 디자인할 때 시각 장애인, 청각 장애인, 노인, 비영어권 화자, 색맹 등 다양한 사람들의 구체적인 필요 사항을 고려해야 한다는 것이다.

24 제목

❶ The most prevalent problem kids report is that they feel like they need to be accessible at all times.

아이들이 이야기하는 가장 일반적인 문제는 그들이 항상 연락될 수 있어야 한다고 느낀다는 것이다.

❷ Because technology allows for it, they feel an obligation.

기술이 그것을 허용하기 때문에, 그들은 의무감을 느낀다.

❸ It's easy for most of us to relate — you probably feel the same pressure in your own life!

우리 대부분은 공감하기 쉬운데, 아마 여러분도 자신의 삶에서 같은 압박을 느낄 것이다!

❹ It is really challenging to deal with the fact that we're human and can't always respond instantly.

우리가 인간이고 항상 즉각적으로 응답할 수 없다는 사실에 대처하는 것은 매우 힘들다.

❺ Here's how this behavior plays out sometimes:

때때로 이 행동이 나타나는 방식은 다음과 같다.

❼ Your child texts one of his friends, and the friend doesn't text back right away.

예를 들어, 여러분의 자녀가 친구 중 한 명에게 문자 메세지를 보내고, 그 친구가 즉시 답장을 보내지 않는다면,

❽ Now it's easy for your child to think, "This person doesn't want to be my friend anymore!"

이제 여러분의 자녀는 "얘는 더 이상 내 친구가 되기를 원하지 않는구나!"라고 생각하기 쉽다.

❾ So he texts again, and again, and again — "blowing up their phone."

그래서 다시, 다시, 그리고 또 다시 문자 메시지를 보내다가, '전화기를 폭파하는(과부하 상태로 만드는) 것'이다.

❿ This can be stress-inducing and even read as aggressive.

이것은 스트레스를 유발하고, 심지어 공격적인 것으로 읽힐수 있다.

⓫ But you can see how easily this could happen.

하지만 여러분은 이것이 얼마나 쉽게 일어날 수 있는지 알 수 있다.

26 일치

❶ Theodore von Karman, a Hungarian-American engineer, was one of the greatest minds of the twentieth century.

Theodore von Karman은 헝가리계 미국인 공학자로, 20세기의 가장 위대한 지성인 중 한 명이었다.

❷ He was born in Hungary and at an early age, he showed a talent for math and science.

그는 헝가리에서 태어나 어린 시절 수학과 과학에 재능을 보였다.

❸ In 1908, he received a doctoral degree in engineering at the University of Gottingen in Germany.

1908년, 독일 University of Gottingen에서 공학 박사 학위를 받았다.

❹ In the 1920s, he began traveling as a lecturer and consultant to industry.

1920년대에, 관련 분야의 강연자 겸 자문 위원으로 다니기 시작했다.

❺ He was invited to the United States to advise engineers on the design of a wind tunnel at California Institute of Technology (Caltech).

미국으로 초청되어 캘리포니아 공과대학(Caltech)에서 공학자들에게 윈드 터널 설계에 관한 조언을 하였다.

❻ He became the director of the Guggenheim Aeronautical Laboratory at Caltech in 1930.

1930년에 Caltech의 Guggenheim Aeronautical Laboratory의 소장이 되었다.

❼ Later, he was awarded the National Medal of Science for his leadership in science and engineering.

나중에는 과학과 공학 분야에서의 리더십으로 National Medal of Science를 받았다.

29 어법

❶ For years, many psychologists have held strongly to the belief that the key to addressing negative health habits is to change behavior.

수년 동안 많은 심리학자들이 부정적인 건강 습관을 해결하기 위한 열쇠는 행동을 바꾸는 것이라는 믿음을 굳게 갖고 있었다.

❷ This, more than values and attitudes, is the part of personality that is easiest to change.

가치관이나 태도보다, 이것이 가장 바꾸기 쉬운 성격의 한 부분이다.

❸ Ingestive habits such as smoking, drinking and various eating behaviors are the most common health concerns targeted for behavioral changes.

흡연, 음주, 그리고 다양한 섭식 행동과 같은 섭취 습관은 행동 변화의 대상이 되는 가장 일반적인 건강 문제이다.

❹ Process-addiction behaviors (workaholism, shopaholism, and the like) fall into this category as well.

과정 중독 행동(일중독, 쇼핑 중독 등) 또한 이 범주에 속한다.

❺ Mental imagery combined with power of suggestion was taken up as the premise of behavioral medicine to help people change negative health behaviors into positive ones.

암시의 힘과 결합된 마음 속 이미지는 사람들이 부정적인 건강 행동을 긍정적인 것으로 바꾸는 데 도움을 주는 행동 의학의 전제가 되었다.

❻ Although this technique alone will not produce changes, when used alongside other behavior modification tactics and coping strategies, behavioral changes have proved effective for some people.

이 기술만으로는 변화를 만들어 내지는 않지만, 다른 행동 수정 기법 및 대응 전략과 함께 사용되면, 행동 변화가 일부 사람들에게는 효과적인 것으로 입증되었다.

❼ What mental imagery does is reinforce a new desired behavior.

마음 속 이미지가 하는 일은 새로운 바람직한 행동을 강화하는 것이다.

❽ Repeated use of images reinforces the desired behavior more strongly over time.

이미지의 반복적 사용은 시간이 지남에 따라 그 바람직한 행동을 더욱 강력하게 강화한다.

30 어휘

❶ Emotion socialization — learning from other people about emotions and how to deal with them — starts early in life and plays a foundational role for emotion regulation development.

다른 사람들로부터 감정과 감정을 다루는 방법을 배우는 감정 사회화는 어릴 때부터 시작되며 감정 조절 발달에 기초적인 역할을 한다.

❷ Although extra-familial influences, such as peers or media, gain in importance during adolescence, parents remain the primary socialization agents.

청소년기에는 또래나 미디어와 같은 가족 이외의 영향이 중요해지지만, 부모는 여전히 주된 사회화 주체이다.

❸ For example, their own responses to emotional situations serve as a role model for emotion regulation, increasing the likelihood that their children will show similar reactions in comparable situations.

예를 들어, 감정적 상황에 대한 부모 자신의 반응이 감정 조절의 롤모델이 되어 자녀가 비슷한 상황에서 유사한 반응을 보일 가능성을 높인다.

❹ Parental practices at times when their children are faced with emotional challenges also impact emotion regulation development.

자녀가 정서적 어려움에 직면했을 때 부모의 (습관적) 행동 또한 감정 조절 발달에 영향을 미친다.

❺ Whereas direct soothing and directive guidance of what to do are beneficial for younger children, they may intrude on adolescents' autonomy striving.

직접적인 위로와 어떻게 해야 하는지에 대한 지시적 안내가 어린 자녀에게는 도움이 되지만, 청소년의 자율성 추구를 방해할 수 있다.

❻ In consequence, adolescents might pull away from, rather than turn toward, their parents in times of emotional crisis, unless parental practices are adjusted.

결과적으로 부모의 행동이 조정되지 않는다면, 청소년은 정서적 위기 상황에서 부모에게 의지하기보다 오히려 부모로부터 멀어질 수 있다.

❼ More suitable in adolescence is indirect support of autonomous emotion regulation, such as through interest in, as well as awareness and nonjudgmental acceptance of, adolescents' emotional experiences, and being available when the adolescent wants to talk.

청소년기에 더 적합한 것은 청소년의 정서적 경험에 대한 인식과 무비판적 수용뿐만 아니라 (그에 대한) 관심, 그리고 청소년이 대화하고 싶을 때 곁에 있어 주는 것과 같은 방법으로 자율적 감정 조절을 간접적으로 지원하는 것이다.

31 빈칸

❶ Dancers often push themselves to the limits of their physical capabilities.

무용수는 종종 자신의 신체 능력의 한계까지 자신을 밀어붙인다.

❷ But that push is misguided if it is directed toward accomplishing something physically impossible.

그러나 그렇게 밀어붙이는 것이 물리적으로 불가능한 것을 달성하는 쪽으로 향하게 된다면, 잘못 이해한 것이다.

❸ For instance, a tall dancer with long feet may wish to perform repetitive vertical jumps to fast music, pointing his feet while in the air and lowering his heels to the floor between jumps.

예를 들어, 키가 크고 발이 긴 무용수가 공중에서 발끝을 뾰족하게 하고 점프 사이에 발 뒤꿈치를 바닥에 내리면서 빠른 음악에 맞춰 반복적인 수직 점프를 수행하고 싶을 수 있다.

❹ That may be impossible no matter how strong the dancer is.

무용수가 아무리 힘이 좋을지라도 그것은 불가능할 수 있다.

❺ Another dancer may be struggling to complete a half-turn in the air.

또 다른 무용수는 공중에서 반 회전을 완성하려고 애쓰고 있을 수 있다.

❻ Understanding the connection between a rapid turn rate and the alignment of the body close to the rotation axis tells her how to accomplish her turn successfully.

빠른 회전 속도와 회전축에 가깝게 몸을 정 렬하는 것의 연관성을 이해하는 것은 그 무용수에게 성공적으로 회전을 해내는 방법을 알려 준다.

❼ In both of these cases, understanding and working within the constraints imposed by nature and described by physical laws allows dancers to work efficiently, minimizing potential risk of injury.

이 두 경우 모두에서, 선천적으로 주어지고 물리적 법칙에 의해 설명되는 제약을 이해하고 그 안에서 움직이는 것은 잠재적인 부상 위험을 최소화하면서 무용수가 효율적으로 움직이게 해 준다.

32 빈칸

❶ We must explore the relationship between children's film production and consumption habits.

우리는 어린이 영화 제작과 소비 습관 사이의 관계를 탐구해야 한다.

❷ The term "children's film" implies ownership by children — their cinema — but films supposedly made for children have always been consumed by audiences of all ages, particularly in commercial cinemas.

'어린이 영화'라는 용어는 어린이에 의한 소유권, 즉 '그들의' 영화를 암시하지만, 소위 어린이를 위해 만들어진 영화는 특히 상업 영화에서, 항상 모든 연령대의 관객들에게 소비되어 왔다.

❸ The considerable crossover in audience composition for children's films can be shown by the fact that, in 2007, eleven Danish children's and youth films attracted 59 per cent of theatrical admissions, and in 2014, German children's films comprised seven out of the top twenty films at the national box office.

어린이 영화의 관객 구성에서 상당한 (연령 간의) 넘나듦이 있다는 것은, 2007년에 11개의 덴마크의 어린이 및 청소년 영화가 극장 입장객의 59퍼센트를 끌어모았고 2014년에는 독일의 어린이 영화가 전국 극장 흥행 수익 상위 20개 영화 중 7개를 차지했다는 사실에 의해 증명될 수 있다.

❹ This phenomenon corresponds with a broader, international embrace of what is seemingly children's culture among audiences of diverse ages.

이 현상은 다양한 연령대의 관객들 사이에서 겉으로는 어린이 문화처럼 보이는 것이 더 광범위하고 국제적으로 수용되는 것과 일치한다.

❺ The old prejudice that children's film is some other realm, separate from (and forever subordinate to) a more legitimate cinema for adults is not supported by the realities of consumption: children's film is at the heart of contemporary popular culture.

어린이 영화가 성인을 위한 더 제대로 된 영화와는 별개의 (그리고 영원히 하위의) 다른 영역이라는 오래된 편견은 소비의 실상에 의해 뒷받침되지 않는다. 즉, 어린이 영화가 현대 대중문화의 중심에 있다.

33 빈칸

❶ Beethoven's drive to create something novel is a reflection of his state of curiosity.

새로운 것을 창작하려는 베토벤의 욕구는 그의 호기심 상태의 반영이다.

❷ Our brains experience a sense of reward when we create something new in the process of exploring something uncertain, such as a musical phrase that we've never played or heard before.

우리의 뇌는 우리가 이전에 연주 하거나 들어본 적이 없는 악절과 같이 불확실한 것을 탐구하는 과정에서 새로운 것을 창작할 때 보상감을 경험한다.

❸ When our curiosity leads to something novel, the resulting reward brings us a sense of pleasure.

우리의 호기심이 새로운 것으로 이어지면, 그 결과로 얻어지는 보상은 우리에게 쾌감을 가져다 준다.

❹ A number of investigators have modeled how curiosity influences musical composition.

많은 연구자들이 음악 작곡에 호기심이 어떻게 영향을 미치는지를 모델링해 왔다.

❺ In the case of Beethoven, computer modeling focused on the thirty-two piano sonatas written after age thirteen revealed that the musical patterns found in all of Beethoven's music decreased in later sonatas, while novel patterns, including patterns that were unique to a particular sonata, increased.

베토벤의 경우, 13세 이후로 작곡된 32개의 피아노 소나타에 초점을 맞춘 컴퓨터 모델링에서 베토벤의 모든 음악에서 발견되는 음악 패턴이 후기 소나타에서는 감소한 반면, 특정 소나타에만 나타나는 패턴을 포함한 새로운 패턴은 증가한 것을 보여 주었다.

❻ In other words, Beethoven's music became less predictable over time as his curiosity drove the exploration of new musical ideas.

다시 말해, 베토벤의 호기심이 새로운 음악적 아이디어의 탐구를 이끌게 됨에 따라 그의 음악은 시간이 지날수록 덜 예측 가능하게 되었다.

❼ Curiosity is a powerful driver of human creativity.

호기심은 인간의 창의성의 강력한 원동력이다

34 빈칸

❶ Technologists are always on the lookout for quantifiable metrics.

기술자들은 항상 정량화할 수 있는 측정 기준을 찾고 있다.

❷ Measurable inputs to a model are their lifeblood, and like a social scientist, a technologist needs to identify concrete measures, or "proxies," for assessing progress.

모델에 측정 가능한 입력(을 하는 것)은 그들의 생명줄이며, 사회 과학자와 마찬가지로 기술자는 진척 상황을 평가하기 위한 구체적인 측정 방법, 즉 '프록시'를 식별할 필요가 있다.

❸ This need for quantifiable proxies produces a bias toward measuring things that are easy to quantify.

이러한 정량화할 수 있는 프록시에 대한 필요성은 정량화하기 쉬운 것들을 측정하는 쪽으로 편향을 만든다.

❹ But simple metrics can take us further away from the important goals we really care about, which may require complicated metrics or be extremely difficult, or perhaps impossible, to reduce to any measure.

하지만 단순한 측정 기준은 우리가 정말로 신경 쓰는 중요한 목표로부터 우리를 더 멀어지게 할 수 있는데, 이 목표는 복잡한 측정 기준을 요구하거나, 또는 (이 목표를) 어떤 하나의 측정 방법만으로 한정(하여 측정)하기가 어렵거나 아마 불가능할 수도 있다.

❺ And when we have imperfect or bad proxies, we can easily fall under the illusion that we are solving for a good end without actually making genuine progress toward a worthy solution.

그리고 우리가 불완전하거나 잘못된 프록시를 가지고 있을 때, 우리는 가치 있는 해결책을 향한 진정한 진전을 실제로 이루지 못하면서 좋은 목적을 위해 문제를 해결하고 있다는 착각에 쉽게 빠질 수 있다.

❻ The problem of proxies results in technologists frequently substituting what is measurable for what is meaningful.

프록시의 문제는 기술자들이 흔히 의미 있는 것을 측정 가능한 것으로 대체하는 결과를 낳는다.

❼ As the saying goes, "Not everything that counts can be counted, and not everything that can be counted counts."

흔히 말하듯이, "중요한 모든 것들이 셀 수 있는 것은 아니고, 셀 수 있는 모든 것들이 중요한 것도 아니다."

35 무관

❶ We are the only species that seasons its food, deliberately altering it with the highly flavored plant parts we call herbs and spices.

우리는 음식에 양념을 하는 유일한 종으로, 허브와 향신료라고 부르는 강한 맛을 내는 식물의 부분을 이용하여 그것(음식)을 의도적으로 바꾼다.

❷ It's quite possible that our taste for spices has an evolutionary root.

향신료에 대한 우리의 미각은 진화적 뿌리를 가지고 있을 가능성이 높다.

❸ Many spices have antibacterial properties — in fact, common seasonings such as garlic, onion, and oregano inhibit the growth of almost every bacterium tested.

많은 향신료가 항균성을 가지고 있는데, 실제로 마늘, 양파, 오레가노와 같은 흔한 조미료들이 거의 모든 확인된 박테리아의 성장을 억제한다.

❹ And the cultures that make the heaviest use of spices — think of the garlic and black pepper of Thai food, the ginger and coriander of India, the chili peppers of Mexico — come from warmer climates, where bacterial spoilage is a bigger issue.

그리고 태국 음식의 마늘과 후추, 인도의 생강과 고수, 멕시코의 고추를 생각해 보면, 향신료를 가장 많이 사용하는 문화권은 더 따뜻한 기후에서 유래하는데, 그곳에서는 박테리아에 의한 (음식의) 부패가 큰 문제이다.

❺ In contrast, the most lightly spiced cuisines — those of Scandinavia and northern Europe — are from cooler climates.

반대로, 스칸디나비아와 북유럽의 요리같이 가장 향신료를 적게 쓰는 요리는 더 서늘한 기후에서 유래한다.

❻ Our uniquely human attention to flavor, in this case the flavor of spices, turns out to have arisen as a matter of life and death.

맛에 대한 인간 특유의 관심, 이 경우 향신료의 맛은 사느냐 죽느냐의 문제로서 생겨난 것으로 드러난다.

36 순서

❶ Development of the human body from a single cell provides many examples of the structural richness that is possible when the repeated production of random variation is combined with nonrandom selection.

단일 세포로부터 인체가 발달하는 것은 무작위적인 변이의 반복적 생성이 비무작위적인 선택과 결합될 때 가능해지는 구조적 풍부함의 많은 예를 제공한다.

❷ All phases of body development from embryo to adult exhibit random activities at the cellular level, and body formation depends on the new possibilities generated by these activities coupled with selection of those outcomes that satisfy previously built-in criteria.

배아에서 성체에 이르기까지 신체 발달의 모든 단계는 15세포 수준에서는 무작위 활동을 보이고, 신체 형성은 이러한 활동(무작위 활동)에 의해 만들어진 새로운 가능성과 더불어, 이전에 확립된 기준을 만족시키는 결과물의 선택에 달려 있다.

❸ Always new structure is based on old structure, and at every stage selection favors some cells and eliminates others.

항상 새로운 구조는 오래된 구조를 기반으로 하며, 모든 단계에서 선택은 일부 세포들을 선호하고 다른 세포들은 제거한다.

❹ The survivors serve to produce new cells that undergo further rounds of selection.

생존한 세포들은 추가적인 선택의 과정을 거치는 새로운 세포들을 만들어 내는 역할을 한다.

❺ Except in the immune system, cells and extensions of cells are not genetically selected during development, but rather, are positionally selected.

면역계를 제외하면 세포와 세포의 확장은 발달 과정에서 유전적으로 선택되는 것이 아니라 위치에 의해 선택된다.

❻ Those in the right place that make the right connections are stimulated, and those that don't are eliminated.
제 자리에서 제대로 된 연결을 만들어 낸 것(세포)들은 활성화 되고, 그렇지 않은 것들은 제거된다.

❼ This process is much like sculpting.
이 과정은 마치 조각을 하는 것과 같다.

❽ A natural consequence of the strategy is great variability from individual to individual at the cell and molecular levels, even though largescale structures are quite similar.
이 전략의 필연적 결과는 전체 구조가 상당히 비슷하더라도 세포와 분자 수준에서 개인마다 큰 변이성이 있다는 것이다.

37 순서

❶ In order to bring the ever-increasing costs of home care for elderly and needy persons under control, managers of home care providers have introduced management systems.

노인과 빈곤층을 위한 재택 간호의 계속적으로 증가하는 비용을 통제하기 위해 재택 간호 제공 업체의 관리자는 관리 시스템을 도입했다.

❷ These systems specify tasks of home care workers and the time and budget available to perform these tasks.

이러한 시스템은 재택 간호 종사자의 업무와 이러한 업무를 수행하는 데 사용할 수 있는 시간과 예산을 명시한다.

❸ Electronic reporting systems require home care workers to report on their activities and the time spent, thus making the distribution of time and money visible and, in the perception of managers, controllable.

전자 보고 시스템은 재택 간호 종사자가 자신의 활동과 소요 시간을 보고하도록 요구하므로 시간과 비용의 분배를 잘 보이게 만들고, 관리자의 입장에서는 통제 가능하게 만든다.

❹ This, in the view of managers, has contributed to the resolution of the problem.

관리자의 관점에서는, 이것이 문제 해결에 기여해 왔다.

❺ The home care workers, on the other hand, may perceive their work not as a set of separate tasks to be performed as efficiently as possible, but as a service to be provided to a client with whom they may have developed a relationship.

반면에, 재택 간호 종사자들은 자신의 업무를 가능한 한 효율적으로 수행되어야 하는 일련의 분리된 업무가 아니라, 그들이 관계를 맺어온 고객에게 제공되는 서비스로 인식할 것이다.

❻ This includes having conversations with clients and enquiring about the person's wellbeing.
이것은 고객과 대화를 나누고 고객의 안부를 묻는 것을 포함한다.

❼ Restricted time and the requirement to report may be perceived as obstacles that make it impossible to deliver the service that is needed.
제한된 시간과 보고를 해야 한다는 요구 사항은 필요한 서비스를 제공하는 것을 불가능하게 하는 장애물로 여겨질 것이다.

❽ If the management systems are too rigid, this may result in home care workers becoming overloaded and demotivated.
만약 관리 시스템이 너무 엄격하면, 이것은 재택 간호 종사자가 너무 많은 부담을 지게 되고 의욕을 잃는 결과를 초래할 것이다.

38 삽입

❶ It is a common assumption that most vagrant birds are ultimately doomed, aside from the rare cases where individuals are able to reorientate and return to their normal ranges.

무리에서 떨어져 헤매는 대부분의 새들은 방향을 다시 잡고 그들의 일반적인 (서식) 범위로 돌아갈 수 있는 드문 경우의 개체들을 제외하고, 궁극적으로 죽을 운명이라는 것이 일반적인 가정이다.

❷ In turn, it is also commonly assumed that vagrancy itself is a relatively unimportant biological phenomenon.

결국, 무리에서 떨어져 헤매는 것 자체가 비교적 중요하지 않은 생물학적 현상이라고 일반적으로 여겨지기도 한다.

❸ This is undoubtedly true for the majority of cases, as the most likely outcome of any given vagrancy event is that the individual will fail to find enough resources, and/or be exposed to inhospitable environmental conditions, and perish.

이것은 의심할 여지 없이 대부분의 경우에 사실인데, 무리에서 떨어져 헤매는 어떤 경우든 가장 가능성 있는 결과는 개체가 충분한 자원을 찾지 못하고/못하거나, 살기 힘든 환경 조건에 노출되어 죽기 때문이다.

❹ However, there are many lines of evidence to suggest that vagrancy can, on rare occasions, dramatically alter the fate of populations, species or even whole ecosystems.

하지만, 드문 경우에, 무리에서 떨어져 헤매는 것이 개체 수, 종, 심지어 생태계 전체의 운명을 극적으로 바꿀 수 있다는 것을 시사하는 많은 증거가 있다.

❺ Despite being infrequent, these events can be extremely important when viewed at the timescales over which ecological and evolutionary processes unfold.

드물기는 하지만, 이러한 경우들은 생태학적이고 진화적인 과정이 진행되는 시간의 관점에서 볼 때 매우 중요할 수 있다.

❻ The most profound consequences of vagrancy relate to the establishment of new breeding sites, new migration routes and wintering locations.
무리에서 떨어져 헤매는 것의 가장 중대한 결과는 새로운 번식지, 새로운 이동 경로 및 월동 장소의 확보와 관련이 있다.

❼ Each of these can occur through different mechanisms, and at different frequencies, and they each have their own unique importance.
이들 각각은 서로 다른 메커니즘을 통해, 서로 다른 빈도로 발생할 수 있으며, 각각 고유한 중요성을 가지고 있다.

39 삽입

❶ Intuition can be great, but it ought to be hard-earned.

직관은 탁월할 수 있지만, 힘들여 얻은 것이어야 한다.

❷ Experts, for example, are able to think on their feet because they've invested thousands of hours in learning and practice: their intuition has become data-driven.

예를 들어, 전문가들은 수천 시간을 학습과 경험에 투자하여, 데이터로부터 직관이 얻어졌기 때문에 즉각적으로 생각할 수 있다.

❸ Only then are they able to act quickly in accordance with their internalized expertise and evidence-based experience.

그래야만 그들이 내재화된 전문 지식과 증거에 기반한 경험에 따라 빠르게 행동할 수 있다.

❹ Yet most people are not experts, though they often think they are.

그러나 대부분의 사람들은 종종 스스로를 전문가라고 생각하지만 실제로는 전문가가 아니다.

❺ Most of us, especially when we interact with others on social media, act with expert-like speed and conviction, offering a wide range of opinions on global crises, without the substance of knowledge that supports it.

우리 중 대부분은, 특히 소셜 미디어에서 다른 사람들과 소통할 때, 전문가와 같은 속도와 확신을 가지고 행동하며, 이를 뒷받침하는 지식의 실체 없이 국제적 위기에 대한 다양한 의견을 제시한다.

❻ And thanks to AI, which ensures that our messages are delivered to an audience more inclined to believing it, our delusions of expertise can be reinforced by our personal filter bubble.

그리고 우리의 메시지가 그것을 더 믿으려는 성향이 있는 독자에게 확실히 전달되도록 하는 인공 지능 덕분에, 전문 지식에 대한 우리의 착각은 개인적 필터 버블(자신의 관심사에 맞게 필터링된 정보만을 접하게 되는 현상)에 의해 강화 될 수 있다.

❼ We have an interesting tendency to find people more open-minded, rational, and sensible when they think just like us.

우리는 남들이 우리와 똑같이 생각할 때 그들을 더 개방적이고 합리적이며 분별 있다고 여기는 흥미로운 경향을 가지고 있다.

40 요약

❶ The fast-growing, tremendous amount of data, collected and stored in large and numerous data repositories, has far exceeded our human ability for understanding without powerful tools.

빠르게 증가하는 엄청난 양의 데이터는, 크고 많은 데이터 저장소에 수집되고 저장되어, 우리 인간이 효과적인 도구 없이는 이해할 수 있는 능력을 훨씬 뛰어 넘었다.

❷ As a result, data collected in large data repositories become "data tombs" — data archives that are hardly visited.

결과적으로, 대규모 데이터 저장소에서 수집된 데이터는 '데이터 무덤', 즉 찾는 사람이 거의 없는 데이터 보관소가 된다.

❸ Important decisions are often made based not on the information-rich data stored in data repositories but rather on a decision maker's instinct, simply because the decision maker does not have the tools to extract the valuable knowledge hidden in the vast amounts of data.

중요한 의사 결정이 종종 데이터 저장소에 저장된 정보가 풍부한 데이터가 아닌 의사 결정자의 직관에 기반하여 내려지기도 하는데, 이는 단지 의사 결정자가 방대한 양의 데이터에 숨겨진 가치 있는 지식을 추출할 수 있는 도구를 가지고 있지 않기 때문이다.

❹ Efforts have been made to develop expert system and knowledge-based technologies, which typically rely on users or domain experts to manually input knowledge into knowledge bases.

전문가 시스템과 지식 기반 기술을 개발하려는 노력이 있어 왔는데, 이는 일반적으로 사용자나 분야(별) 전문가가 지식을 '수동으로' 지식 기반에 입력하는 것에 의존한다.

❺ However, this procedure is likely to cause biases and errors and is extremely costly and time consuming.

하지만, 이 방법은 편견과 오류를 일으키기 쉽고 비용과 시간이 엄청나게 든다.

❻ The widening gap between data and information calls for the systematic development of tools that can turn data tombs into "golden nuggets" of knowledge.
점점 더 벌어지는 데이터와 정보 간의 격차로 인해 데이터 무덤을 지식의 '금괴'로 바꿀 수 있는 도구의 체계적인 개발이 요구된다.

41~42　제목, 어휘

❶ It's untrue that teens can focus on two things at once — what they're doing is shifting their attention from one task to another.

십대들이 동시에 두 가지 일에 집중할 수 있다는 것은 사실이 아니며, 그들이 하고 있는 것은 한 작업에서 다른 작업으로 주의를 전환하는 것이다.

❷ In this digital age, teens wire their brains to make these shifts very quickly, but they are still, like everyone else, paying attention to one thing at a time, sequentially.

디지털 시대에, 십대의 뇌는 매우 빠르게 작업을 전환하도록 발달하지만, 여전히 다른 모든 사람들과 마찬가지로 십 대들도 한 번에 한 가지씩 순차적으로 주의를 기울이고 있다.

❸ Common sense tells us multitasking should increase brain activity, but Carnegie Mellon University scientists using the latest brain imaging technology find it doesn't.

상식적으로 멀티태스킹이 뇌 활동을 증가시킬 것이라고 생각하지만, Carnegie Mellon 대학의 과학자들은 최신 뇌 영상 기술을 사용하여 그렇지 않다는 것을 발견했다.

❹ As a matter of fact, they discovered that multitasking actually decreases brain activity.

사실, 그들은 멀티태스킹이 실제로는 두뇌 활동을 감소시킨다는 것을 발견했다.

❺ Neither task is done as well as if each were performed individually.

어느 작업도 각각 개별적으로 수행될 때만큼 잘 되지 못한다.

❻ Fractions of a second are lost every time we make a switch, and a person's interrupted task can take 50 percent longer to finish, with 50 percent more errors.

우리가 (작업을) 전환할 때마다 시간이 아주 조금씩 낭비되며, 중단된 작업은 완료하기까지 50퍼센트 더 오래 걸리고, 50퍼센트 더 많은 오류가 발생할 수 있다.

❼ Turns out the latest brain research supports the old advice "one thing at a time."

최신 뇌 연구가 '한 번에 한 가지 일만 하라'는 오래된 조언을 뒷받침하는 것으로 드러났다.

❽ It's not that kids can't do some tasks simultaneously.

아이들이 동시에 여러 작업을 할 수 없다는 것은 아니다.

❾ But if two tasks are performed at once, one of them has to be familiar.

하지만 동시에 두 가지 작업이 수행된다면, 그 중 하나는 익숙한 작업이어야 한다.

❿ Our brains perform a familiar task on "automatic pilot" while really paying attention to the other one.

우리의 뇌는 익숙한 작업은 '자동 조종' 상태에서 수행하고 실제로는 다른 작업에 주의를 기울인다.

⓫ That's why insurance companies consider talking on a cell phone and driving to be as dangerous as driving while drunk— it's the driving that goes on "automatic pilot" while the conversation really holds our attention.

그것이 보험 회사가 휴대 전화로 통화하면서 운전하는 것을 술에 취한 상태에서 운전하는 것만큼 위험한 것으로 간주하는 이유이다. 대화가 실제로 우리의 주의를 끌고 있는 동안 '자동 조종' 상태에서 수행되는 것은 운전이다.

⓬ Our kids may be living in the Information Age but our brains have not been redesigned yet.

우리 아이들이 정보화 시대에 살고 있을지 모르지만, 우리의 뇌는 아직 (정보화 시대에 맞게) 재설계되지 않았다.

43~45 순서, 지칭, 세부 내용

❶ Christine was a cat owner who loved her furry companion, Leo.

Christine은 고양이 주인으로 그녀의 털북숭이 반려동물인 Leo를 사랑한다.

❷ One morning, she noticed that Leo was not feeling well.

어느 날 아침, 그녀는 Leo의 몸 상태가 좋지 않다는 것을 알게 되었다.

❸ Concerned for her beloved cat, Christine decided to take him to the animal hospital.

사랑하는 고양이가 걱정되어서, Christine은 Leo를 동물병원에 데려가기로 결심했다.

❹ As she always brought Leo to this hospital, she was certain that the vet knew well about Leo.

그녀가 항상 Leo를 이 병원에 데려왔기 때문에, 수의사가 Leo에 대해 잘 알고 있을 것이라고 그녀는 확신했다.

❺ She desperately hoped Leo got the necessary care as soon as possible.

Leo가 필요한 보살핌을 가능한 한 빨리 받기를 그녀는 간절히 바랐다.

❻ The waiting room was filled with other pet owners.
대기실은 다른 반려동물의 주인들로 꽉 차 있었다.

❼ Finally, it was Leo's turn to see the vet.
마침내, Leo가 수의사를 만날 차례가 되었다.

❽ Christine watched as the vet gently examined him.
Christine은 수의사가 Leo를 조심스럽게 진찰하는 모습을 지켜보았다.

❾ The vet said, "I think Leo has a minor infection."
"저는 Leo에게 경미한 감염이 있다고 생각합니다." 수의사가 말했다.

❿ "Infection? Will he be okay?" asked Christine.
"감염이요? Leo는 괜찮을까요?" Christine이 물었다.

⓫ "We need to do some tests to see if he is infected.
"감염 여부를 알기 위해 우리는 몇 가지 검사를 할 필요가 있습니다.

❶ But for the tests, it's best for Leo to stay here," replied the vet.
하지만 검사를 위해서 Leo가 여기 머무는 것이 가장 좋습니다." 수의사가 대답했다.

❸ It was heartbreaking for Christine to leave Leo at the animal hospital, but she had to accept it was for the best.
Leo를 동물병원에 두고 가는 것이 Christine에게는 가슴 아팠지만, 그녀는 그 것이 최선이라는 것을 받아들여야만 했다.

❹ "I'll call you with updates as soon as we know anything," said the vet.
"저희가 뭔가 알게 되는 즉시 당신에게 전화로 새로운 소식을 알려 드리겠습니다."라고 수의사가 말했다.

❺ Throughout the day, Christine anxiously awaited news about Leo.
그날 내내 Christine은 초조하게 Leo에 대한 소식을 기다렸다.

❻ Later that day, the phone rang and it was the vet.
그날 늦게 전화가 울렸고 그것(전화를 건 사람)은 수의사였다.

❼ "The tests revealed a minor infection.
"검사 결과 경미한 감염이 발견되었습니다.

❽ Relieved to hear the news, Christine rushed back to the animal hospital to pick up Leo.
그 소식을 듣고 안도하며, Christine은 Leo를 데리러 동물병원으로 서둘러 되돌아갔다.

❾ The vet provided detailed instructions on how to administer the medication and shared tips for a speedy recovery.
수의사는 약을 투여하는 방법을 자세히 설명해 주고 빠른 회복을 위한 조언을 했다.

❿ Back at home, Christine created a comfortable space for Leo to rest and heal.
집으로 돌아와서, Christine은 Leo가 쉬고 회복할 수 있는 편안한 공간을 만들었다.

⓫ She patted him with love and attention, ensuring that he would recover in no time.
그녀는 Leo가 금방 회복할 수 있도록 사랑과 관심으로 Leo를 쓰다듬어 주었다.

⓬ As the days passed, Leo gradually regained his strength and playful spirit.
며칠이 지나자, Leo는 점차 체력과 장난기 넘치는 활기를 되찾았다.

18

Dear Art Crafts People of Greenville,
For the [**annual / annually**]¹⁾ Crafts Fair on May 25 from 1 p.m. to 6 p.m., the Greenville Community Center is providing booth spaces to rent as in [**precious / previous**]²⁾ years. To reserve your space, please visit our website and [**complete / to complete**]³⁾ a registration form by April 20. The rental fee is $50. All the money we receive from rental fees [**go / goes**]⁴⁾ to support upcoming activities throughout the year. We expect all available spaces to be [**full / fully**]⁵⁾ booked soon, so don't get [**leaving / left**]⁶⁾ out. We hope to see you at the fair.

친애하는 Greenville의 공예가들에게 5월 25일 오후 1시부터 6시까지 열리는 연례 공예 품 박람회를 위해서, Greenville 커 뮤니티 센터에서는 지난 몇 년간처럼 대여 부스 공간을 제공합니다. 공간 을 예약하려면 저희 웹사이트를 방문하여 4월 20일까지 신청서를 작성하시기 바랍니다. 대여 요금은 50달러입니다. 부스 대여료로 받은 모든 돈은 연중 예정된 활동을 지원하는 데 사용됩니다. 모든 이용할 수 있는 공간이 곧 모두 예약될 것으로 예상되니 놓치지 마세요. 박람회에서 뵙기를 바랍니다.

19

Sarah, a young artist with a love for painting, [**entered / entered into**]⁷⁾ a local art contest. As she looked at the amazing artworks made by [**others / the others**]⁸⁾, her [**confidence / coincidence**]⁹⁾ dropped. She quietly thought, 'I might not win an award.' The moment of judgment arrived, and the judges began announcing winners one by one. It wasn't until the end [**that / what**]¹⁰⁾ she heard her name. The head of the judges said, "Congratulations, Sarah Parker! You won first prize. We loved the uniqueness of your work." Sarah was [**overcame / overcome**]¹¹⁾ with joy, and she couldn't stop [**smiling / to smile**]¹²⁾. This experience meant more than just winning; it [**confirmed / conformed**]¹³⁾ her identity as an artist.

그림 그리기를 좋아하는 젊은 예술가 Sarah는 지역 미술 대회에 참가했다. 다른 사람들이 만든 놀라운 예술 작품들을 보 면서 그녀의 자신감은 떨어졌다. 그녀는 '내가 상을 받지 못할 수도 있겠네.'라고 조용히 생각했다. 심사의 순간이 다가왔 고, 심사위원들은 수상자를 한 명씩 발표하기 시작했다. 그녀는 마지막에야 자신의 이름을 들었다. 심사위원장이 "축하해 요, Sarah Parker! 당신이 1등을 했습니다. 당신 작품의 독창성이 정말 좋았습니다."라고 말했다. Sarah는 기쁨에 휩싸였고 미소가 가시지 않았다. 이 경험은 단순한 우승이상의 의미를 지녔고, 그녀에게 예술가로서의 정체성을 확인해 주었다.

20

Too many times people, especially in today's generation, [**expect / expecting**]¹⁴⁾ things to just happen overnight. When we have these false expectations, it tends to discourage us from [**continue / continuing**]¹⁵⁾ to move forward. [**Because / Because of**]¹⁶⁾ this is a high tech society, everything we want [**have / has**]¹⁷⁾ to be within the parameters of our comfort and [**convenient / convenience**]¹⁸⁾. If it doesn't happen fast enough, we're tempted to lose interest. So many people don't want to take the time it requires to be [**successful / successive**]¹⁹⁾. Success is not a matter of [**mere / merely**]²⁰⁾ desire; you should develop patience in order to achieve it. Have you fallen prey [**for / to**]²¹⁾ impatience? Great things take time to build.

너무나 많은 경우에, 사람들, 특히 오늘날의 세대는, 일이 하룻밤 사이에 일어나기를 기대한다. 우리가 이러한 잘못된 기대를 가질 때, 그것은 우리가 계속해서 앞으로 나아가는 것을 방해하는 경향이 있다. 지금은 첨단 기술 사회이기 때문에, 우리가 원하는 모든 것은 편안함과 편리함이라는 제한 내에 있어야 한다. 그 일이 충분히 빨리 일어나지 않으면, 우리는 흥미를 잃게끔 유혹을 받는다. 그래서 많은 사람들은 성공하는 데 필요한 시간을 들이는 것을 원하지 않는다. 성공은 단순한 욕망의 문제가 아니다. 여러분은 그것(성공)을 이루기 위해 인내심을 길러야 한다. 여러분은 조바심의 먹잇감이 되어 본 적이 있는가? 위대한 일이 이루어지는 데에는 시간이 걸린다.

21

If you [**had** / **have**]22) wanted to create a "self-driving" car in the 1950s, your best option might have been to strap a brick to the accelerator. Yes, the vehicle would have been able to move forward on its own, but it could not slow down, stop, or turn to avoid barriers. Obviously not [**ideal** / **ideally**]23). But does that mean the entire concept of the self-driving car is not worth [**pursuing** / **to pursue**]24)? No, it only means [**that** / **what**]25) at the time we did not yet have the tools we now [**possess** / **obsess**]26) to help enable vehicles to operate both [**autonomous** / **autonomously**]27) and [**safe** / **safely.**]28) This once-distant dream now seems within our reach. It is [**more** / **much**]29) the same story in medicine. Two decades ago, we were still taping bricks to accelerators. Today, we are approaching the point [**where** / **which**]30) we can begin to bring some appropriate technology to bear in ways that [**advance** / **advances**]31) our understanding of patients as unique individuals. In fact, many patients are already wearing devices that [**monitor** / **monitors**]32) their conditions in real time, [**which** / **that**]33) allows doctors to talk to their patients in a specific, refined, and feedback-driven way that was not even possible a decade ago.

만약 '자율 주행' 자동차를 1950년대에 만들고 싶었다면, 가장 좋은 선택은 가속 페달에 벽돌을 끈으로 묶는 것이었을 것이다. 물론, 자동차가 스스로 앞으로 나아갈 수는 있었겠지만, 속도를 줄이거나 멈추거나 또는 장애물을 피하기 위해 방향을 전환할 수는 없었다. 분명히, 이상적이지는 않다. 그러나 그것이 자율주행 자동차라는 전체 개념이 추구할 만한 가치가 없다는 의미일까? 아니다, 그것은 단지 우리가 지금은 갖고 있는, 자동차를 자율적이고도 안전하게 작동할 수 있도록 해 주는 도구를, 그 당시에는 우리가 아직 갖고 있지 않았다는 것을 의미할 뿐이다. 한때 멀게만 느껴졌던 이 꿈이 이제 우리의 손이 닿는 곳에 있는 것처럼 보인다. 이는 의학에서도 마찬가지이다. 20년 전에, 우리는 여전히 가속 페달에 벽돌을 테이프로 묶어 두고 있었다. 오늘날, 우리는 환자를 고유한 개인으로서 이해하는 것을 증진하는 방식에 맞는 적절한 기술을 도입하기 시작하는 지점에 접근하고 있다. 사실, 많은 환자들이 이미 자신의 상태를 실시간으로 관찰하는 장치를 착용하고 있는데, 이는 의사가 구체적이고도 정제되었으며 피드백을 기반으로 하는, 십 년 전에는 전혀 가능하지 않았던 방식으로 환자에게 말할 수 있도록 해 주었다.

22

We tend to [**overrate** / **underrate**]34) the impact of new technologies in part [**because** / **because of**]35) older technologies have become absorbed into the furniture of our lives, so as to be almost [**invisible** / **visible**]36). Take the baby bottle. Here is a simple implement [**that** / **what**]37) has transformed a [**fundamental** / **fundamentally**]38) human experience for vast numbers of infants and mothers, yet it finds no place in our histories of technology. This technology might be thought of as a classic time-shifting device, as it enables mothers to exercise [**less** / **more**]39) control over the timing of feeding. It can also function to save time, as bottle feeding [**allow** / **allows**]40) for someone else to substitute for the mother's time. Potentially, therefore, it has huge implications for the management of time in everyday life, yet it is entirely [**overlooking** / **overlooked**]41) in discussions of high-speed society.

우리는 새로운 기술의 영향을 과대평가하는 경향이 있는데, 부분적으로 그 이유는 기존 기술이 눈에 거의 보이지 않을 만큼 우리 삶의 일부로 흡수되었기 때문이다. 젖병을 예로 들어 보자. 여기에 수많은 영유아와 엄마들의 인간으로서의 근본적인 경험을 바꿨으나, 기술의 역사에서 그 자리를 찾지 못한 단순한 도구가 있다. 이 기술은 전형적으로 시간을 조절하는 장치라고 여겨지는데 이는 엄마가 수유 시간에 대해 더 많은 통제력을 발휘할 수 있게 하기 때문이다. 또한 젖병 수유는 시간을 절약하는 기능도 하는데, 이는 다른 사람이 엄마의 (수유) 시간을 대신하도록 허락하기 때문이다. 따라서, 잠재적으로 그것(젖병)은 일상생활의 시간 관리에 큰 영향을 미치지만, 빠른 속도의 사회적 논의에서는 완전히 간과되고 있다.

23

Empathy is frequently listed as one of the most desired [**skill / skills**]⁴²⁾ in an employer or employee, although without [**specify / specifying**]⁴³⁾ exactly what is meant by empathy. Some businesses stress cognitive empathy, [**emphasizing / to emphasize**]⁴⁴⁾ the need for leaders to understand the perspective of employees and customers when negotiating deals and [**making / to make**]⁴⁵⁾ decisions. [**Another / Others**]⁴⁶⁾ stress affective empathy and empathic concern, emphasizing the ability of leaders to gain trust [**from / in**]⁴⁷⁾ employees and customers by treating [**them / themselves**]⁴⁸⁾ with real concern and compassion. When some consultants argue that [**successful / successive**]⁴⁹⁾ companies foster empathy, what that [**translate / translates**]⁵⁰⁾ to is that companies should conduct good market research. In other words, an "empathic" company understands the needs and wants of [**its / their**]⁵¹⁾ customers and [**seek / seeks**]⁵²⁾ to fulfill those needs and wants. When some people speak of design with empathy, [**what / where**]⁵³⁾ that translates to is that companies should take into account the [**broad / specific**]⁵⁴⁾ needs of [**different / similar**]⁵⁵⁾ populations — the blind, the deaf, the elderly, non-English speakers, the color-blind, and so on — when designing products.

'공감'이 무엇을 의미하는지 정확히 밝히지는 않지만, 공감은 고용주나 직원에게 가장 바라는 기술 중 하나로 목록에 종종 오른다. 일부 기업은 인지적 공감을 강조하여 리더가 거래를 협상하고 결정을 내릴 때 직원과 고객의 관점을 이해할 필요성에 중점을 둔다. 다른 기업은 정서적 공감과 공감적 관심을 강조하여 진정한 관심과 동정심으로 직원과 고객을 대함으로써 그들의 신뢰를 얻는 리더의 능력에 중점을 둔다. 일부 자문 위원이 성공하려는 기업은 공감 능력을 길러야 한다고 주장할 때, 그것이 의미하는 바는 기업이 시장조사를 잘 수행해야 한다는 것이다. 다시 말해, '공감적인' 기업은 고객의 필요와 요구를 이해하고, 그 필요와 요구를 충족시키기 위해 노력한다. 일부 사람들이 공감을 담은 디자인을 말할 때, 그것이 의미하는 바는 회사가 제품을 디자인할 때 시각 장애인, 청각 장애인, 노인, 비영어권 화자, 색맹 등 다양한 사람들의 구체적인 필요 사항을 고려해야 한다는 것이다.

24

The most prevalent problem kids report is [**that / what**]⁵⁶⁾ they feel like they need to be accessible at all times. [**Because / Because of**]⁵⁷⁾ technology allows for it, they feel an obligation. It's easy for most of us to relate — you probably feel the same pressure in your own life! It is really challenging to deal with the fact [**that / where**]⁵⁸⁾ we're human and can't always respond [**instant / instantly**]⁵⁹⁾. For a teen or tween who's still learning the ins and outs of social interactions, it's even [**better / worse**]⁶⁰⁾. Here's how this behavior plays out sometimes: Your child [**texts / texting**]⁶¹⁾ one of his friends, and the friend doesn't text back right away. Now it's easy for your child to think, "This person doesn't want to be my friend anymore!" So he texts again, and again, and again — "[**blowing / blows**]⁶²⁾ up their phone." This can be stress-[**induced / inducing**]⁶³⁾ and even read as [**aggressive / progressive**]⁶⁴⁾ . But you can see how [**east / easily**]⁶⁵⁾ this could happen.

아이들이 이야기하는 가장 일반적인 문제는 그들이 항상 연락될 수 있어야 한다고 느낀다는 것이다. 기술이 그것을 허용하기 때문에, 그들은 의무감을 느낀다. 우리 대부분은 공감하기 쉬운데, 아마 여러분도 자신의 삶에서 같은 압박을 느낄 것이다! 우리가 인간이고 항상 즉각적으로 응답할 수 없다는 사실에 대처하는 것은 매우 힘들다. 아직 사회적 상호 작용의 세부적인 것들을 배우고 있는 십대나 십대 초반의 아동에게 상황은 훨씬 더 심각하다. 때때로 이 행동이 나타나는 방식은 다음과 같다. 예를 들어, 여러분의 자녀가 친구 중 한 명에게 문자메세지를 보내고, 그 친구가 즉시 답장을 보내지 않는다면, 이제 여러분의 자녀는 "얘는 더 이상 내 친구가 되기를 원하지 않는구나!"라고 생각하기 쉽다. 그래서 다시, 다시, 그리고 또 다시 문자 메시지를 보내다가, '전화기를 폭파하는(과부하 상태로 만드는) 것'이다. 이것은 스트레스를 유발하고, 심지어 공격적인 것으로 읽힐 수 있다. 하지만 여러분은 이것이 얼마나 쉽게 일어날 수 있는지 알 수 있다.

25

The graph above shows the animal protein consumption [**measuring** / **measured**]66) as the average daily [**supply** / **supplement**]67) per person in three different countries in 2020. The U.S. showed the largest amount of total animal protein consumption per person among the three countries. Eggs and Dairy was the top animal protein consumption source among four categories in the U.S., [**followed** / **following**]68) by Meat and Poultry at 22.4g and 20.6g, [**respective** / **respectively**]69). Unlike the U.S., Brazil consumed the most animal protein from Meat, with Eggs and Dairy being the second most. Japan had less than 50g of the total animal protein consumption per person, [**which** / **that**]70) was the smallest among the three countries. Fish and Seafood, which was the [**least** / **less**]71) consumed animal protein consumption source in the U.S. and Brazil, [**ranked** / **ranking**]72) the highest in Japan.

위 그래프는 2020년 3개국의 1인당 일일 평균 공급량으로 측정한 동물성 단백질 섭취량을 나타낸다. 미국은 3개국 중 1인당 총 동물성 단백질 섭취량이 가장 많은 것으로 나타났다. 계란과 유제품이 미국에서 네 가지 범주 가운데 가장 많은 동물성 단백질 공급원이었고, 육류와 가금류가 각각 22.4g과 20.6g으로 그 뒤를 이었다. 미국과 달리, 브라질은 가장 많은 동물성 단백질을 육류로부터 섭취했고, 계란과 유제품을 두 번째로 많이 섭취했다. 일본은 1인당 50g 미만의 총 동물 단백질을 섭취했고, 이는 세 나라 중 가장 적은 양이었다. 생선과 해산물은 미국과 브라질에서 가장 적게 섭취한 동물성 단백질 섭취원이었는데, 일본에서는 첫 번째로 높은 순위를 차지했다.

26

Theodore von Kármán, a Hungarian-American engineer, was one of the greatest [**mind** / **minds**]73) of the twentieth century. He was born in Hungary and [**at** / **in**]74) an early age, he showed a talent [**for** / **at**]75) math and science. In 1908, he [**received** / **has received**]76) a doctoral degree in engineering at the University of Göttingen in Germany. In the 1920s, he began traveling as a lecturer and consultant to industry. He was invited to the United States to advise engineers [**in** / **on**]77) the design of a wind tunnel at California Institute of Technology (Caltech). He became the director of the Guggenheim Aeronautical Laboratory at Caltech in 1930. Later, he was [**awarded** / **rewarded**]78) the National Medal of Science [**for** / **in**]79) his leadership in science and engineering.

Theodore von Kármán은 헝가리계 미국인 공학자로, 20세기의 가장 위대한 지성인 중 한 명이었다. 그는 헝가리에서 태어나 어린 시절 수학과 과학에 재능을 보였다. 1908년, 독일 University of Göttingen에서 공학 박사 학위를 받았다. 1920년대에, 관련 분야의 강연자 겸 자문 위원으로 다니기 시작했다. 미국으로 초청되어 캘리포니아 공과대학(Caltech)에서 공학자들에게 윈드 터널 설계에 관한 조언을 하였다. 1930년에 Caltech의 Guggenheim Aeronautical Laboratory의 소장이 되었다. 나중에는 과학과 공학 분야에서의 리더십으로 National Medal of Science를 받았다.

29

For years, many psychologists [**had / have**]80) held [**strong / strongly**]81) to the belief that the key to [**address / addressing**]82) negative health habits is to change behavior. This, more than values and attitudes, [**are / is**]83) the part of personality that is easiest to change. Ingestive habits such as smoking, drinking and various eating behaviors are the most common health concerns [**targeted / targeting**]84) for behavioral changes. Process-addiction behaviors (workaholism, shopaholism, and the like) fall into this category as well. [**Mental / Physical**]85) imagery combined with power of suggestion was taken up as the premise of behavioral medicine to help people [**change / changing**]86) negative health behaviors into positive ones. Although this technique alone will not produce changes, when used alongside [**another / other**]87) behavior modification tactics and coping strategies, behavioral changes have proved [**affective / effective**]88) for some people. What mental imagery does is [**force / reinforce**]89) a new desired behavior. Repeated use of images [**reinforce / reinforces**]90) the desired behavior more [**stronger / strongly**]91) over time.

수년 동안 많은 심리학자들이 부정적인 건강 습관을 해결하기 위한 열쇠는 행동을 바꾸는 것이라는 믿음을 굳게 갖고 있었다. 가치관이나 태도보다, 이것이 가장 바꾸기 쉬운 성격의 한 부분이다. 흡연, 음주, 그리고 다양한 섭식 행동과 같은 섭취 습관은 행동 변화의 대상이 되는 가장 일반적인 건강 문제이다. 과정 중독행동(일중독, 쇼핑 중독 등) 또한 이 범주에 속한다. 암시의 힘과 결합된 마음 속 이미지는 사람들이 부정적인 건강 행동을 긍정적인 것으로 바꾸는 데 도움을 주는 행동 의학의 전제가 되었다. 이 기술만으로는 변화를 만들어 내지는 않지만, 다른 행동 수정 기법 및 대응 전략과 함께 사용되면, 행동 변화가 일부 사람들에게는 효과적인 것으로 입증되었다. 마음 속 이미지가 하는 일은 새로운 바람직한 행동을 강화하는 것이다. 이미지의 반복적 사용은 시간이 지남에 따라 그 바람직한 행동을 더욱 강력하게 강화한다.

30

Emotion socialization — learning from [**another / other**]92) people about emotions and how to deal with them — starts early in life and plays a foundational role for emotion regulation development. Although extra-familial influences, such as peers or media, [**gain / gaining**]93) in importance during adolescence, parents remain the primary socialization agents. For example, their own responses to emotional situations [**serve / serves**]94) as a role model for emotion regulation, [**increase / increasing**]95) the likelihood that their children will show similar reactions in [**comparable / comparative**]96) situations. Parental practices at times when their children are faced with emotional challenges also [**impact / impacts**]97) emotion regulation development. Whereas direct soothing and directive guidance of [**what / when**]98) to do are beneficial for younger children, they may [**intrude / intrigue**]99) on adolescents' [**autonomous / autonomy**]100) striving. In consequence, adolescents might pull away from, rather than turn toward, their parents in times of emotional crisis, [**if / unless**]101) parental practices are adjusted. More suitable in adolescence is [**direct / indirect**]102) support of autonomous emotion regulation, such as through interest in, as well as awareness and nonjudgmental acceptance of, adolescents' emotional experiences, and being available when the adolescent wants to talk.

다른 사람들로부터 감정과 감정을 다루는 방법을 배우는 감정 사회화는 어릴 때부터 시작되며 감정 조절발달에 기초적인 역할을 한다. 청소년기에는 또래나 미디어와 같은 가족 이외의 영향이 중요해지지만, 부모는 여전히 주된 사회화 주체이다. 예를 들어, 감정적 상황에 대한 부모 자신의 반응이 감정 조절의 롤모델이 되어 자녀가 비슷한 상황에서 유사한 반응을 보일 가능성을 높인다. 자녀가 정서적 어려움에 직면했을 때 부모의 (습관적) 행동 또한 감정 조절 발달에 영향을 미친다. 직접적인 위로와 어떻게 해야 하는지에 대한 지시적 안내가 어린 자녀에게는 도움이 되지만, 청소년의 자율성 추구를 방해할 수 있다. 결과적으로 부모의 행동이 조정되지 않는다면, 청소년은 정서적 위기 상황에서 부모에게 의지하기보다 오히려 부모로부터 멀어질 수 있다. 청소년기에 더 적합한 것은 청소년의 정서적 경험에 대한 인식과 무비판적 수용뿐만 아니라 (그에 대한) 관심, 그리고 청소년이 대화하고 싶을 때 곁에 있어 주는 것과 같은 방법으로 자율적 감정 조절을 간접적으로 지원하는 것이다.

31

Dancers often push [**them / themselves**]103) to the limits of their physical capabilities. But that push is [**guided / misguided**]104) if it is directed toward accomplishing something [**emotionally / physically**]105) impossible. For instance, a tall dancer with long feet may wish to perform repetitive [**horizontal / vertical**]106) jumps to fast music, pointing his feet [**during / while**]107) in the air and [**lowering / lowers**]108) his heels to the floor between jumps. That may be impossible no matter [**how / what**]109) strong the dancer is. But a short-footed dancer may have no trouble! [**Another / Other**]110) dancer may be struggling to [**compete / complete**]111) a half-turn in the air. Understanding the connection between a rapid turn rate and the alignment of the body close to the rotation axis [**tell / tells**]112) her how to accomplish her turn successfully. In [**both / either**]113) of these cases, understanding and working within the constraints imposed by nature and described by physical laws [**allow / allows**]114) dancers to work efficiently, [**maximizing / minimizing**]115) potential risk of injury.

무용수는 종종 자신의 신체 능력의 한계까지 자신을 밀어붙인다. 그러나 그렇게 밀어붙이는 것이 물리적으로 불가능한 것을 달성하는 쪽으로 향하게 된다면, 잘못 이해한 것이다. 예를 들어, 키가 크고 발이 긴 무용수가 공중에서 발끝을 뾰족하게 하고 점프 사이에 발뒤꿈치를 바닥에 내리면서 빠른 음악에 맞춰 반복적인 수직 점프를 수행하고 싶을 수 있다. 무용수가 아무리 힘이 좋을지라도 그것은 불가능할 수 있다. 하지만 발이 짧은 무용수는 전혀 문제가 없을 것이다! 또 다른 무용수는 공중에서 반 회전을 완성하려고 애쓰고 있을 수 있다. 빠른 회전 속도와 회전축에 가깝게 몸을 정렬하는 것의 연관성을 이해하는 것은 그 무용수에게 성공적으로 회전을 해내는 방법을 알려 준다. 이 두 경우 모두에서, 선천적으로 주어지고 물리적 법칙에 의해 설명되는 제약을 이해하고 그 안에서 움직이는 것은 잠재적인 부상 위험을 최소화하면서 무용수가 효율적으로 움직이게 해 준다.

32

We must [**deplore / explore**]116) the relationship between children's film production and consumption habits. The term "children's film" implies ownership by children — their cinema — but films [**suppose / supposedly**]117) made for children have always been consumed by audiences of all ages, particularly in commercial cinemas. The [**considerable / considerate**]118) crossover in audience composition for children's films can be shown by the fact that, in 2007, eleven Danish children's and youth films [**attracted / were attracted**]119) 59 percent of theatrical admissions, and in 2014, German children's films comprised seven out of the top twenty films at the national box office. This phenomenon corresponds with a broader, international embrace of [**that / what**]120) is seemingly children's culture among audiences of [**diverse / similar**]121) ages. The old prejudice that children's film is some other realm, [**separate / separating**]122) from (and forever subordinate to) a more legitimate cinema for adults [**are / is**]123) not supported by the realities of consumption: children's film is at the heart of [**contemporary / temporary**]124) popular culture.

우리는 어린이 영화 제작과 소비 습관 사이의 관계를 탐구해야 한다. '어린이 영화'라는 용어는 어린이에 의한 소유권, 즉 '그들의' 영화를 암시하지만, 소위 어린이를 위해 만들어진 영화는 특히 상업 영화에서, 항상 모든 연령대의 관객들에게 소비되어 왔다. 어린이 영화의 관객 구성에서 상당한 (연령 간의) 넘나듦이 있다는 것은, 2007년에 11개의 덴마크의 어린이 및 청소년 영화가 극장 입장객의 59퍼센트를 끌어 모았고 2014년에는 독일의 어린이영화가 전국 극장 흥행 수익 상위 20개 영화 중 7개를 차지했다는 사실에 의해 증명될 수 있다. 이 현상은 다양한 연령대의 관객들 사이에서 겉으로는 어린이 문화처럼 보이는 것이 더 광범위하고 국제적으로 수용되는 것과 일치한다. 어린이 영화가 성인을 위한 더 제대로 된 영화와는 별개의(그리고 영원히 하위의) 다른 영역이라는 오래된 편견은 소비의 실상에 의해 뒷받침되지 않는다. 즉, 어린이영화가 현대 대중문화의 중심에 있다.

33

Beethoven's drive to create something [**noble** / **novel**]125) is a reflection of his state of curiosity. Our brains experience a sense of reward when we create [**new something** / **something new**]126) in the process of exploring something [**certain** / **uncertain**]127), such as a musical phrase that we've never played or heard before. When our curiosity leads to something novel, the resulting [**toward** / **reward**]128) brings us a sense of pleasure. [**A** / **The**]129) number of investigators have modeled how curiosity influences musical composition. In the case of Beethoven, computer modeling [**focused** / **focusing**]130) on the thirty-two piano sonatas written after age thirteen [**revealed** / **revealing**]131) that the musical patterns found in all of Beethoven's music [**decreased** / **increased**]132) in later sonatas, [**during** / **while**]133) novel patterns, including patterns that were unique to a particular sonata, increased. In other words, Beethoven's music became [**less** / **more**]134) predictable over time as his curiosity drove the [**exploration** / **exploitation**]135) of new musical ideas. Curiosity is a powerful driver of human creativity.

새로운 것을 창작하려는 베토벤의 욕구는 그의 호기심 상태의 반영이다. 우리의 뇌는 우리가 이전에 연주하거나 들어본 적이 없는 악절과 같이 불확실한 것을 탐구하는 과정에서 새로운 것을 창작할 때 보상감을 경험한다. 우리의 호기심이 새로운 것으로 이어지면, 그 결과로 얻어지는 보상은 우리에게 쾌감을 가져다준다. 많은 연구자들이 음악 작곡에 호기심이 어떻게 영향을 미치는지를 모델링해 왔다. 베토벤의 경우, 13세 이후로 작곡된 32개의 피아노 소나타에 초점을 맞춘 컴퓨터 모델링에서 베토벤의 모든 음악에서 발견되는 음악 패턴이 후기 소나타에서는 감소한 반면, 특정 소나타에만 나타나는 패턴을 포함한 새로운 패턴은 증가한 것을 보여 주었다. 다시 말해, 베토벤의 호기심이 새로운 음악적 아이디어의 탐구를 이끌게 됨에 따라 그의 음악은 시간이 지날수록 덜 예측 가능하게 되었다. 호기심은 인간의 창의성의 강력한 원동력이다.

34

Technologists are always on the lookout for [**qualifiable** / **quantifiable**]136) metrics. Measurable inputs to a model [**are** / **is**]137) their lifeblood, and like a social scientist, a technologist needs to [**identify** / **identifying**]138) concrete measures, or "proxies," for [**accessing** / **assessing**]139) progress. This need for quantifiable proxies [**produce** / **produces**]140) a bias toward measuring things that are [**difficult** / **easy**]141) to quantify. But simple metrics can take us further away from the important goals we really care about, [**which** / **that**]142) may require [**complicated** / **complicating**]143) metrics or be extremely difficult, or perhaps impossible, to reduce to any measure. And when we have imperfect or bad proxies, we can easily fall under the illusion [**that** / **what**]144) we are solving for a good end without actually making genuine [**process** / **progress**]145) toward a worthy solution. The problem of proxies results [**from** / **in**]146) technologists frequently substituting [**that** / **what**]147) is measurable for what is meaningful. As the saying goes, "Not everything that counts can be counted, and not everything that can be counted counts."

기술자들은 항상 정량화할 수 있는 측정 기준을 찾고 있다. 모델에 측정 가능한 입력(을 하는 것)은 그들의 생명줄이며, 사회 과학자와 마찬가지로 기술자는 진척 상황을 평가하기 위한 구체적인 측정 방법, 즉 '프록시'를 식별할 필요가 있다. 이러한 정량화할 수 있는 프록시에 대한 필요성은 정량화하기 쉬운 것들을 측정하는 쪽으로 편향을 만든다. 하지만 단순한 측정기준은 우리가 정말로 신경 쓰는 중요한 목표로부터 우리를 더 멀어지게 할 수 있는데, 이 목표는 복잡한 측정 기준을 요구하거나, 또는 (이 목표를) 어떤 하나의 측정 방법만으로 한정(하여 측정)하기가 어렵거나 아마 불가능할 수도 있다. 그리고 우리가 불완전하거나 잘못된 프록시를 가지고 있을 때, 우리는 가치 있는 해결책을 향한 진정한 진전을 실제로 이루지 못하면서 좋은 목적을 위해 문제를 해결하고 있다는 착각에 쉽게 빠질 수 있다. 프록시의 문제는 기술자들이 흔히 의미 있는 것을 측정 가능한 것으로 대체하는 결과를 낳는다. 흔히 말하듯이, "중요한 모든 것들이 셀 수 있는 것은 아니고, 셀 수 있는 모든 것들이 중요한 것도 아니다."

35

We are the only species that [**season / seasons**]148) its food, deliberately altering it with the [**high / highly**]149) flavored plant parts we call herbs and spices. It's quite possible that our taste for spices has an evolutionary root. Many spices have antibacterial properties — in fact, common seasonings such as garlic, onion, and oregano [**inhabit / inhibit**]150) the growth of almost every bacterium tested. And the cultures that make the heaviest use of spices — think of the garlic and black pepper of Thai food, the ginger and coriander of India, the chili peppers of Mexico — [**come / comes**]151) from warmer climates, where bacterial spoilage is a [**bigger / minor**]152) issue. In contrast, the most lightly [**spiced / spicing**]153) cuisines — [**that / those**]154) of Scandinavia and northern Europe — are from cooler climates. Our [**unique / uniquely**]155) human attention to flavor, in this case the flavor of spices, turns out to [**had / have**]156) arisen as a matter of life and death.

우리는 음식에 양념을 하는 유일한 종으로, 허브와 향신료라고 부르는 강한 맛을 내는 식물의 부분을 이용하여 그것(음식)을 의도적으로 바꾼다. 향신료에 대한 우리의 미각은 진화적 뿌리를 가지고 있을 가능성이 높다. 많은 향신료가 항균성을 가지고 있는데, 실제로 마늘, 양파, 오레가노와 같은 흔한 조미료들이 거의 모든 확인된 박테리아의 성장을 억제한다. 그리고 태국 음식의 마늘과 후추, 인도의 생강과 고수, 멕시코의 고추를 생각해 보면, 향신료를 가장 많이 사용하는 문화권은 더 따뜻한 기후에서 유래하는데, 그곳에서는 박테리아에 의한 (음식의) 부패가 큰 문제이다. 반대로, 스칸디나비아와 북유럽의 요리같이 가장 향신료를 적게 쓰는 요리는 더 서늘한 기후에서 유래한다. 맛에 대한 인간 특유의 관심, 이 경우 향신료의 맛은 사느냐 죽느냐의 문제로서 생겨난 것으로 드러난다.

36

Development of the human body from a single cell provides many examples of the structural richness [**that / what**]157) is possible when the repeated production of random variation is combined with nonrandom selection. All phases of body development from embryo [**into / to**]158) adult exhibit random activities at the cellular level, and body formation [**depend / depends**]159) on the new possibilities generated by these activities coupled with selection of those outcomes that [**satisfies / satisfy**]160) previously builtin criteria. Always new structure is based on old structure, and at every stage selection [**favor / favors**]161) some cells and eliminates others. The survivors serve to produce new cells that undergo [**farther / further**]162) rounds of selection. Except in the immune system, cells and extensions of cells are not genetically [**selected / selecting**]163) during development, but rather, are positionally selected. Those in the right place [**that / what**]164) make the right connections are stimulated, and those that don't are eliminated. This process is much [**alike / like**]165) sculpting. A natural consequence of the strategy is great variability from individual to individual at the cell and molecular levels, even though large-scale structures are quite [**different / similar**]166).

단일 세포로부터 인체가 발달하는 것은 무작위적인 변이의 반복적 생성이 비무작위적인 선택과 결합될 때 가능해지는 구조적 풍부함의 많은 예를 제공한다. 배아에서 성체에 이르기까지 신체 발달의 모든 단계는 세포 수준에서는 무작위 활동을 보이고, 신체 형성은 이러한 활동(무작위 활동)에 의해 만들어진 새로운 가능성과 더불어, 이전에 확립된 기준을 만족시키는 결과물의 선택에 달려 있다. 항상 새로운 구조는 오래된 구조를 기반으로 하며, 모든 단계에서 선택은 일부 세포들을 선호하고 다른 세포들은 제거한다. 생존한 세포들은 추가적인 선택의 과정을 거치는 새로운 세포들을 만들어 내는 역할을 한다. 면역계를 제외하면 세포와 세포의 확장은 발달 과정에서 유전적으로 선택되는 것이 아니라 위치에 의해 선택된다. 제 자리에서 제대로 된 연결을 만들어 낸 것(세포)들은 활성화되고, 그렇지 않은 것들은 제거된다. 이 과정은 마치 조각을 하는 것과 같다. 이 전략의 필연적 결과는 전체 구조가 상당히 비슷하더라도 세포와 분자 수준에서 개인마다 큰 변이성이 있다는 것이다.

37

In order to bring the ever-increasing costs of home care for elderly and [**need / needy**]167) persons under control, managers of home care providers have introduced management systems. These systems specify tasks of home care workers and the time and [**budget / to budget**]168) available to perform these tasks. Electronic reporting systems require home care workers to report [**in / on**]169) their activities and the time spent, thus making the [**contribution / distribution**]170) of time and money [**visible / invisible**]171) and, in the perception of managers, controllable. This, in the view of managers, has contributed to the resolution of the problem. The home care workers, on the other hand, may perceive their work not as a set of [**combined / separate**]172) tasks to be performed as [**efficient / efficiently**]173) as possible, but as a service to [**be provided / provided**]174) to a client with whom they may have developed a relationship. This includes having [**conversations / reservations**]175) with clients and enquiring about the person's wellbeing. [**Restricting / Restricted**]176) time and the requirement to report may be perceived as obstacles that [**make / makes**]177) it impossible to deliver the service that is needed. If the management systems are too rigid, this may result [**from / in**]178) home care workers [**become / becoming**]179) overloaded and demotivated.

노인과 빈곤층을 위한 재택 간호의 계속적으로 증가하는 비용을 통제하기 위해 재택 간호 제공 업체의 관리자는 관리 시스템을 도입했다. 이러한 시스템은 재택 간호 종사자의 업무와 이러한 업무를 수행하는데 사용할 수 있는 시간과 예산을 명시한다. 전자 보고 시스템은 재택 간호 종사자가 자신의 활동과 소요시간을 보고하도록 요구하므로 시간과 비용의 분배를 잘 보이게 만들고, 관리자의 입장에서는 통제 가능하게 만든다. 관리자의 관점에서는, 이것이 문제 해결에 기여해 왔다. 반면에, 재택 간호 종사자들은 자신의 업무를 가능한 한 효율적으로 수행되어야 하는 일련의 분리된 업무가 아니라, 그들이 관계를 맺어온 고객에게 제공되는 서비스로 인식할 것이다. 이것은 고객과 대화를 나누고 고객의 안부를 묻는 것을 포함한다. 제한된 시간과 보고를 해야 한다는 요구 사항은 필요한 서비스를 제공하는 것을 불가능하게 하는 장애물로 여겨질 것이다. 만약 관리 시스템이 너무 엄격하면, 이것은 재택 간호 종사자가 너무 많은 부담을 지게 되고 의욕을 잃는 결과를 초래할 것이다.

38

It is a common assumption [**that / what**]180) most vagrant birds are ultimately doomed, aside from the rare cases where individuals are able to reorientate and return to their normal ranges. In turn, it is also commonly assumed that vagrancy itself is a [**relative / relatively**]181) unimportant biological phenomenon. This is undoubtedly true for the majority of cases, as the [**least / most**]182) likely outcome of any given vagrancy event is that the individual will fail to find enough resources, and/or be exposed to [**hospitable / inhospitable**]183) environmental conditions, and perish. However, there are many lines of evidence to suggest that vagrancy can, on rare occasions, dramatically [**alter / preserve**]184) the fate of populations, species or even whole ecosystems. Despite being [**frequent / infrequent**]185), these events can be extremely important when [**viewed / viewing**]186) at the timescales over which ecological and evolutionary processes unfold. The most profound consequences of vagrancy [**relate / relates**]187) to the establishment of new breeding sites, new migration routes and wintering locations. Each of these can occur through [**different / similar**]188) mechanisms, and at different frequencies, and they each have their own unique importance.

무리에서 떨어져 헤매는 대부분의 새들은 방향을 다시 잡고 그들의 일반적인 (서식) 범위로 돌아갈 수 있는 드문 경우의 개체들을 제외하고, 궁극적으로 죽을 운명이라는 것이 일반적인 가정이다. 결국, 무리에서 떨어져 헤매는 것 자체가 비교적 중요하지 않은 생물학적 현상이라고 일반적으로 여겨지기도 한다. 이것은 의심할 여지없이 대부분의 경우에 사실인데, 무리에서 떨어져 헤매는 어떤 경우든 가장 가능성 있는 결과는 개체가 충분한 자원을 찾지 못하고/못하거나, 살기 힘든 환경 조건에 노출되어 죽기 때문이다. 하지만, 드문 경우에, 무리에서 떨어져 헤매는 것이 개체 수, 종, 심지어 생태계 전체의 운명을 극적으로 바꿀 수 있다는 것을 시사하는 많은 증거가 있다. 드물기는 하지만, 이러한 경우들은 생태학적이고 진화적인 과정이 진행되는 시간의 관점에서 볼 때 매우 중요할 수 있다. 무리에서 떨어져 헤매는 것의 가장 중대한 결과는 새로운 번식지, 새로운 이동 경로 및 월동 장소의 확보와 관련이 있다. 이들 각각은 서로 다른 메커니즘을 통해, 서로 다른 빈도로 발생할 수 있으며, 각각 고유한 중요성을 가지고 있다.

39

Intuition can be great, but it ought to be hard-earned. Experts, for example, are able to think on their feet [**because / because of**]189) they've invested thousands of hours in learning and practice: their intuition has become data-driven. Only then are they able to act quickly in accordance with their [**externalized / internalized**]190) expertise and evidence-based experience. Yet most people are not experts, though they often think they [**are / do**]191). Most of us, especially when we interact with others [**in / on**]192) social media, act with expert-like speed and conviction, [**offer / offering**]193) a wide range of opinions on global crises, without the substance of knowledge that supports [**it / them**]194). And thanks to AI, which ensures that our messages [**are delivered / delivered**]195) to an audience more inclined to [**believe / believing**]196) it, our delusions of expertise can be reinforced by our personal filter bubble. We have an interesting tendency to [**find / finding**]197) people more open-minded, rational, and sensible when they think just like us.

직관은 탁월할 수 있지만, 힘들여 얻은 것이어야 한다. 예를 들어, 전문가들은 수천 시간을 학습과 경험에 투자하여, 데이터로부터 직관이 얻어졌기 때문에 즉각적으로 생각할 수 있다. 그래야만 그들이 내재화된 전문 지식과 증거에 기반한 경험에 따라 빠르게 행동할 수 있다. 그러나 대부분의 사람들은 종종 스스로를 전문가라고 생각하지만 실제로는 전문가가 아니다. 우리 중 대부분은, 특히 소셜 미디어에서 다른 사람들과 소통할 때, 전문가와 같은 속도와 확신을 가지고 행동하며, 이를 뒷받침하는 지식의 실체 없이 국제적 위기에 대한 다양한 의견을 제시한다. 그리고 우리의 메시지가 그것을 더 믿으려는 성향이 있는 독자에게 확실히 전달되도록 하는 인공 지능 덕분에, 전문 지식에 대한 우리의 착각은 개인적 필터 버블(자신의 관심사에 맞게 필터링된 정보만을 접하게 되는 현상)에 의해 강화될 수 있다. 우리는 남들이 우리와 똑같이 생각할 때 그들을 더 개방적이고 합리적이며 분별 있다고 여기는 흥미로운 경향을 가지고 있다.

40

The fast-growing, tremendous amount of data, collected and stored in large and numerous data repositories, has far [**exceeded / exceeding**]198) our human ability for understanding without powerful tools. As a result, data collected in large data repositories [**become / becomes**]199) "data tombs" — data archives that are [**frequently / hardly**]200) visited. Important decisions are often made based not on the information–rich data stored in data repositories but [**rather / rather than**]201) on a decision maker's instinct, simply because the decision maker does not have the tools to [**contract / extract**]202) the valuable knowledge hidden in the vast amounts of data. Efforts have been made to develop expert system and knowledge-based technologies, which typically rely on users or domain experts to [**manual / manually**]203) input knowledge into knowledge bases. However, this procedure is likely to cause biases and errors and is extremely costly and time consuming. The [**widened / widening**]204) gap between data and information calls for the systematic development of tools that can turn data tombs into "golden nuggets" of knowledge.

빠르게 증가하는 엄청난 양의 데이터는, 크고 많은 데이터 저장소에 수집되고 저장되어, 우리 인간이 효과적인 도구 없이는 이해할 수 있는 능력을 훨씬 뛰어 넘었다. 결과적으로, 대규모 데이터 저장소에서 수집된 데이터는 '데이터 무덤', 즉 찾는 사람이 거의 없는 데이터 보관소가 된다. 중요한 의사 결정이 종종 데이터 저장소에 저장된 정보가 풍부한 데이터가 아닌 의사결정자의 직관에 기반하여 내려지기도 하는데, 이는 단지 의사 결정자가 방대한 양의 데이터에 숨겨진 가치 있는 지식을 추출할 수 있는 도구를 가지고 있지않기 때문이다. 전문가 시스템과 지식 기반 기술을 개발하려는 노력이 있어 왔는데, 이는 일반적으로 사용자나 분야(별) 전문가가 지식을 '수동으로' 지식 기반에 입력하는 것에 의존한다. 이 방법은 편견과 오류를 일으키기 쉽고 비용과 시간이 엄청나게 든다. 점점 더 벌어지는 데이터와 정보 간의 격차로 인해 데이터 무덤을 지식의 '금괴'로 바꿀 수 있는 도구의 체계적인 개발이 요구된다.

41 ~ 42

It's [**true** / untrue]²⁰⁵⁾ that teens can focus on two things at once — what they're doing is shifting their attention from one task to another. In this digital age, teens wire their brains to make these shifts very quickly, but they are still, like everyone else, paying attention to one thing at a time, sequentially. Common sense tells us multitasking should increase brain activity, but Carnegie Mellon University scientists using the [last / **latest**]²⁰⁶⁾ brain imaging technology find it doesn't. As a matter of fact, they discovered that multitasking actually decreases brain activity. [Either / **Neither**]²⁰⁷⁾ task is done as well as if each were performed [individual / **individually**]²⁰⁸⁾. Fractions of a second are lost every time we make a switch, and a person's interrupted task can take 50 percent longer to finish, with 50 percent more errors. Turns out the latest brain research supports the old advice "one thing at a time."

It's not that kids can't do some tasks [simultaneous / **simultaneously**]²⁰⁹⁾. But if two tasks are performed at once, one of them has to be familiar. Our brains perform a familiar task on "automatic pilot" [during / **while**]²¹⁰⁾ really paying attention to the other one. That's [because / **why**]²¹¹⁾ insurance companies consider talking on a cell phone and driving to be as [**dangerous** / dangerously]²¹²⁾ as driving while drunk — it's the driving that goes on "automatic pilot" while the conversation really holds our attention. Our kids may be living in the Information Age but our brains have not [been redesigned / **redesigned**]²¹³⁾ yet.

십대들이 동시에 두 가지 일에 집중할 수 있다는 것은 사실이 아니며, 그들이 하고 있는 것은 한 작업에서 다른 작업으로 주의를 전환하는 것이다. 디지털 시대에, 십대의 뇌는 매우 빠르게 작업을 전환하도록 발달하지만, 여전히 다른 모든 사람들과 마찬가지로 십대들도 한 번에 한 가지씩 순차적으로 주의를 기울이고 있다. 상식적으로 멀티태스킹이 뇌 활동을 증가시킬 것이라고 생각하지만, Carnegie Mellon 대학의 과학자들은 최신 뇌 영상 기술을 사용하여 그렇지 않다는 것을 발견했다. 사실, 그들은 멀티태스킹이 실제로는 두뇌 활동을 감소시킨다는 것을 발견했다. 어느 작업도 각각 개별적으로 수행될 때만큼 잘 되지 못한다. 우리가 (작업을) 전환할 때마다 시간이 아주 조금씩 낭비되며, 중단된 작업은 완료하기까지 50퍼센트 더 오래 걸리고, 50퍼센트 더 많은 오류가 발생할 수 있다. 최신 뇌 연구가 '한 번에 한 가지 일만 하라'는 오래된 조언을 뒷받침하는 것으로 드러났다.

아이들이 동시에 여러 작업을 할 수 없다는 것은 아니다. 하지만 동시에 두 가지 작업이 수행된다면, 그 중 하나는 익숙한 작업이어야 한다. 우리의 뇌는 익숙한 작업은 '자동 조종' 상태에서 수행하고 실제로는 다른 작업에 주의를 기울인다. 그것이 보험 회사가 휴대전화로 통화하면서 운전하는 것을 술에 취한 상태에서 운전하는 것만큼 위험한 것으로 간주하는 이유이다. 대화가 실제로 우리의 주의를 끌고 있는 동안 '자동조종' 상태에서 수행되는 것은 운전이다. 우리 아이들이 정보화 시대에 살고 있을지 모르지만, 우리의 뇌는 아직 (정보화 시대에 맞게) 재설계되지 않았다.

43 ~ 45

Christine was a cat owner who loved her furry companion, Leo. One morning, she noticed that Leo was not feeling well. Concerned for her beloved cat, Christine decided to take him to the animal hospital. As she always brought Leo to this hospital, she was certain [**that / what**]214) the vet knew well about Leo. She desperately hoped Leo got the necessary care as soon as possible. The waiting room was filled with [**other / the other**]215) pet owners. Finally, it was Leo's turn to see the vet. Christine watched as the vet gently examined him. The vet said, "I think Leo has a minor infection." "Infection? Will he be okay?" asked Christine. "We need to do some tests to see if he is infected. But for the tests, it's best for Leo to stay here," [**implied / replied**]216) the vet. It was [**heartbroken / heartbreaking**]217) for Christine to leave Leo at the animal hospital, but she had to accept it was for the best. "I'll call you with updates as soon as we know anything," said the vet. Throughout the day, Christine anxiously awaited news about Leo. Later that day, the phone rang and it was the vet. "The tests [**released / revealed**]218) a minor infection. Leo needs some [**mediation / medication**]219) and rest, but he'll be back to his playful self soon." Relieved to hear the news, Christine rushed back to the animal hospital to pick up Leo. The vet provided detailed instructions on how to administer the medication and shared tips for a speedy recovery. Back at home, Christine created a comfortable space for Leo to rest and heal. She patted him with love and attention, [**ensured / ensuring**]220) that he would recover in no time. As the days passed, Leo gradually regained his strength and playful spirit.

Christine은 고양이 주인으로 그녀의 털북숭이 반려동물인 Leo를 사랑한다. 어느 날 아침, 그녀는 Leo의 몸 상태가 좋지 않다는 것을 알게 되었다. 사랑하는 고양이가 걱정되어서, Christine은 Leo를 동물병원에 데려가기로 결심했다. 그녀가 항상 Leo를 이 병원에 데려왔기 때문에, 수의사가 Leo에 대해 잘 알고 있을 것이라고 그녀는 확신했다. Leo가 필요한 보살핌을 가능한 한 빨리 받기를 그녀는 간절히 바랐다. 대기실은 다른 반려동물의 주인들로 꽉 차 있었다. 마침내, Leo가 수의사를 만날 차례가 되었다. Christine은 수의사가 Leo를 조심스럽게 진찰하는 모습을 지켜보았다. "저는 Leo에게 경미한 감염이 있다고 생각합니다." 수의사가 말했다. "감염이요? Leo는 괜찮을까요?" Christine이 물었다. "감염 여부를 알기위해 우리는 몇 가지 검사를 할 필요가 있습니다. 하지만 검사를 위해서 Leo가 여기 머무는 것이 가장 좋습니다." 수의사가 대답했다. Leo를 동물병원에 두고 가는 것이 Christine에게는 가슴 아팠지만, 그녀는 그것이 최선이라는 것을 받아들여야만 했다. "저희가 뭔가 알게 되는 즉시 당신에게 전화로 새로운 소식을 알려 드리겠습니다."라고 수의사가 말했다. 그날 내내 Christine은 초조하게 Leo에 대한 소식을 기다렸다. 그날 늦게 전화가 울렸고 그것(전화를 건사람)은 수의사였다. "검사 결과 경미한 감염이 발견되었습니다. Leo는 약간의 약물 치료와 휴식이 필요하긴 하지만 곧 장난기 넘치는 모습으로 돌아올 거예요." 그 소식을 듣고 안도하며, Christine은 Leo를 데리러 동물병원으로 서둘러 되돌아갔다. 수의사는 약을 투여하는 방법을 자세히 설명해주고 빠른 회복을 위한 조언을 했다. 집으로 돌아와서, Christine은 Leo가 쉬고 회복할 수 있는 편안한 공간을 만들었다. 그녀는 Leo가 금방 회복할 수 있도록 사랑과 관심으로 Leo를 쓰다듬어 주었다. 며칠이 지나자, Leo는 점차 체력과 장난기 넘치는 활기를 되찾았다.

2024 고2 3월 모의고사　　❷ 회차 :　　　점 / 220점

❶ voca　❷ text　❸ [/]　❹ ____　❺ quiz 1　❻ quiz 2　❼ quiz 3　❽ quiz 4　❾ quiz 5

18

Dear Art Crafts People of Greenville, / For the [**annual / annually**]¹⁾ Crafts Fair on May 25 from 1 p.m. to 6 p.m., the Greenville Community Center is providing booth spaces to rent as in [**precious / previous**]²⁾ years. To reserve your space, please visit our website and [**complete / to complete**]³⁾ a registration form by April 20. The rental fee is $50. All the money we receive from rental fees [**go / goes**]⁴⁾ to support upcoming activities throughout the year. We expect all available spaces to be [**full / fully**]⁵⁾ booked soon, so don't get [**leaving / left**]⁶⁾ out. We hope to see you at the fair.

19

Sarah, a young artist with a love for painting, [**entered / entered into**]⁷⁾ a local art contest. As she looked at the amazing artworks made by [**others / the others**]⁸⁾, her [**confidence / coincidence**]⁹⁾ dropped. She quietly thought, 'I might not win an award.' The moment of judgment arrived, and the judges began announcing winners one by one. It wasn't until the end [**that / what**]¹⁰⁾ she heard her name. The head of the judges said, "Congratulations, Sarah Parker! You won first prize. We loved the uniqueness of your work." Sarah was [**overcame / overcome**]¹¹⁾ with joy, and she couldn't stop [**smiling / to smile**]¹²⁾. This experience meant more than just winning; it [**confirmed / conformed**]¹³⁾ her identity as an artist.

20

Too many times people, especially in today's generation, [**expect / expecting**]¹⁴⁾ things to just happen overnight. When we have these false expectations, it tends to discourage us from [**continue / continuing**]¹⁵⁾ to move forward. [**Because / Because of**]¹⁶⁾ this is a high tech society, everything we want [**have / has**]¹⁷⁾ to be within the parameters of our comfort and [**convenient / convenience**]¹⁸⁾. If it doesn't happen fast enough, we're tempted to lose interest. So many people don't want to take the time it requires to be [**successful / successive**]¹⁹⁾. Success is not a matter of [**mere / merely**]²⁰⁾ desire; you should develop patience in order to achieve it. Have you fallen prey [**for / to**]²¹⁾ impatience? Great things take time to build.

21

If you [**had / have**]²²⁾ wanted to create a "self-driving" car in the 1950s, your best option might have been to strap a brick to the accelerator. Yes, the vehicle would have been able to move forward on its own, but it could not slow down, stop, or turn to avoid barriers. Obviously not [**ideal / ideally**]²³⁾. But does that mean the entire concept of the self-driving car is not worth [**pursuing / to pursue**]²⁴⁾? No, it only means [**that / what**]²⁵⁾ at the time we did not yet have the tools we now [**possess / obsess**]²⁶⁾ to help enable vehicles to operate both [**autonomous / autonomously**]²⁷⁾ and [**safe / safely.**]²⁸⁾ This once-distant dream now seems within our reach. It is [**more / much**]²⁹⁾ the same story in medicine. Two decades ago, we were still taping bricks to accelerators. Today, we are approaching the point [**where / which**]³⁰⁾ we can begin to bring some appropriate technology to bear in ways that [**advance / advances**]³¹⁾ our understanding of patients as unique individuals. In fact, many patients are already wearing devices that [**monitor / monitors**]³²⁾ their conditions in real time, [**which / that**]³³⁾ allows doctors to talk to their patients in a specific, refined, and feedback-driven way that was not even possible a decade ago.

22

We tend to [**overrate / underrate**]³⁴⁾ the impact of new technologies in part [**because / because of**]³⁵⁾ older technologies have become absorbed into the furniture of our lives, so as to be almost [**invisible / visible**]³⁶⁾. Take the baby bottle. Here is a simple implement [**that / what**]³⁷⁾ has transformed a [**fundamental / fundamentally**]³⁸⁾ human experience for vast numbers of infants and mothers, yet it finds no place in our histories of technology. This technology might be thought of as a classic time-shifting device, as it enables mothers to exercise [**less / more**]³⁹⁾ control over the timing of feeding. It can also function to save time, as bottle feeding [**allow / allows**]⁴⁰⁾ for someone else to substitute for the mother's time. Potentially, therefore, it has huge implications for the management of time in everyday life, yet it is entirely [**overlooking / overlooked**]⁴¹⁾ in discussions of high-speed society.

23

Empathy is frequently listed as one of the most desired [**skill / skills**]⁴²⁾ in an employer or employee, although without [**specify / specifying**]⁴³⁾ exactly what is meant by empathy. Some businesses stress cognitive empathy, [**emphasizing / to emphasize**]⁴⁴⁾ the need for leaders to understand the perspective of employees and customers when negotiating deals and [**making / to make**]⁴⁵⁾ decisions. [**Another / Others**]⁴⁶⁾ stress affective empathy and empathic concern, emphasizing the ability of leaders to gain trust [**from / in**]⁴⁷⁾ employees and customers by treating [**them / themselves**]⁴⁸⁾ with real concern and compassion. When some consultants argue that [**successful / successive**]⁴⁹⁾ companies foster empathy, what that [**translate / translates**]⁵⁰⁾ to is that companies should conduct good market research. In other words, an "empathic" company understands the needs and wants of [**its / their**]⁵¹⁾ customers and [**seek / seeks**]⁵²⁾ to fulfill those needs and wants. When some people speak of design with empathy, [**what / where**]⁵³⁾ that translates to is that companies should take into account the [**broad / specific**]⁵⁴⁾ needs of [**different / similar**]⁵⁵⁾ populations — the blind, the deaf, the elderly, non-English speakers, the color-blind, and so on — when designing products.

24

The most prevalent problem kids report is [**that / what**]⁵⁶⁾ they feel like they need to be accessible at all times. [**Because / Because of**]⁵⁷⁾ technology allows for it, they feel an obligation. It's easy for most of us to relate — you probably feel the same pressure in your own life! It is really challenging to deal with the fact [**that / where**]⁵⁸⁾ we're human and can't always respond [**instant / instantly**]⁵⁹⁾. For a teen or tween who's still learning the ins and outs of social interactions, it's even [**better / worse**]⁶⁰⁾. Here's how this behavior plays out sometimes: Your child [**texts / texting**]⁶¹⁾ one of his friends, and the friend doesn't text back right away. Now it's easy for your child to think, "This person doesn't want to be my friend anymore!" So he texts again, and again, and again — "[**blowing / blows**]⁶²⁾ up their phone." This can be stress-[**induced / inducing**]⁶³⁾ and even read as [**aggressive / progressive**]⁶⁴⁾ . But you can see how [**east / easily**]⁶⁵⁾ this could happen.

25

The graph above shows the animal protein consumption [**measuring** / **measured**]66) as the average daily [**supply** / **supplement**]67) per person in three different countries in 2020. The U.S. showed the largest amount of total animal protein consumption per person among the three countries. Eggs and Dairy was the top animal protein consumption source among four categories in the U.S., [**followed** / **following**]68) by Meat and Poultry at 22.4g and 20.6g, [**respective** / **respectively**]69). Unlike the U.S., Brazil consumed the most animal protein from Meat, with Eggs and Dairy being the second most. Japan had less than 50g of the total animal protein consumption per person, [**which** / **that**]70) was the smallest among the three countries. Fish and Seafood, which was the [**least** / **less**]71) consumed animal protein consumption source in the U.S. and Brazil, [**ranked** / **ranking**]72) the highest in Japan.

26

Theodore von Kármán, a Hungarian-American engineer, was one of the greatest [**mind** / **minds**]73) of the twentieth century. He was born in Hungary and [**at** / **in**]74) an early age, he showed a talent [**for** / **at**]75) math and science. In 1908, he [**received** / **has received**]76) a doctoral degree in engineering at the University of Göttingen in Germany. In the 1920s, he began traveling as a lecturer and consultant to industry. He was invited to the United States to advise engineers [**in** / **on**]77) the design of a wind tunnel at California Institute of Technology (Caltech). He became the director of the Guggenheim Aeronautical Laboratory at Caltech in 1930. Later, he was [**awarded** / **rewarded**]78) the National Medal of Science [**for** / **in**]79) his leadership in science and engineering.

29

For years, many psychologists [**had** / **have**]80) held [**strong** / **strongly**]81) to the belief that the key to [**address** / **addressing**]82) negative health habits is to change behavior. This, more than values and attitudes, [**are** / **is**]83) the part of personality that is easiest to change. Ingestive habits such as smoking, drinking and various eating behaviors are the most common health concerns [**targeted** / **targeting**]84) for behavioral changes. Process-addiction behaviors (workaholism, shopaholism, and the like) fall into this category as well. [**Mental** / **Physical**]85) imagery combined with power of suggestion was taken up as the premise of behavioral medicine to help people [**change** / **changing**]86) negative health behaviors into positive ones. Although this technique alone will not produce changes, when used alongside [**another** / **other**]87) behavior modification tactics and coping strategies, behavioral changes have proved [**affective** / **effective**]88) for some people. What mental imagery does is [**force** / **reinforce**]89) a new desired behavior. Repeated use of images [**reinforce** / **reinforces**]90) the desired behavior more [**stronger** / **strongly**]91) over time.

30

Emotion socialization — learning from [**another** / **other**]92) people about emotions and how to deal with them — starts early in life and plays a foundational role for emotion regulation development. Although extra-familial influences, such as peers or media, [**gain** / **gaining**]93) in importance during adolescence, parents remain the primary socialization agents. For example, their own responses to emotional situations [**serve** / **serves**]94) as a role model for emotion regulation, [**increase** / **increasing**]95) the likelihood that their children will show similar reactions in [**comparable** / **comparative**]96) situations. Parental practices at times when their children are faced with emotional challenges also [**impact** / **impacts**]97) emotion regulation development. Whereas direct soothing and directive guidance of [**what** / **when**]98) to do are beneficial for younger children, they may [**intrude** / **intrigue**]99) on adolescents' [**autonomous** / **autonomy**]100) striving. In consequence, adolescents might pull away from, rather than turn toward, their parents in times of emotional crisis, [**if** / **unless**]101) parental practices are adjusted. More suitable in adolescence is [**direct** / **indirect**]102) support of autonomous emotion regulation, such as through interest in, as well as awareness and nonjudgmental acceptance of, adolescents' emotional experiences, and being available when the adolescent wants to talk.

31

Dancers often push [**them / themselves**]103) to the limits of their physical capabilities. But that push is [**guided / misguided**]104) if it is directed toward accomplishing something [**emotionally / physically**]105) impossible. For instance, a tall dancer with long feet may wish to perform repetitive [**horizontal / vertical**]106) jumps to fast music, pointing his feet [**during / while**]107) in the air and [**lowering / lowers**]108) his heels to the floor between jumps. That may be impossible no matter [**how / what**]109) strong the dancer is. But a short-footed dancer may have no trouble! [**Another / Other**]110) dancer may be struggling to [**compete / complete**]111) a half-turn in the air. Understanding the connection between a rapid turn rate and the alignment of the body close to the rotation axis [**tell / tells**]112) her how to accomplish her turn successfully. In [**both / either**]113) of these cases, understanding and working within the constraints imposed by nature and described by physical laws [**allow / allows**]114) dancers to work efficiently, [**maximizing / minimizing**]115) potential risk of injury.

32

We must [**deplore / explore**]116) the relationship between children's film production and consumption habits. The term "children's film" implies ownership by children — their cinema — but films [**suppose / supposedly**]117) made for children have always been consumed by audiences of all ages, particularly in commercial cinemas. The [**considerable / considerate**]118) crossover in audience composition for children's films can be shown by the fact that, in 2007, eleven Danish children's and youth films [**attracted / were attracted**]119) 59 percent of theatrical admissions, and in 2014, German children's films comprised seven out of the top twenty films at the national box office. This phenomenon corresponds with a broader, international embrace of [**that / what**]120) is seemingly children's culture among audiences of [**diverse / similar**]121) ages. The old prejudice that children's film is some other realm, [**separate / separating**]122) from (and forever subordinate to) a more legitimate cinema for adults [**are / is**]123) not supported by the realities of consumption: children's film is at the heart of [**contemporary / temporary**]124) popular culture.

33

Beethoven's drive to create something [**noble / novel**]125) is a reflection of his state of curiosity. Our brains experience a sense of reward when we create [**new something / something new**]126) in the process of exploring something [**certain / uncertain**]127), such as a musical phrase that we've never played or heard before. When our curiosity leads to something novel, the resulting [**toward / reward**]128) brings us a sense of pleasure. [**A / The**]129) number of investigators have modeled how curiosity influences musical composition. In the case of Beethoven, computer modeling [**focused / focusing**]130) on the thirty-two piano sonatas written after age thirteen [**revealed / revealing**]131) that the musical patterns found in all of Beethoven's music [**decreased / increased**]132) in later sonatas, [**during / while**]133) novel patterns, including patterns that were unique to a particular sonata, increased. In other words, Beethoven's music became [**less / more**]134) predictable over time as his curiosity drove the [**exploration / exploitation**]135) of new musical ideas. Curiosity is a powerful driver of human creativity.

34

Technologists are always on the lookout for [**qualifiable** / **quantifiable**]136) metrics. Measurable inputs to a model [**are** / **is**]137) their lifeblood, and like a social scientist, a technologist needs to [**identify** / **identifying**]138) concrete measures, or "proxies," for [**accessing** / **assessing**]139) progress. This need for quantifiable proxies [**produce** / **produces**]140) a bias toward measuring things that are [**difficult** / **easy**]141) to quantify. But simple metrics can take us further away from the important goals we really care about, [**which** / **that**]142) may require [**complicated** / **complicating**]143) metrics or be extremely difficult, or perhaps impossible, to reduce to any measure. And when we have imperfect or bad proxies, we can easily fall under the illusion [**that** / **what**]144) we are solving for a good end without actually making genuine [**process** / **progress**]145) toward a worthy solution. The problem of proxies results [**from** / **in**]146) technologists frequently substituting [**that** / **what**]147) is measurable for what is meaningful. As the saying goes, "Not everything that counts can be counted, and not everything that can be counted counts."

35

We are the only species that [**season** / **seasons**]148) its food, deliberately altering it with the [**high** / **highly**]149) flavored plant parts we call herbs and spices. It's quite possible that our taste for spices has an evolutionary root. Many spices have antibacterial properties — in fact, common seasonings such as garlic, onion, and oregano [**inhabit** / **inhibit**]150) the growth of almost every bacterium tested. And the cultures that make the heaviest use of spices — think of the garlic and black pepper of Thai food, the ginger and coriander of India, the chili peppers of Mexico — [**come** / **comes**]151) from warmer climates, where bacterial spoilage is a [**bigger** / **minor**]152) issue. In contrast, the most lightly [**spiced** / **spicing**]153) cuisines — [**that** / **those**]154) of Scandinavia and northern Europe — are from cooler climates. Our [**unique** / **uniquely**]155) human attention to flavor, in this case the flavor of spices, turns out to [**had** / **have**]156) arisen as a matter of life and death.

36

Development of the human body from a single cell provides many examples of the structural richness [**that** / **what**]157) is possible when the repeated production of random variation is combined with nonrandom selection. All phases of body development from embryo [**into** / **to**]158) adult exhibit random activities at the cellular level, and body formation [**depend** / **depends**]159) on the new possibilities generated by these activities coupled with selection of those outcomes that [**satisfies** / **satisfy**]160) previously builtin criteria. Always new structure is based on old structure, and at every stage selection [**favor** / **favors**]161) some cells and eliminates others. The survivors serve to produce new cells that undergo [**farther** / **further**]162) rounds of selection. Except in the immune system, cells and extensions of cells are not genetically [**selected** / **selecting**]163) during development, but rather, are positionally selected. Those in the right place [**that** / **what**]164) make the right connections are stimulated, and those that don't are eliminated. This process is much [**alike** / **like**]165) sculpting. A natural consequence of the strategy is great variability from individual to individual at the cell and molecular levels, even though large-scale structures are quite [**different** / **similar**]166).

37

In order to bring the ever-increasing costs of home care for elderly and [**need / needy**]¹⁶⁷⁾ persons under control, managers of home care providers have introduced management systems. These systems specify tasks of home care workers and the time and [**budget / to budget**]¹⁶⁸⁾ available to perform these tasks. Electronic reporting systems require home care workers to report [**in / on**]¹⁶⁹⁾ their activities and the time spent, thus making the [**contribution / distribution**]¹⁷⁰⁾ of time and money [**visible / invisible**]¹⁷¹⁾ and, in the perception of managers, controllable. This, in the view of managers, has contributed to the resolution of the problem. The home care workers, on the other hand, may perceive their work not as a set of [**combined / separate**]¹⁷²⁾ tasks to be performed as [**efficient / efficiently**]¹⁷³⁾ as possible, but as a service to [**be provided / provided**]¹⁷⁴⁾ to a client with whom they may have developed a relationship. This includes having [**conversations / reservations**]¹⁷⁵⁾ with clients and enquiring about the person's wellbeing. [**Restricting / Restricted**]¹⁷⁶⁾ time and the requirement to report may be perceived as obstacles that [**make / makes**]¹⁷⁷⁾ it impossible to deliver the service that is needed. If the management systems are too rigid, this may result [**from / in**]¹⁷⁸⁾ home care workers [**become / becoming**]¹⁷⁹⁾ overloaded and demotivated.

38

It is a common assumption [**that / what**]¹⁸⁰⁾ most vagrant birds are ultimately doomed, aside from the rare cases where individuals are able to reorientate and return to their normal ranges. In turn, it is also commonly assumed that vagrancy itself is a [**relative / relatively**]¹⁸¹⁾ unimportant biological phenomenon. This is undoubtedly true for the majority of cases, as the [**least / most**]¹⁸²⁾ likely outcome of any given vagrancy event is that the individual will fail to find enough resources, and/or be exposed to [**hospitable / inhospitable**]¹⁸³⁾ environmental conditions, and perish. However, there are many lines of evidence to suggest that vagrancy can, on rare occasions, dramatically [**alter / preserve**]¹⁸⁴⁾ the fate of populations, species or even whole ecosystems. Despite being [**frequent / infrequent**]¹⁸⁵⁾, these events can be extremely important when [**viewed / viewing**]¹⁸⁶⁾ at the timescales over which ecological and evolutionary processes unfold. The most profound consequences of vagrancy [**relate / relates**]¹⁸⁷⁾ to the establishment of new breeding sites, new migration routes and wintering locations. Each of these can occur through [**different / similar**]¹⁸⁸⁾ mechanisms, and at different frequencies, and they each have their own unique importance.

39

Intuition can be great, but it ought to be hard-earned. Experts, for example, are able to think on their feet [**because / because of**]¹⁸⁹⁾ they've invested thousands of hours in learning and practice: their intuition has become data-driven. Only then are they able to act quickly in accordance with their [**externalized / internalized**]¹⁹⁰⁾ expertise and evidence-based experience. Yet most people are not experts, though they often think they [**are / do**]¹⁹¹⁾. Most of us, especially when we interact with others [**in / on**]¹⁹²⁾ social media, act with expert-like speed and conviction, [**offer / offering**]¹⁹³⁾ a wide range of opinions on global crises, without the substance of knowledge that supports [**it / them**]¹⁹⁴⁾. And thanks to AI, which ensures that our messages [**are delivered / delivered**]¹⁹⁵⁾ to an audience more inclined to [**believe / believing**]¹⁹⁶⁾ it, our delusions of expertise can be reinforced by our personal filter bubble. We have an interesting tendency to [**find / finding**]¹⁹⁷⁾ people more open-minded, rational, and sensible when they think just like us.

40

The fast-growing, tremendous amount of data, collected and stored in large and numerous data repositories, has far **[exceeded / exceeding]**198) our human ability for understanding without powerful tools. As a result, data collected in large data repositories **[become / becomes]**199) "data tombs" — data archives that are **[frequently / hardly]**200) visited. Important decisions are often made based not on the information–rich data stored in data repositories but **[rather / rather than]**201) on a decision maker's instinct, simply because the decision maker does not have the tools to **[contract / extract]**202) the valuable knowledge hidden in the vast amounts of data. Efforts have been made to develop expert system and knowledge-based technologies, which typically rely on users or domain experts to **[manual / manually]**203) input knowledge into knowledge bases. However, this procedure is likely to cause biases and errors and is extremely costly and time consuming. The **[widened / widening]**204) gap between data and information calls for the systematic development of tools that can turn data tombs into "golden nuggets" of knowledge.

41 ~ 42

It's **[true / untrue]**205) that teens can focus on two things at once — what they're doing is shifting their attention from one task to another. In this digital age, teens wire their brains to make these shifts very quickly, but they are still, like everyone else, paying attention to one thing at a time, sequentially. Common sense tells us multitasking should increase brain activity, but Carnegie Mellon University scientists using the **[last / latest]**206) brain imaging technology find it doesn't. As a matter of fact, they discovered that multitasking actually decreases brain activity. **[Either / Neither]**207) task is done as well as if each were performed **[individual / individually]**208). Fractions of a second are lost every time we make a switch, and a person's interrupted task can take 50 percent longer to finish, with 50 percent more errors. Turns out the latest brain research supports the old advice "one thing at a time."
It's not that kids can't do some tasks **[simultaneous / simultaneously]**209). But if two tasks are performed at once, one of them has to be familiar. Our brains perform a familiar task on "automatic pilot" **[during / while]**210) really paying attention to the other one. That's **[because / why]**211) insurance companies consider talking on a cell phone and driving to be as **[dangerous / dangerously]**212) as driving while drunk — it's the driving that goes on "automatic pilot" while the conversation really holds our attention. Our kids may be living in the Information Age but our brains have not **[been redesigned / redesigned]**213) yet.

43 ~ 45

Christine was a cat owner who loved her furry companion, Leo. One morning, she noticed that Leo was not feeling well. Concerned for her beloved cat, Christine decided to take him to the animal hospital. As she always brought Leo to this hospital, she was certain **[that / what]**²¹⁴⁾ the vet knew well about Leo. She desperately hoped Leo got the necessary care as soon as possible. The waiting room was filled with **[other / the other]**²¹⁵⁾ pet owners. Finally, it was Leo's turn to see the vet. Christine watched as the vet gently examined him. The vet said, "I think Leo has a minor infection." "Infection? Will he be okay?" asked Christine. "We need to do some tests to see if he is infected. But for the tests, it's best for Leo to stay here," **[implied / replied]**²¹⁶⁾ the vet. It was **[heartbroken / heartbreaking]**²¹⁷⁾ for Christine to leave Leo at the animal hospital, but she had to accept it was for the best. "I'll call you with updates as soon as we know anything," said the vet. Throughout the day, Christine anxiously awaited news about Leo. Later that day, the phone rang and it was the vet. "The tests **[released / revealed]**²¹⁸⁾ a minor infection. Leo needs some **[mediation / medication]**²¹⁹⁾ and rest, but he'll be back to his playful self soon." Relieved to hear the news, Christine rushed back to the animal hospital to pick up Leo. The vet provided detailed instructions on how to administer the medication and shared tips for a speedy recovery. Back at home, Christine created a comfortable space for Leo to rest and heal. She patted him with love and attention, **[ensured / ensuring]**²²⁰⁾ that he would recover in no time. As the days passed, Leo gradually regained his strength and playful spirit.

2024 고2 3월 모의고사 ❶ 회차 : 점 / 350점

18

Dear Art Crafts People of Greenville,
For the a_____1) Crafts Fair on May 25 from 1 p.m. to 6 p.m., the Greenville Community Center is p_____2) booth spaces to rent as in previous years. To r_____3) your space, please visit our website and complete a r_____4) form by April 20. The rental fee is $50. All the money we receive from rental f_____5) goes to support upcoming activities throughout the year. We expect all a_____6) spaces to be fully b_____7) soon, so don't get l_____8) out. We hope to see you at the f_____9) .

친애하는 Greenville의 공예가들에게 5월 25일 오후 1시부터 6시까지 열리는 연례 공예 품 박람회를 위해서, Greenville 커뮤니티 센터에서는 지난 몇 년간처럼 대여 부스 공간을 제공합니다. 공간 을 예약하려면 저희 웹사이트를 방문하여 4월 20일까지 신청서를 작성하시기 바랍니다. 대여 요금은 50달러입니다. 부스 대여료로 받은 모든 돈은 연중 예정된 활동을 지원하는 데 사용됩니다. 모든 이용할 수 있는 공간이 곧 모두 예약될 것으로 예상되니 놓치지 마세요. 박람회에서 뵙기를 바랍니다.

19

Sarah, a young artist with a love for painting, e_____10) a local art contest. As she looked at the amazing artworks made by others, her c_____11) dropped. She q_____12) thought, 'I might not win an a_____13) .' The moment of j_____14) arrived, and the judges began a_____15) winners one by one. It wasn't until the end t_____16) she heard her name. The head of the judges said, "Congratulations, Sarah Parker! You won first prize. We loved the u_____17) of your work." Sarah was o_____18) with joy, and she couldn't stop smiling. This experience m_____19) more than just winning; it c_____20) her i_____21) as an artist.

그림 그리기를 좋아하는 젊은 예술가 Sarah는 지역 미술 대회에 참가했다. 다른 사람들이 만든 놀라운 예술 작품들을 보면서 그녀의 자신감은 떨어졌다. 그녀는 '내가 상을 받지 못할 수도 있겠네.'라고 조용히 생각했다. 심사의 순간이 다가왔고, 심사위원들은 수상자를 한 명씩 발표하기 시작했다. 그녀는 마지막에야 자신의 이름을 들었다. 심사위원장이 "축하해요, Sarah Parker! 당신이 1등을 했습니다. 당신 작품의 독창성이 정말 좋았습니다."라고 말했다. Sarah는 기쁨에 휩싸였고 미소가 가시지 않았다. 이 경험은 단순한 우승이상의 의미를 지녔고, 그녀에게 예술가로서의 정체성을 확인해 주었다.

20

Too many times people, especially in today's g_____22) , expect things to just happen overnight. When we have these f_____23) expectations, it tends to d_____24) us from c_____25) to move forward. Because this is a high tech society, everything we want has to be within the p_____26) of our c_____27) and c_____28) . If it doesn't happen fast enough, we're t_____29) to lose interest. So many people don't want to take the time it r_____30) to be s_____31) . Success is not a matter of mere d_____32) ; you should develop p_____33) in order to achieve it. Have you fallen p_____34) to i_____35) ? Great things take time to build.

너무나 많은 경우에, 사람들, 특히 오늘날의 세대는, 일이 하룻밤 사이에 일어나기를 기대한다. 우리가 이러한 잘못된 기대를 가질 때, 그것은 우리가 계속해서 앞으로 나아가는 것을 방해하는 경향이 있다. 지금은 첨단 기술 사회이기 때문에, 우리가 원하는 모든 것은 편안함과 편리함이라는 제한 내에 있어야 한다. 그 일이 충분히 빨리 일어나지 않으면, 우리는 흥미를 잃게끔 유혹을 받는다. 그래서 많은 사람들은 성공하는 데 필요한 시간을 들이는 것을 원하지 않는다. 성공은 단순한 욕망의 문제가 아니다. 여러분은 그것(성공)을 이루기 위해 인내심을 길러야 한다. 여러분은 조바심의 먹잇감이 되어 본 적이 있는가? 위대한 일이 이루어지는 데에는 시간이 걸린다.

21

If you had wanted to create a "self-driving" car in the 1950s, your best option might have been to s_____36) a b_____37) to the a_____38) . Yes, the v_____39) would have been able to move forward on its own, but it could not slow down, stop, or turn to avoid barriers. Obviously not i_____40) . But does that mean the entire concept of the self-driving car is not worth p_____41) ? No, it only means that at the time we did not yet have the tools we now p_____42) to help e_____43) vehicles to operate both a_____44) and safely. This once-distant dream now seems within our r_____45) . It is much the same story in medicine. Two decades ago, we were still t_____46) bricks to accelerators. Today, we are a_____47) the point where we can begin to bring some appropriate technology to b_____48) in ways that a_____49) our understanding of patients as u_____50) individuals. In fact, many patients are already wearing devices that monitor their conditions in real time, w_____51) allows doctors to talk to their patients in a specific, refined, and feedback-driven way that was not even possible a decade ago.

만약 '자율 주행' 자동차를 1950년대에 만들고 싶었다면, 가장 좋은 선택은 가속 페달에 벽돌을 끈으로 묶는 것이었을 것이다. 물론, 자동차가 스스로 앞으로 나아갈 수는 있었겠지만, 속도를 줄이거나 멈추거나 또는 장애물을 피하기 위해 방향을 전환할 수는 없었다. 분명히, 이상적이지는 않다. 그러나 그것이 자율주행 자동차라는 전체 개념이 추구할 만한 가치가 없다는 의미일까? 아니다, 그것은 단지 우리가 지금은 갖고 있는, 자동차를 자율적이고도 안전하게 작동할 수 있도록 해주는 도구를, 그 당시에는 우리가 아직 갖고 있지 않았다는 것을 의미할 뿐이다. 한때 멀게만 느껴졌던 이 꿈이 이제 우리의 손이 닿는 곳에 있는 것처럼 보인다. 이는 의학에서도 마찬가지이다. 20년 전에, 우리는 여전히 가속 페달에 벽돌을 테이프로 묶어 두고 있었다. 오늘날, 우리는 환자를 고유한 개인으로서 이해하는 것을 증진하는 방식에 맞는 적절한 기술을 도입하기 시작하는 지점에 접근하고 있다. 사실, 많은 환자들이 이미 자신의 상태를 실시간으로 관찰하는 장치를 착용하고 있는데, 이는 의사가 구체적이고도 정제되었으며 피드백을 기반으로 하는, 십 년 전에는 전혀 가능하지 않았던 방식으로 환자에게 말할 수 있도록 해 주었다.

22

We tend to o_____52) the impact of new technologies in part because older technologies have become a_____53) into the f_____54) of our lives, so as to be almost i_____55) . Take the baby bottle. Here is a simple i_____56) that has t_____57) a fundamental human experience for vast numbers of infants and mothers, yet it finds no place in our histories of technology. This technology might be thought of as a classic t_____58) device, as it enables mothers to e_____59) more c_____60) over the timing of feeding. It can also f_____61) to s_____62) time, as bottle feeding allows for someone else to s_____63) for the mother's time. Potentially, therefore, it has huge i_____64) for the m_____65) of time in everyday life, yet it is entirely o_____66) in discussions of high-speed society.

우리는 새로운 기술의 영향을 과대평가하는 경향이 있는데, 부분적으로 그 이유는 기존 기술이 눈에 거의 보이지 않을 만큼 우리 삶의 일부로 흡수되었기 때문이다. 젖병을 예로 들어 보자. 여기에 수많은 영유아와 엄마들의 인간으로서의 근본적인 경험을 바꿨으나, 기술의 역사에서 그 자리를 찾지 못한 단순한 도구가 있다. 이 기술은 전형적으로 시간을 조절하는 장치라고 여겨지는데 이는 엄마가 수유 시간에 대해 더 많은 통제력을 발휘할 수 있게 하기 때문이다. 또한 젖병 수유는 시간을 절약하는 기능도 하는데, 이는 다른 사람이 엄마의 (수유) 시간을 대신하도록 허락하기 때문이다. 따라서, 잠재적으로 그것(젖병)은 일상생활의 시간 관리에 큰 영향을 미치지만, 빠른 속도의 사회적 논의에서는 완전히 간과되고 있다.

23

E_____ 67) is frequently listed as one of the most d_____ 68) skills in an employer or employee, although without s_____ 69) exactly what is meant by empathy. Some businesses stress c_____ 70) empathy, emphasizing the need for leaders to understand the p_____ 71) of employees and customers when n_____ 72) deals and making decisions. Others stress a_____ _73) empathy and empathic concern, emphasizing the ability of leaders to gain trust from employees and customers by treating them with real c_____ 74) and c_____ 75) . When some consultants argue that successful companies f_____ 76) empathy, what that t_____ 77) to is that companies should conduct good market research. In other words, an "empathic" c_____ 78) understands the needs and wants of its customers and seeks to f_____ 79) those needs and wants. When some people speak of design with empathy, what that t_____ 80) to is that companies should take into a_____ 81) the specific needs of different populations — the blind, the deaf, the elderly, non-English speakers, the color-blind, and so on — when designing products.

'공감'이 무엇을 의미하는지 정확히 밝히지는 않지만, 공감은 고용주나 직원에게 가장 바라는 기술 중 하나로 목록에 종종 오른다. 일부 기업은 인지적 공감을 강조하여 리더가 거래를 협상하고 결정을 내릴 때 직원과 고객의 관점을 이해할 필요성에 중점을 둔다. 다른 기업은 정서적 공감과 공감적 관심을 강조하여 진정한 관심과 동정심으로 직원과 고객을 대함으로써 그들의 신뢰를 얻는 리더의 능력에 중점을 둔다. 일부 자문 위원이 성공하려는 기업은 공감 능력을 길러야 한다고 주장할 때, 그것이 의미하는 바는 기업이 시장조사를 잘 수행해야 한다는 것이다. 다시 말해, '공감적인' 기업은 고객의 필요와 요구를 이해하고, 그 필요와 요구를 충족시키기 위해 노력한다. 일부 사람들이 공감을 담은 디자인을 말할 때, 그것이 의미하는 바는 회사가 제품을 디자인할 때 시각 장애인, 청각 장애인, 노인, 비영어권 화자, 색맹 등 다양한 사람들의 구체적인 필요 사항을 고려해야 한다는 것이다.

24

The most p_____ 82) problem kids report is that they feel like they need to be a_____ 83) at all times. Because technology allows for it, they feel an o_____ 84) . It's easy for most of us to r_____ 85) — you probably feel the same p_____ 86) in your own life! It is really challenging to deal with the fact that we're human and can't always respond i_____ 87) . For a teen or tween who's still learning the ins and outs of social i_____ 88) , it's even worse. Here's how this behavior plays out sometimes: Your child texts one of his friends, and the friend doesn't text back right away. Now it's easy for your child to think, "This person doesn't want to be my friend anymore!" So he texts again, and again, and again — "_____ 89) up their phone." This can be stress-inducing and even read as a_____ 90) . But you can see how e_____ 91) this could happen.

아이들이 이야기하는 가장 일반적인 문제는 그들이 항상 연락될 수 있어야 한다고 느낀다는 것이다. 기술이 그것을 허용하기 때문에, 그들은 의무감을 느낀다. 우리 대부분은 공감하기 쉬운데, 아마 여러분도 자신의 삶에서 같은 압박을 느낄 것이다! 우리가 인간이고 항상 즉각적으로 응답할 수 없다는 사실에 대처하는 것은 매우 힘들다. 아직 사회적 상호 작용의 세부적인 것들을 배우고 있는 십대나 십대 초반의 아동에게 상황은 훨씬 더 심각하다. 때때로 이 행동이 나타나는 방식은 다음과 같다. 예를 들어, 여러분의 자녀가 친구 중 한 명에게 문자메세지를 보내고, 그 친구가 즉시 답장을 보내지 않는다면, 이제 여러분의 자녀는 "얘는 더 이상 내 친구가 되기를 원하지 않는구나!"라고 생각하기 쉽다. 그래서 다시, 다시, 그리고 또 다시 문자 메시지를 보내다가, '전화기를 폭파하는(과부하 상태로 만드는) 것'이다. 이것은 스트레스를 유발하고, 심지어 공격적인 것으로 읽힐 수 있다. 하지만 여러분은 이것이 얼마나 쉽게 일어날 수 있는지 알 수 있다.

26

Theodore von Kármán, a Hungarian-American engineer, was one of the greatest **m_____ 92)** of the twentieth century. He was born in Hungary and at an early age, he showed a **t_____ 93)** for math and science. In 1908, he received a **d_____ 94)** degree in engineering at the University of Göttingen in Germany. In the 1920s, he began traveling as a lecturer and **c_____ 95)** to industry. He was invited to the United States to advise engineers on the design of a wind tunnel at California Institute of Technology (Caltech). He became the director of the Guggenheim Aeronautical Laboratory at Caltech in 1930. Later, he was **a_____ 96)** the National Medal of Science for his leadership in science and engineering.

Theodore von Kármán은 헝가리계 미국인 공학자로, 20세기의 가장 위대한 지성인 중 한 명이었다. 그는 헝가리에서 태어나 어린 시절 수학과 과학에 재능을 보였다. 1908년, 독일 University of Göttingen에서 공학 박사 학위를 받았다. 1920년대에, 관련 분야의 강연자 겸 자문 위원으로 다니기 시작했다. 미국으로 초청되어 캘리포니아 공과대학(Caltech)에서 공학자들에게 윈드 터널 설계에 관한 조언을 하였다. 1930년에 Caltech의 Guggenheim Aeronautical Laboratory의 소장이 되었다. 나중에는 과학과 공학 분야에서의 리더십으로 National Medal of Science를 받았다.

29

For years, many psychologists have held strongly to the **b_____ 97)** that the key to **a_____ 98)** negative health **h_____ 99)** is to change behavior. This, more than values and **a_____ 100)** , is the part of **p_____ 101)** that is easiest to change. **l_____ 102)** habits such as smoking, drinking and various eating behaviors are the most common health **c_____ 103)** targeted for behavioral changes. **P_____ 104)** behaviors (workaholism, shopaholism, and the like) fall into this category as well. Mental imagery combined with power of suggestion was taken up as the **p_____ 105)** of behavioral **m_____ 106)** to help people change negative health behaviors into positive ones. Although this technique alone will not produce changes, when used **a_____ 107)** other behavior **m_____ 108) t_____ 109)** and **c_____ 110) s_____ 111)** , behavioral changes have proved **e_____ 112)** for some people. What mental imagery **d_____ 113)** is **r_____ 114)** a new desired behavior. **R_____ 115)** use of images **r_____ 116)** the desired behavior more **s_____ 117)** over time.

수년 동안 많은 심리학자들이 부정적인 건강 습관을 해결하기 위한 열쇠는 행동을 바꾸는 것이라는 믿음을 굳게 갖고 있었다. 가치관이나 태도보다, 이것이 가장 바꾸기 쉬운 성격의 한 부분이다. 흡연, 음주, 그리고 다양한 섭식 행동과 같은 섭취 습관은 행동 변화의 대상이 되는 가장 일반적인 건강 문제이다. 과정 중독행동(일중독, 쇼핑 중독 등) 또한 이 범주에 속한다. 암시의 힘과 결합된 마음 속 이미지는 사람들이 부정적인 건강 행동을 긍정적인 것으로 바꾸는 데 도움을 주는 행동 의학의 전제가 되었다. 이 기술만으로는 변화를 만들어 내지는 않지만, 다른 행동 수정 기법 및 대응 전략과 함께 사용되면, 행동 변화가 일부 사람들에게는 효과적인 것으로 입증되었다. 마음 속 이미지가 하는 일은 새로운 바람직한 행동을 강화하는 것이다. 이미지의 반복적 사용은 시간이 지남에 따라 그 바람직한 행동을 더욱 강력하게 강화한다.

30

Emotion s_____118) — learning from other people about emotions and how to deal with them — starts early in life and plays a f_____119) role for emotion r_____120) development. Although extra-familial influences, such as peers or media, g_____121) in importance during adolescence, parents remain the p_____122) socialization agents. For example, their own responses to emotional situations s_____123) as a role model for emotion regulation, increasing the l_____124) that their children will show similar reactions in c_____125) situations. Parental practices at times when their children are faced with emotional challenges also i_____126) emotion regulation development. Whereas direct s_____127) and directive g_____128) of what to do are b_____129) for younger children, they may i_____130) on adolescents' a_____131) s_____132). In consequence, adolescents might pull away from rather than turn toward, their parents in times of emotional crisis, unless parental practices are a_____133). More s_____134) in adolescence is i_____135) support of autonomous emotion regulation, such as through interest in, as well as awareness and n_____136) a_____137) of, adolescents' emotional experiences, and being available when the adolescent wants to talk.

다른 사람들로부터 감정과 감정을 다루는 방법을 배우는 감정 사회화는 어릴 때부터 시작되며 감정 조절발달에 기초적인 역할을 한다. 청소년기에는 또래나 미디어와 같은 가족 이외의 영향이 중요해지지만, 부모는 여전히 주된 사회화 주체이다. 예를 들어, 감정적 상황에 대한 부모 자신의 반응이 감정 조절의 롤모델이 되어 자녀가 비슷한 상황에서 유사한 반응을 보일 가능성을 높인다. 자녀가 정서적 어려움에 직면했을 때 부모의 (습관적) 행동 또한 감정 조절 발달에 영향을 미친다. 직접적인 위로와 어떻게 해야 하는지에 대한 지시적 안내가 어린 자녀에게는 도움이 되지만, 청소년의 자율성 추구를 방해할 수 있다. 결과적으로 부모의 행동이 조정되지 않는다면, 청소년은 정서적 위기 상황에서 부모에게 의지하기보다 오히려 부모로부터 멀어질 수 있다. 청소년기에 더 적합한 것은 청소년의 정서적 경험에 대한 인식과 무비판적 수용뿐만 아니라 (그에 대한) 관심, 그리고 청소년이 대화하고 싶을 때 곁에 있어 주는 것과 같은 방법으로 자율적 감정 조절을 간접적으로 지원하는 것이다.

31

Dancers often push themselves to the l_____138) of their physical capabilities. But that push is m_____139) if it is directed toward a_____140) something physically impossible. For instance, a tall dancer with long feet may wish to perform repetitive v_____141) jumps to fast music, pointing his feet while in the air and l_____142) his heels to the floor between jumps. That may be impossible no matter how strong the dancer is. But a short-footed dancer may have no trouble! Another dancer may be struggling to complete a half-turn in the air. Understanding the c_____143) between a rapid turn rate and the a_____144) of the body close to the r_____145) a_____146) tells her how to accomplish her turn s_____147). In both of these cases, understanding and working within the c_____148) i_____149) by nature and described by physical laws allows dancers to work efficiently, m_____150) potential risk of injury.

무용수는 종종 자신의 신체 능력의 한계까지 자신을 밀어붙인다. 그러나 그렇게 밀어붙이는 것이 물리적으로 불가능한 것을 달성하는 쪽으로 향하게 된다면, 잘못 이해한 것이다. 예를 들어, 키가 크고 발이 긴 무용수가 공중에서 발끝을 뾰족하게 하고 점프 사이에 발뒤꿈치를 바닥에 내리면서 빠른 음악에 맞춰 반복적인 수직 점프를 수행하고 싶을 수 있다. 무용수가 아무리 힘이 좋을지라도 그것은 불가능할 수 있다. 하지만 발이 짧은 무용수는 전혀 문제가 없을 것이다! 또 다른 무용수는 공중에서 반 회전을 완성하려고 애쓰고 있을 수 있다. 빠른 회전 속도와 회전축에 가깝게 몸을 정렬하는 것의 연관성을 이해하는 것은 그 무용수에게 성공적으로 회전을 해내는 방법을 알려 준다. 이 두 경우 모두에서, 선천적으로 주어지고 물리적 법칙에 의해 설명되는 제약을 이해하고 그 안에서 움직이는 것은 잠재적인 부상 위험을 최소화하면서 무용수가 효율적으로 움직이게 해 준다.

32

We must **e**_____151) the relationship between children's film production and **c**_____152) habits. The term "children's film" implies **o**_____153) by children —their cinema — but films supposedly made for children have always been **c**_____154) by audiences of all ages, particularly in commercial cinemas. The **c**_____155) crossover in audience **c**_____156) for children's films can be shown by the fact that, in 2007, eleven Danish children's and youth films **a**_____157) 59 percent of theatrical admissions, and in 2014, German children's films **c**_____158) seven out of the top twenty films at the national box office. This phenomenon **c**_____159) with a **b**_____160) , international **e**_____161) of what is seemingly children's culture among audiences of **d**_____ _162) ages. The old **p**_____163) that children's film is some other **r**_____164) , **s**_____165) from (and forever subordinate to) a more **l**_____166) cinema for adults is not supported by the realities of consumption: children's film is at the heart of **c**_____167) popular culture.

우리는 어린이 영화 제작과 소비 습관 사이의 관계를 탐구해야 한다. '어린이 영화'라는 용어는 어린이에 의한 소유권, 즉 '그들의' 영화를 암시하지만, 소위 어린이를 위해 만들어진 영화는 특히 상업 영화에서, 항상 모든 연령대의 관객들에게 소비되어 왔다. 어린이 영화의 관객 구성에서 상당한 (연령 간의) 넘나듦이 있다는 것은, 2007년에 11개의 덴마크의 어린이 및 청소년 영화가 극장 입장객의 59퍼센트를 끌어 모았고 2014년에는 독일의 어린이영화가 전국 극장 흥행 수익 상위 20개 영화 중 7개를 차지했다는 사실에 의해 증명될 수 있다. 이 현상은 다양한 연령대의 관객들 사이에서 겉으로는 어린이 문화처럼 보이는 것이 더 광범위하고 국제적으로 수용되는 것과 일치한다. 어린이 영화가 성인을 위한 더 제대로 된 영화와는 별개의(그리고 영원히 하위의) 다른 영역이라는 오래된 편견은 소비의 실상에 의해 뒷받침되지 않는다. 즉, 어린이영화가 현대 대중문화의 중심에 있다.

33

Beethoven's **d**_____168) to create something **n**_____169) is a **r**_____170) of his state of **c**_____171) . Our brains experience a sense of reward when we create something new in the process of exploring something **u**_____172) , such as a musical phrase that we've never played or heard before. When our **c**_____173) leads to something novel, the **r**_____174) reward brings us a sense of **p**_____175) . A number of investigators have **m**_____176) how curiosity influences musical **c**_____177) . In the case of Beethoven, computer modeling focused on the thirty-two piano sonatas **w**_____178) after age thirteen revealed that the musical patterns found in all of Beethoven's music **d**_____179) in later sonatas, while **n**_____180) patterns, including patterns that were unique to a particular sonata, increased. In other words, Beethoven's music became less **p**_____181) over time as his curiosity drove the **e**_____182) of new musical ideas. Curiosity is a powerful driver of human **c**_____183) .

새로운 것을 창작하려는 베토벤의 욕구는 그의 호기심 상태의 반영이다. 우리의 뇌는 우리가 이전에 연주하거나 들어본 적이 없는 악절과 같이 불확실한 것을 탐구하는 과정에서 새로운 것을 창작할 때 보상감을 경험한다. 우리의 호기심이 새로운 것으로 이어지면, 그 결과로 얻어지는 보상은 우리에게 쾌감을 가져다준다. 많은 연구자들이 음악 작곡에 호기심이 어떻게 영향을 미치는지를 모델링해 왔다. 베토벤의 경우, 13세 이후로 작곡된 32개의 피아노 소나타에 초점을 맞춘 컴퓨터 모델링에서 베토벤의 모든 음악에서 발견되는 음악 패턴이 후기 소나타에서는 감소한 반면, 특정 소나타에만 나타나는 패턴을 포함한 새로운 패턴은 증가한 것을 보여 주었다. 다시 말해, 베토벤의 호기심이 새로운 음악적 아이디어의 탐구를 이끌게 됨에 따라 그의 음악은 시간이 지날수록 덜 예측 가능하게 되었다. 호기심은 인간의 창의성의 강력한 원동력이다.

34

Technologists are always on the lookout for q_____184) metrics. M_____185) i_____186) to a model are their l_____187) , and like a social scientist, a technologist needs to i_____188) c_____189) m_____190) , or "proxies," for a_____191) p_____192) . This need for q_____193) proxies produces a b_____194) toward measuring things that are easy to q_____195) . But simple m_____196) can take us further away from the important goals we really care about, which may require c_____197) metrics or be extremely difficult, or perhaps impossible, to r_____198) to any measure. And when we have i_____199) or bad proxies, we can easily fall under the i_____200) that we are solving for a good end without actually making g_____201) progress toward a worthy solution. The problem of proxies r_____202) in technologists frequently s_____203) what is measurable for what is meaningful. As the saying goes, "Not everything that c_____204) can be c_____205) , and not everything that can be c_____206) c_____207) ."

기술자들은 항상 정량화할 수 있는 측정 기준을 찾고 있다. 모델에 측정 가능한 입력(을 하는 것)은 그들의 생명줄이며, 사회 과학자와 마찬가지로 기술자는 진척 상황을 평가하기 위한 구체적인 측정 방법, 즉 '프록시'를 식별할 필요가 있다. 이러한 정량화할 수 있는 프록시에 대한 필요성은 정량화하기 쉬운 것들을 측정하는 쪽으로 편향을 만든다. 하지만 단순한 측정기준은 우리가 정말로 신경 쓰는 중요한 목표로부터 우리를 더 멀어지게 할 수 있는데, 이 목표는 복잡한 측정 기준을 요구하거나, 또는 (이 목표를) 어떤 하나의 측정 방법만으로 한정(하여 측정)하기가 어렵거나 아마 불가능할 수도 있다. 그리고 우리가 불완전하거나 잘못된 프록시를 가지고 있을 때, 우리는 가치 있는 해결책을 향한 진정한 진전을 실제로 이루지 못하면서 좋은 목적을 위해 문제를 해결하고 있다는 착각에 쉽게 빠질 수 있다. 프록시의 문제는 기술자들이 흔히 의미 있는 것을 측정 가능한 것으로 대체하는 결과를 낳는다. 흔히 말하듯이, "중요한 모든 것들이 셀 수 있는 것은 아니고, 셀 수 있는 모든 것들이 중요한 것도 아니다."

35

We are the only species that s_____208) its food, d_____209) a_____210) it with the highly f_____211) plant parts we call herbs and spices. It's quite possible that our taste for spices has an e_____212) root. Many spices have a_____213) p_____214) — in fact, common seasonings such as garlic, onion, and oregano i_____215) the growth of almost every b_____216) t_____217) . And the cultures that make the heaviest use of spices — think of the garlic and black pepper of Thai food, the ginger and coriander of India, the chili peppers of Mexico — come from warmer climates, where b_____218) s_____219) is a bigger issue. In contrast, the most lightly spiced c_____220) — those of Scandinavia and northern Europe — are from c_____221) climates. Our uniquely human attention to flavor, in this case the flavor of spices, turns out to have a_____222) as a matter of life and death.

우리는 음식에 양념을 하는 유일한 종으로, 허브와 향신료라고 부르는 강한 맛을 내는 식물의 부분을 이용하여 그것(음식)을 의도적으로 바꾼다. 향신료에 대한 우리의 미각은 진화적 뿌리를 가지고 있을 가능성이 높다. 많은 향신료가 항균성을 가지고 있는데, 실제로 마늘, 양파, 오레가노와 같은 흔한 조미료들이 거의 모든 확인된 박테리아의 성장을 억제한다. 그리고 태국 음식의 마늘과 후추, 인도의 생강과 고수, 멕시코의 고추를 생각해 보면, 향신료를 가장 많이 사용하는 문화권은 더 따뜻한 기후에서 유래하는데, 그곳에서는 박테리아에 의한 (음식의) 부패가 큰 문제이다. 반대로, 스칸디나비아와 북유럽의 요리같이 가장 향신료를 적게 쓰는 요리는 더 서늘한 기후에서 유래한다. 맛에 대한 인간 특유의 관심, 이 경우 향신료의 맛은 사느냐 죽느냐의 문제로서 생겨난 것으로 드러난다.

36

Development of the human body from a single cell provides many examples of the s_____ 223) r_____ 224) that is possible when the r_____ 225) production of random v_____ 226) is combined with nonrandom s_____ 227) . All p_____ 228) of body development from e_____ 229) to adult e_____ 230) r_____ 231) activities at the cellular level, and body f_____ 232) depends on the new possibilities g_____ 233) by these activities c_____ 234) with s_____ 235) of those outcomes that s_____ 236) previously b_____ 237) criteria. Always new structure is based on old structure, and at every stage selection f_____ 238) some cells and e_____ 239) others. The survivors serve to produce new cells that undergo further rounds of selection. Except in the immune system, cells and extensions of cells are not g_____ 240) selected during development, but rather, are positionally selected. Those in the right place that make the right connections are s_____ 241) , and those that d_____ 242) are eliminated. This process is much like s_____ 243) . A natural consequence of the strategy is great v_____ 244) from individual to individual at the cell and m_____ 245) levels, even though large-scale structures are quite s_____ 246) .

단일 세포로부터 인체가 발달하는 것은 무작위적인 변이의 반복적 생성이 비무작위적인 선택과 결합될 때 가능해지는 구조적 풍부함의 많은 예를 제공한다. 배아에서 성체에 이르기까지 신체 발달의 모든 단계는 세포 수준에서는 무작위 활동을 보이고, 신체 형성은 이러한 활동(무작위 활동)에 의해 만들어진 새로운 가능성과 더불어, 이전에 확립된 기준을 만족시키는 결과물의 선택에 달려 있다. 항상 새로운 구조는 오래된 구조를 기반으로 하며, 모든 단계에서 선택은 일부 세포들을 선호하고 다른 세포들은 제거한다. 생존한 세포들은 추가적인 선택의 과정을 거치는 새로운 세포들을 만들어 내는 역할을 한다. 면역계를 제외하면 세포와 세포의 확장은 발달 과정에서 유전적으로 선택되는 것이 아니라 위치에 의해 선택된다. 제 자리에서 제대로 된 연결을 만들어 낸 것(세포)들은 활성화되고, 그렇지 않은 것들은 제거된다. 이 과정은 마치 조각을 하는 것과 같다. 이 전략의 필연적 결과는 전체 구조가 상당히 비슷하더라도 세포와 분자 수준에서 개인마다 큰 변이성이 있다는 것이다.

37

In order to bring the ever-increasing costs of home care for e_____ 247) and n_____ 248) persons under control, managers of home care providers have i_____ 249) management systems. These systems s_____ 250) tasks of home care workers and the time and budget available to p_____ 251) these tasks. Electronic r_____ 252) systems r_____ 253) home care workers to report on their activities and the time spent, thus making the d_____ 254) of time and money v_____ 255) and, in the p_____ 256) of managers, c_____ 257) . This, in the view of managers, has contributed to the r_____ 258) of the problem. The home care workers, on the other hand, may p_____ 259) their work not as a set of separate tasks to be performed as e_____ 260) as possible, but as a service to be p_____ 261) to a client with whom they may have developed a relationship. This includes having conversations with clients and e_____ 262) about the person's wellbeing. R_____ 263) time and the requirement to report may be perceived as o_____ 264) that make it impossible to deliver the service that is needed. If the management systems are too r_____ 265) , this may result in home care workers becoming o_____ 266) and d_____ 267) .

노인과 빈곤층을 위한 재택 간호의 계속적으로 증가하는 비용을 통제하기 위해 재택 간호 제공 업체의 관리자는 관리 시스템을 도입했다. 이러한 시스템은 재택 간호 종사자의 업무와 이러한 업무를 수행하는데 사용할 수 있는 시간과 예산을 명시한다. 전자 보고 시스템은 재택 간호 종사자가 자신의 활동과 소요시간을 보고하도록 요구하므로 시간과 비용의 분배를 잘 보이게 만들고, 관리자의 입장에서는 통제 가능하게 만든다. 관리자의 관점에서는, 이것이 문제 해결에 기여해 왔다. 반면에, 재택 간호 종사자들은 자신의 업무를 가능한 한 효율적으로 수행되어야 하는 일련의 분리된 업무가 아니라, 그들이 관계를 맺어온 고객에게 제공되는 서비스로 인식할 것이다. 이것은 고객과 대화를 나누고 고객의 안부를 묻는 것을 포함한다. 제한된 시간과 보고를 해야 한다는 요구 사항은 필요한 서비스를 제공하는 것을 불가능하게 하는 장애물로 여겨질 것이다. 만약 관리 시스템이 너무 엄격하면, 이것은 재택 간호 종사자가 너무 많은 부담을 지게 되고 의욕을 잃는 결과를 초래할 것이다.

38

It is a common assumption that most v_____268) birds are ultimately d_____269), aside from the rare cases w_____270) individuals are able to r_____271) and return to their normal ranges. In turn, it is also commonly assumed that v_____272) itself is a relatively u_____273) b_____274) phenomenon. This is undoubtedly true for the majority of cases, as the most likely outcome of any given v_____275) event is that the individual will fail to find enough resources, and/or be exposed to i_____276) environmental conditions, and p_____277) . However, there are many lines of evidence to suggest that v_____278) can, on rare occasions, dramatically a_____279) the fate of populations, species or even whole ecosystems. Despite being infrequent, these events can be extremely important when viewed at the timescales over which ecological and evolutionary processes u_____280) . The most profound consequences of v_____281) relate to the e_____282) of new breeding sites, new m_____283) routes and w_____284) locations. Each of these can occur through different m_____285) , and at different f_____286) , and they each have their own unique i_____287) .

무리에서 떨어져 헤매는 대부분의 새들은 방향을 다시 잡고 그들의 일반적인 (서식) 범위로 돌아갈 수 있는 드문 경우의 개체들을 제외하고, 궁극적으로 죽을 운명이라는 것이 일반적인 가정이다. 결국, 무리에서 떨어져 헤매는 것 자체가 비교적 중요하지 않은 생물학적 현상이라고 일반적으로 여겨지기도 한다. 이것은 의심할 여지없이 대부분의 경우에 사실인데, 무리에서 떨어져 헤매는 어떤 경우든 가장 가능성 있는 결과는 개체가 충분한 자원을 찾지 못하고/못하거나, 살기 힘든 환경 조건에 노출되어 죽기 때문이다. 하지만, 드문 경우에, 무리에서 떨어져 헤매는 것이 개체 수, 종, 심지어 생태계 전체의 운명을 극적으로 바꿀 수 있다는 것을 시사하는 많은 증거가 있다. 드물기는 하지만, 이러한 경우들은 생태학적이고 진화적인 과정이 진행되는 시간의 관점에서 볼 때 매우 중요할 수 있다. 무리에서 떨어져 헤매는 것의 가장 중대한 결과는 새로운 번식지, 새로운 이동 경로 및 월동 장소의 확보와 관련이 있다. 이들 각각은 서로 다른 메커니즘을 통해, 서로 다른 빈도로 발생할 수 있으며, 각각 고유한 중요성을 가지고 있다.

39

I_____288) can be great, but it ought to be h_____289) . Experts, for example, are able to think on their f_____290) because they've i_____291) thousands of hours in learning and practice: their intuition has become data-driven. Only then are t_____292) a_____293) to act quickly in a_____294) with their i_____295) e_____296) and evidence-based experience. Yet most people are not experts, though they often think they a_____297) . Most of us, especially when we i_____298) with others on social media, act with expert-like speed and c_____299), offering a wide range of opinions on global crises, without the substance of knowledge that supports it. And thanks to AI, which e_____300) that our messages are delivered to an audience more inclined to believing it, our d_____301) of expertise can be r_____302) by our personal filter bubble. We have an interesting tendency to find people more open-minded, rational, and s_____303) when they think just like us.

직관은 탁월할 수 있지만, 힘들여 얻은 것이어야 한다. 예를 들어, 전문가들은 수천 시간을 학습과 경험에 투자하여, 데이터로부터 직관이 얻어졌기 때문에 즉각적으로 생각할 수 있다. 그래야만 그들이 내재화된 전문 지식과 증거에 기반한 경험에 따라 빠르게 행동할 수 있다. 그러나 대부분의 사람들은 종종 스스로를 전문가라고 생각하지만 실제로는 전문가가 아니다. 우리 중 대부분은, 특히 소셜 미디어에서 다른 사람들과 소통할 때, 전문가와 같은 속도와 확신을 가지고 행동하며, 이를 뒷받침하는 지식의 실체 없이 국제적 위기에 대한 다양한 의견을 제시한다. 그리고 우리의 메시지가 그것을 더 믿으려는 성향이 있는 독자에게 확실히 전달되도록 하는 인공 지능 덕분에, 전문 지식에 대한 우리의 착각은 개인적 필터 버블(자신의 관심사에 맞게 필터링된 정보만을 접하게 되는 현상)에 의해 강화될 수 있다. 우리는 남들이 우리와 똑같이 생각할 때 그들을 더 개방적이고 합리적이며 분별 있다고 여기는 흥미로운 경향을 가지고 있다.

40

The fast-growing, tremendous amount of data, collected and stored in large and numerous data r_____304), has far e_____305) our human ability for understanding without powerful tools. As a result, data collected in large data repositories become "data tombs" — data a_____306) that are h_____307) visited. Important decisions are often made based not on the information–rich data stored in data repositories but rather on a decision maker's i_____308), simply because the decision maker does not have the tools to e_____309) the valuable knowledge h_____310) in the vast amounts of data. Efforts have been made to develop expert system and knowledge-based technologies, which typically rely on users or domain experts to manually i_____311) knowledge into knowledge bases. However, this p_____312) is likely to cause b_____313) and errors and is extremely c_____314) and time consuming. The w_____315) gap between data and information calls for the systematic development of tools that can turn data tombs into "golden nuggets" of k_____316).

빠르게 증가하는 엄청난 양의 데이터는, 크고 많은 데이터 저장소에 수집되고 저장되어, 우리 인간이 효과적인 도구 없이는 이해할 수 있는 능력을 훨씬 뛰어 넘었다. 결과적으로, 대규모 데이터 저장소에서 수집된 데이터는 '데이터 무덤', 즉 찾는 사람이 거의 없는 데이터 보관소가 된다. 중요한 의사 결정이 종종 데이터 저장소에 저장된 정보가 풍부한 데이터가 아닌 의사결정자의 직관에 기반하여 내려지기도 하는데, 이는 단지 의사 결정자가 방대한 양의 데이터에 숨겨진 가치 있는 지식을 추출할 수 있는 도구를 가지고 있지않기 때문이다. 전문가 시스템과 지식 기반 기술을 개발하려는 노력이 있어 왔는데, 이는 일반적으로 사용자나 분야(별) 전문가가 지식을 '수동으로' 지식 기반에 입력하는 것에 의존한다. 이 방법은 편견과 오류를 일으키기 쉽고 비용과 시간이 엄청나게 든다. 점점 더 벌어지는 데이터와 정보 간의 격차로 인해 데이터 무덤을 지식의 '금괴'로 바꿀 수 있는 도구의 체계적인 개발이 요구된다.

41 ~42

It's untrue that teens can focus on two things at once — what they're doing is s_____317) their attention from one task to another. In this digital age, teens w_____318) their brains to make these shifts very quickly, but they are still, like everyone else, paying attention to one thing at a time, s_____319). Common sense tells us m_____320) should increase brain activity, but Carnegie Mellon University scientists using the l_____321) brain imaging technology find it d_____322). As a matter of fact, they discovered that multitasking actually d_____323) brain activity. N_____324) task is done as well as if each w_____325) performed individually. Fractions of a second are l_____326) every time we make a switch, and a person's i_____327) task can take 50 percent longer to finish, with 50 percent more errors. Turns out the l_____328) brain research supports the old advice "one thing at a time."

It's not that kids can't do some tasks s_____329). But if two tasks are performed at once, one of them has to be f_____330). Our brains perform a familiar task on "_____331) pilot" while really paying attention to the other one. That's why i_____332) companies consider talking on a cell phone and driving to be as dangerous as driving while d_____333) — it's the driving that goes on "automatic pilot" while the conversation really holds our attention. Our kids may be living in the Information Age but our brains have not been r_____334) yet.

십대들이 동시에 두 가지 일에 집중할 수 있다는 것은 사실이 아니며, 그들이 하고 있는 것은 한 작업에서 다른 작업으로 주의를 전환하는 것이다. 디지털 시대에, 십대의 뇌는 매우 빠르게 작업을 전환하도록 발달하지만, 여전히 다른 모든 사람들과 마찬가지로 십대들도 한 번에 한 가지씩 순차적으로 주의를 기울이고 있다. 상식적으로 멀티태스킹이 뇌 활동을 증가시킬 것이라고 생각하지만, Carnegie Mellon 대학의 과학자들은 최신 뇌 영상 기술을 사용하여 그렇지 않다는 것을 발견했다. 사실, 그들은 멀티태스킹이 실제로는 두뇌 활동을 감소시킨다는 것을 발견했다. 어느 작업도 각각 개별적으로 수행될 때만큼 잘 되지 못한다. 우리가 (작업을) 전환할 때마다 시간이 아주 조금씩 낭비되며, 중단된 작업은 완료하기까지 50퍼센트 더 오래 걸리고, 50퍼센트 더 많은 오류가 발생할 수 있다. 최신 뇌 연구가 '한 번에 한 가지 일만 하라'는 오래된 조언을 뒷받침하는 것으로 드러났다.

아이들이 동시에 여러 작업을 할 수 없다는 것은 아니다. 하지만 동시에 두 가지 작업이 수행된다면, 그 중 하나는 익숙한 작업이어야 한다. 우리의 뇌는 익숙한 작업은 '자동 조종' 상태에서 수행하고 실제로는 다른 작업에 주의를 기울인다. 그것이 보험 회사가 휴대전화로 통화하면서 운전하는 것을 술에 취한 상태에서 운전하는 것만큼 위험한 것으로 간주하는 이유이다. 대화가 실제로 우리의 주의를 끌고 있는 동안 '자동조종' 상태에서 수행되는 것은 운전이다. 우리 아이들이 정보화 시대에 살고 있을지 모르지만, 우리의 뇌는 아직 (정보화 시대에 맞게) 재설계되지 않았다.

43 ~ 45

Christine was a cat owner who loved her furry companion, Leo. One morning, she noticed that Leo was not feeling w_____335) . C_____336) for her b_____337) cat, Christine decided to take him to the animal hospital. As she always brought Leo to this hospital, she was certain that the v_____338) knew well about Leo. She d_____339) hoped Leo got the necessary care as soon as possible. The waiting room was f_____340) with other pet owners. Finally, it was Leo's turn to see the vet. Christine watched as the vet gently e_____341) him. The vet said, "I think Leo has a minor i_____342) ." "Infection? Will he be okay?" asked Christine. "We need to do some tests to see if he is infected. But for the tests, it's best for Leo to stay here," replied the vet. It was heartbreaking for Christine to leave Leo at the animal hospital, but she had to accept it was for the best. "I'll call you with updates as soon as we know anything," said the vet. Throughout the day, Christine anxiously a_____343) news about Leo. Later that day, the phone rang and it was the vet. "The tests r_____344) a minor infection. Leo needs some m_____345) and rest, but he'll be back to his playful self soon." R_____346) to hear the news, Christine rushed back to the animal hospital to pick up Leo. The vet provided detailed i_____347) on how to a_____348) the medication and shared tips for a speedy recovery. Back at home, Christine created a comfortable space for Leo to rest and heal. She p_____349) him with love and attention, e_____350) that he would recover in no time. As the days passed, Leo gradually regained his strength and playful spirit.

Christine은 고양이 주인으로 그녀의 털북숭이 반려동물인 Leo를 사랑한다. 어느 날 아침, 그녀는 Leo의 몸 상태가 좋지 않다는 것을 알게 되었다. 사랑하는 고양이가 걱정되어서, Christine은 Leo를 동물병원에 데려가기로 결심했다. 그녀가 항상 Leo를 이 병원에 데려왔기 때문에, 수의사가 Leo에 대해 잘 알고 있을 것이라고 그녀는 확신했다. Leo가 필요한 보살핌을 가능한 한 빨리 받기를 그녀는 간절히 바랐다. 대기실은 다른 반려동물의 주인들로 꽉 차 있었다. 마침내, Leo가 수의사를 만날 차례가 되었다. Christine은 수의사가 Leo를 조심스럽게 진찰하는 모습을 지켜보았다. "저는 Leo에게 경미한 감염이 있다고 생각합니다." 수의사가 말했다. "감염이요? Leo는 괜찮을까요?" Christine이 물었다. "감염 여부를 알기위해 우리는 몇 가지 검사를 할 필요가 있습니다. 하지만 검사를 위해서 Leo가 여기 머무는 것이 가장 좋습니다." 수의사가 대답했다. Leo를 동물병원에 두고 가는 것이 Christine에게는 가슴 아팠지만, 그녀는 그것이 최선이라는 것을 받아들여야만 했다. "저희가 뭔가 알게 되는 즉시 당신에게 전화로 새로운 소식을 알려 드리겠습니다."라고 수의사가 말했다. 그날 내내 Christine은 초조하게 Leo에 대한 소식을 기다렸다. 그날 늦게 전화가 울렸고 그것(전화를 건사람)은 수의사였다. "검사 결과 경미한 감염이 발견되었습니다. Leo는 약간의 약물 치료와 휴식이 필요하긴 하지만 곧 장난기 넘치는 모습으로 돌아올 거예요." 그 소식을 듣고 안도하며, Christine은 Leo를 데리러 동물병원으로 서둘러 되돌아갔다. 수의사는 약을 투여하는 방법을 자세히 설명해주고 빠른 회복을 위한 조언을 했다. 집으로 돌아와서, Christine은 Leo가 쉬고 회복할 수 있는 편안한 공간을 만들었다. 그녀는 Leo가 금방 회복할 수 있도록 사랑과 관심으로 Leo를 쓰다듬어 주었다. 며칠이 지나자, Leo는 점차 체력과 장난기 넘치는 활기를 되찾았다.

18

Dear Art Crafts People of Greenville,

For the **a**_____¹⁾ Crafts Fair on May 25 from 1 p.m. to 6 p.m., the Greenville Community Center is **p**_____²⁾ booth spaces to rent as in previous years. To **r**_____³⁾ your space, please visit our website and complete a **r**_____⁴⁾ form by April 20. The rental fee is $50. All the money we receive from rental **f**_____⁵⁾ goes to support upcoming activities throughout the year. We expect all **a**_____⁶⁾ spaces to be fully **b**_____⁷⁾ soon, so don't get **l**_____⁸⁾ out. We hope to see you at the **f**_____⁹⁾ .

19

Sarah, a young artist with a love for painting, **e**_____¹⁰⁾ a local art contest. As she looked at the amazing artworks made by others, her **c**_____¹¹⁾ dropped. She **q**_____¹²⁾ thought, 'I might not win an **a**_____¹³⁾ .' The moment of **j**_____¹⁴⁾ arrived, and the judges began **a**_____¹⁵⁾ winners one by one. It wasn't until the end **t**_____¹⁶⁾ she heard her name. The head of the judges said, "Congratulations, Sarah Parker! You won first prize. We loved the **u**_____¹⁷⁾ of your work." Sarah was **o**_____¹⁸⁾ with joy, and she couldn't stop smiling. This experience **m**_____¹⁹⁾ more than just winning; it **c**_____²⁰⁾ her **i**_____²¹⁾ as an artist.

20

Too many times people, especially in today's **g**_____²²⁾ , expect things to just happen overnight. When we have these **f**_____²³⁾ expectations, it tends to **d**_____²⁴⁾ us from **c**_____²⁵⁾ to move forward. Because this is a high tech society, everything we want has to be within the **p**_____²⁶⁾ of our **c**_____²⁷⁾ and **c**_____²⁸⁾ . If it doesn't happen fast enough, we're **t**_____²⁹⁾ to lose interest. So many people don't want to take the time it **r**_____³⁰⁾ to be **s**_____³¹⁾ . Success is not a matter of mere **d**_____³²⁾ ; you should develop **p**_____³³⁾ in order to achieve it. Have you fallen **p**_____³⁴⁾ to **i**_____³⁵⁾ ? Great things take time to build.

21

If you had wanted to create a "self-driving" car in the 1950s, your best option might have been to s_____36) a b_____37) to the a_____38) . Yes, the v_____39) would have been able to move forward on its own, but it could not slow down, stop, or turn to avoid barriers. Obviously not i_____40) . But does that mean the entire concept of the self-driving car is not worth p_____41) ? No, it only means that at the time we did not yet have the tools we now p_____42) to help e_____43) vehicles to operate both a_____44) and safely. This once-distant dream now seems within our r_____45) . It is much the same story in medicine. Two decades ago, we were still t_____46) bricks to accelerators. Today, we are a_____47) the point where we can begin to bring some appropriate technology to b_____48) in ways that a_____49) our understanding of patients as u_____50) individuals. In fact, many patients are already wearing devices that monitor their conditions in real time, w_____51) allows doctors to talk to their patients in a specific, refined, and feedback-driven way that was not even possible a decade ago.

22

We tend to o_____52) the impact of new technologies in part because older technologies have become a_____53) into the f_____54) of our lives, so as to be almost i_____55) . Take the baby bottle. Here is a simple i_____56) that has t_____57) a fundamental human experience for vast numbers of infants and mothers, yet it finds no place in our histories of technology. This technology might be thought of as a classic t_____58) device, as it enables mothers to e_____59) more c_____60) over the timing of feeding. It can also f_____61) to s_____62) time, as bottle feeding allows for someone else to s_____63) for the mother's time. Potentially, therefore, it has huge i_____64) for the m_____65) of time in everyday life, yet it is entirely o_____66) in discussions of high-speed society.

23

E_____67) is frequently listed as one of the most d_____68) skills in an employer or employee, although without s_____69) exactly what is meant by empathy. Some businesses stress c_____70) empathy, emphasizing the need for leaders to understand the p_____71) of employees and customers when n_____72) deals and making decisions. Others stress a_____73) empathy and empathic concern, emphasizing the ability of leaders to gain trust from employees and customers by treating them with real c_____74) and c_____75) . When some consultants argue that successful companies f_____76) empathy, what that t_____77) to is that companies should conduct good market research. In other words, an "empathic" c_____78) understands the needs and wants of its customers and seeks to f_____79) those needs and wants. When some people speak of design with empathy, what that t_____80) to is that companies should take into a_____81) the specific needs of different populations — the blind, the deaf, the elderly, non-English speakers, the color-blind, and so on — when designing products.

24

The most **p**_____82) problem kids report is that they feel like they need to be **a**_____83) at all times. Because technology allows for it, they feel an **o**_____84) . It's easy for most of us to **r**_____85) — you probably feel the same **p**_____86) in your own life! It is really challenging to deal with the fact that we're human and can't always respond **i**_____87) . For a teen or tween who's still learning the ins and outs of social **i**_____88) , it's even worse. Here's how this behavior plays out sometimes: Your child texts one of his friends, and the friend doesn't text back right away. Now it's easy for your child to think, "This person doesn't want to be my friend anymore!" So he texts again, and again, and again — "_____89) up their phone." This can be stress-inducing and even read as **a**_____90) . But you can see how **e**_____91) this could happen.

26

Theodore von Kármán, a Hungarian-American engineer, was one of the greatest **m**_____92) of the twentieth century. He was born in Hungary and at an early age, he showed a **t**_____93) for math and science. In 1908, he received a **d**_____94) degree in engineering at the University of Göttingen in Germany. In the 1920s, he began traveling as a lecturer and **c**_____95) to industry. He was invited to the United States to advise engineers on the design of a wind tunnel at California Institute of Technology (Caltech). He became the director of the Guggenheim Aeronautical Laboratory at Caltech in 1930. Later, he was **a**_____96) the National Medal of Science for his leadership in science and engineering.

29

For years, many psychologists have held strongly to the **b**_____97) that the key to **a**_____98) negative health **h**_____99) is to change behavior. This, more than values and **a**_____100) , is the part of **p**_____101) that is easiest to change. **l**_____102) habits such as smoking, drinking and various eating behaviors are the most common health **c**_____103) targeted for behavioral changes. **P**_____104) behaviors (workaholism, shopaholism, and the like) fall into this category as well. Mental imagery combined with power of suggestion was taken up as the **p**_____105) of behavioral **m**_____106) to help people change negative health behaviors into positive ones. Although this technique alone will not produce changes, when used **a**_____107) other behavior **m**_____108) **t**_____109) and **c**_____110) **s**_____111) , behavioral changes have proved **e**_____112) for some people. What mental imagery **d**_____113) is **r**_____114) a new desired behavior. **R**_____115) use of images **r**_____116) the desired behavior more **s**_____117) over time.

30

Emotion s_____118) — learning from other people about emotions and how to deal with them — starts early in life and plays a f_____119) role for emotion r_____120) development. Although extra-familial influences, such as peers or media, g_____121) in importance during adolescence, parents remain the p_____122) socialization agents. For example, their own responses to emotional situations s_____123) as a role model for emotion regulation, increasing the l_____124) that their children will show similar reactions in c_____125) situations. Parental practices at times when their children are faced with emotional challenges also i_____126) emotion regulation development. Whereas direct s_____127) and directive g_____128) of what to do are b_____129) for younger children, they may i_____130) on adolescents' a_____131) s_____132) . In consequence, adolescents might pull away from rather than turn toward, their parents in times of emotional crisis, unless parental practices are a_____133) . More s_____134) in adolescence is i_____135) support of autonomous emotion regulation, such as through interest in, as well as awareness and n_____136) a_____137) of, adolescents' emotional experiences, and being available when the adolescent wants to talk.

31

Dancers often push themselves to the l_____138) of their physical capabilities. But that push is m_____139) if it is directed toward a_____140) something physically impossible. For instance, a tall dancer with long feet may wish to perform repetitive v_____141) jumps to fast music, pointing his feet while in the air and l_____142) his heels to the floor between jumps. That may be impossible no matter how strong the dancer is. But a short-footed dancer may have no trouble! Another dancer may be struggling to complete a half-turn in the air. Understanding the c_____143) between a rapid turn rate and the a_____144) of the body close to the r_____145) a_____146) tells her how to accomplish her turn s_____147) . In both of these cases, understanding and working within the c_____148) i_____149) by nature and described by physical laws allows dancers to work efficiently, m_____150) potential risk of injury.

32

We must e_____151) the relationship between children's film production and c_____152) habits. The term "children's film" implies o_____153) by children —their cinema — but films supposedly made for children have always been c_____154) by audiences of all ages, particularly in commercial cinemas. The c_____155) crossover in audience c_____156) for children's films can be shown by the fact that, in 2007, eleven Danish children's and youth films a_____157) 59 percent of theatrical admissions, and in 2014, German children's films c_____158) seven out of the top twenty films at the national box office. This phenomenon c_____159) with a b_____160) , international e_____161) of what is seemingly children's culture among audiences of d_____162) ages. The old p_____163) that children's film is some other r_____164) , s_____165) from (and forever subordinate to) a more l_____166) cinema for adults is not supported by the realities of consumption: children's film is at the heart of c_____167) popular culture.

33

Beethoven's d_____168) to create something n_____169) is a r_____170) of his state of c_____171) . Our brains experience a sense of reward when we create something new in the process of exploring something u_____172) , such as a musical phrase that we've never played or heard before. When our c_____173) leads to something novel, the r_____174) reward brings us a sense of p_____175) . A number of investigators have m_____176) how curiosity influences musical c_____177) . In the case of Beethoven, computer modeling focused on the thirty-two piano sonatas w_____178) after age thirteen revealed that the musical patterns found in all of Beethoven's music d_____179) in later sonatas, while n_____180) patterns, including patterns that were unique to a particular sonata, increased. In other words, Beethoven's music became less p_____181) over time as his curiosity drove the e_____182) of new musical ideas. Curiosity is a powerful driver of human c_____183) .

34

Technologists are always on the lookout for q_____184) metrics. M_____185) i_____186) to a model are their l_____187) , and like a social scientist, a technologist needs to i_____188) c_____189) m_____190) , or "proxies," for a_____191) p_____192) . This need for q_____193) proxies produces a b_____194) toward measuring things that are easy to q_____195) . But simple m_____196) can take us further away from the important goals we really care about, which may require c_____197) metrics or be extremely difficult, or perhaps impossible, to r_____198) to any measure. And when we have i_____199) or bad proxies, we can easily fall under the i_____200) that we are solving for a good end without actually making g_____201) progress toward a worthy solution. The problem of proxies r_____202) in technologists frequently s_____203) what is measurable for what is meaningful. As the saying goes, "Not everything that c_____204) can be c_____205) , and not everything that can be c_____206) c_____207) ."

35

We are the only species that s_____208) its food, d_____209) a_____210) it with the highly f_____211) plant parts we call herbs and spices. It's quite possible that our taste for spices has an e_____212) root. Many spices have a_____213) p_____214) — in fact, common seasonings such as garlic, onion, and oregano i_____215) the growth of almost every b_____216) t_____217) . And the cultures that make the heaviest use of spices — think of the garlic and black pepper of Thai food, the ginger and coriander of India, the chili peppers of Mexico — come from warmer climates, where b_____218) s_____219) is a bigger issue. In contrast, the most lightly spiced c_____220) — those of Scandinavia and northern Europe — are from c_____221) climates. Our uniquely human attention to flavor, in this case the flavor of spices, turns out to have a_____222) as a matter of life and death.

36

Development of the human body from a single cell provides many examples of the s_____ 223) r_____ 224) that is possible when the r_____ 225) production of random v_____ 226) is combined with nonrandom s_____ 227) . All p_____ 228) of body development from e_____ 229) to adult e_____ 230) r_____ 231) activities at the cellular level, and body f_____ 232) depends on the new possibilities g_____ 233) by these activities c_____ 234) with s_____ 235) of those outcomes that s_____ 236) previously b_____ 237) criteria. Always new structure is based on old structure, and at every stage selection f_____ 238) some cells and e_____ 239) others. The survivors serve to produce new cells that undergo further rounds of selection. Except in the immune system, cells and extensions of cells are not g_____ 240) selected during development, but rather, are positionally selected. Those in the right place that make the right connections are s_____ 241) , and those that d_____ 242) are eliminated. This process is much like s_____ 243) . A natural consequence of the strategy is great v_____ 244) from individual to individual at the cell and m_____ 245) levels, even though large-scale structures are quite s_____ 246) .

37

In order to bring the ever-increasing costs of home care for e_____ 247) and n_____ 248) persons under control, managers of home care providers have i_____ 249) management systems. These systems s_____ 250) tasks of home care workers and the time and budget available to p_____ 251) these tasks. Electronic r_____ 252) systems r_____ 253) home care workers to report on their activities and the time spent, thus making the d_____ 254) of time and money v_____ 255) and, in the p_____ 256) of managers, c_____ 257) . This, in the view of managers, has contributed to the r_____ 258) of the problem. The home care workers, on the other hand, may p_____ 259) their work not as a set of separate tasks to be performed as e_____ 260) as possible, but as a service to be p_____ 261) to a client with whom they may have developed a relationship. This includes having conversations with clients and e_____ 262) about the person's wellbeing. R_____ 263) time and the requirement to report may be perceived as o_____ 264) that make it impossible to deliver the service that is needed. If the management systems are too r_____ 265) , this may result in home care workers becoming o_____ 266) and d_____ 267) .

38

It is a common assumption that most v_____ 268) birds are ultimately d_____ 269) , aside from the rare cases w_____ 270) individuals are able to r_____ 271) and return to their normal ranges. In turn, it is also commonly assumed that v_____ 272) itself is a relatively u_____ 273) b_____ 274) phenomenon. This is undoubtedly true for the majority of cases, as the most likely outcome of any given v_____ 275) event is that the individual will fail to find enough resources, and/or be exposed to i_____ 276) environmental conditions, and p_____ 277) . However, there are many lines of evidence to suggest that v_____ 278) can, on rare occasions, dramatically a_____ 279) the fate of populations, species or even whole ecosystems. Despite being infrequent, these events can be extremely important when viewed at the timescales over which ecological and evolutionary processes u_____ 280) . The most profound consequences of v_____ 281) relate to the e_____ 282) of new breeding sites, new m_____ 283) routes and w_____ 284) locations. Each of these can occur through different m_____ 285) , and at different f_____ 286) , and they each have their own unique i_____ 287) .

39

I_____288) can be great, but it ought to be h_____289) . Experts, for example, are able to think on their f_____290) because they've i_____291) thousands of hours in learning and practice: their intuition has become data-driven. Only then are t_____292) a_____293) to act quickly in a_____294) with their i_____295) e_____296) and evidence-based experience. Yet most people are not experts, though they often think they a_____297) . Most of us, especially when we i_____298) with others on social media, act with expert-like speed and c_____299) , offering a wide range of opinions on global crises, without the substance of knowledge that supports it. And thanks to AI, which e_____300) that our messages are delivered to an audience more inclined to believing it, our d_____301) of expertise can be r_____302) by our personal filter bubble. We have an interesting tendency to find people more open-minded, rational, and s_____303) when they think just like us.

40

The fast-growing, tremendous amount of data, collected and stored in large and numerous data r_____304) , has far e_____305) our human ability for understanding without powerful tools. As a result, data collected in large data repositories become "data tombs" — data a_____306) that are h_____307) visited. Important decisions are often made based not on the information–rich data stored in data repositories but rather on a decision maker's i_____308) , simply because the decision maker does not have the tools to e_____309) the valuable knowledge h_____310) in the vast amounts of data. Efforts have been made to develop expert system and knowledge-based technologies, which typically rely on users or domain experts to manually i_____311) knowledge into knowledge bases. However, this p_____312) is likely to cause b_____313) and errors and is extremely c_____314) and time consuming. The w_____315) gap between data and information calls for the systematic development of tools that can turn data tombs into "golden nuggets" of k_____316) .

41 ~42

It's untrue that teens can focus on two things at once — what they're doing is s_____ 317) their attention from one task to another. In this digital age, teens w_____ 318) their brains to make these shifts very quickly, but they are still, like everyone else, paying attention to one thing at a time, s_____ 319) . Common sense tells us m_____ 320) should increase brain activity, but Carnegie Mellon University scientists using the l_____ 321) brain imaging technology find it d_____ 322) . As a matter of fact, they discovered that multitasking actually d_____ 323) brain activity. N_____ 324) task is done as well as if each w_____ 325) performed individually. Fractions of a second are l_____ 326) every time we make a switch, and a person's i_____ 327) task can take 50 percent longer to finish, with 50 percent more errors. Turns out the l_____ 328) brain research supports the old advice "one thing at a time."

It's not that kids can't do some tasks s_____ 329) . But if two tasks are performed at once, one of them has to be f_____ 330) . Our brains perform a familiar task on "_____ 331) pilot" while really paying attention to the other one. That's why i_____ 332) companies consider talking on a cell phone and driving to be as dangerous as driving while d_____ 333) — it's the driving that goes on "automatic pilot" while the conversation really holds our attention. Our kids may be living in the Information Age but our brains have not been r_____ 334) yet.

43 ~45

Christine was a cat owner who loved her furry companion, Leo. One morning, she noticed that Leo was not feeling w_____ 335) . C_____ 336) for her b_____ 337) cat, Christine decided to take him to the animal hospital. As she always brought Leo to this hospital, she was certain that the v_____ 338) knew well about Leo. She d_____ 339) hoped Leo got the necessary care as soon as possible. The waiting room was f_____ 340) with other pet owners. Finally, it was Leo's turn to see the vet. Christine watched as the vet gently e_____ 341) him. The vet said, "I think Leo has a minor i_____ 342) ." "Infection? Will he be okay?" asked Christine. "We need to do some tests to see if he is infected. But for the tests, it's best for Leo to stay here," replied the vet. It was heartbreaking for Christine to leave Leo at the animal hospital, but she had to accept it was for the best. "I'll call you with updates as soon as we know anything," said the vet. Throughout the day, Christine anxiously a_____ 343) news about Leo. Later that day, the phone rang and it was the vet. "The tests r_____ 344) a minor infection. Leo needs some m_____ 345) and rest, but he'll be back to his playful self soon." R_____ 346) to hear the news, Christine rushed back to the animal hospital to pick up Leo. The vet provided detailed i_____ 347) on how to a_____ 348) the medication and shared tips for a speedy recovery. Back at home, Christine created a comfortable space for Leo to rest and heal. She p_____ 349) him with love and attention, e_____ 350) that he would recover in no time. As the days passed, Leo gradually regained his strength and playful spirit.

2024 고2 3월 모의고사

❶ voca ❷ text ❸ [/] ❹ _____ ❺ quiz 1 ❻ quiz 2 ❼ quiz 3 ❽ quiz 4 ❾ quiz 5

☑ **다음 글을 읽고 물음에 답하시오.** (18)

All the money we receive from rental fees goes to support upcoming activities throughout the year.

Dear Art Crafts People of Greenville, For the annual Crafts Fair on May 25 from 1 p.m. to 6 p.m., the Greenville Community Center is providing booth spaces to rent as in previous years.(①) To reserve your space, please visit our website and complete a registration form by April 20.(②) The rental fee is $50.(③) We expect all available spaces to be fully booked soon, so don't get left out.(④) We hope to see you at the fair.(⑤)

1. 1)글의 흐름으로 보아, 주어진 문장이 들어가기에 가장 적절한 곳은?

☑ **다음 글을 읽고 물음에 답하시오.** (19)

It wasn't until the end that she heard her name.

Sarah, a young artist with a love for painting, entered a local art contest.(①) As she looked at the amazing artworks made by others, her confidence dropped.(②) She quietly thought, 'I might not win an award'. The moment of judgment arrived, and the judges began announcing winners one by one.(③) The head of the judges said, "Congratulations, Sarah Parker! You won first prize.(④) We loved the uniqueness of your work". Sarah was overcome with joy, and she couldn't stop smiling.(⑤) This experience meant more than just winning; it confirmed her identity as an artist.

2. 2)글의 흐름으로 보아, 주어진 문장이 들어가기에 가장 적절한 곳은?

☑ **다음 글을 읽고 물음에 답하시오.** (20)

Because this is a high tech society, everything we want has to be within the parameters of our comfort and convenience.

Too many times people, especially in today's generation, expect things to just happen overnight.(①) When we have these false expectations, it tends to discourage us from continuing to move forward.(②) If it doesn't happen fast enough, we're tempted to lose interest.(③) So many people don't want to take the time it requires to be successful.(④) Success is not a matter of mere desire; you should develop patience in order to achieve it.(⑤) Have you fallen prey to impatience? Great things take time to build.

3. 3)글의 흐름으로 보아, 주어진 문장이 들어가기에 가장 적절한 곳은?

☑ **다음 글을 읽고 물음에 답하시오.** (21)

In fact, many patients are already wearing devices that monitor their conditions in real time, which allows doctors to talk to their patients in a specific, refined, and feedback-driven way that was not even possible a decade ago.

If you had wanted to create a "self-driving" car in the 1950s, your best option might have been to strap a brick to the accelerator.(①) Yes, the vehicle would have been able to move forward on its own, but it could not slow down, stop, or turn to avoid barriers. Obviously not ideal.(②) But does that mean the entire concept of the self-driving car is not worth pursuing? No, it only means that at the time we did not yet have the tools we now possess to help enable vehicles to operate both autonomously and safely.(③) This once-distant dream now seems within our reach.(④) It is much the same story in medicine. Two decades ago, we were still taping bricks to accelerators.(⑤) Today, we are approaching the point where we can begin to bring some appropriate technology to bear in ways that advance our understanding of patients as unique individuals.

4. 4)글의 흐름으로 보아, 주어진 문장이 들어가기에 가장 적절한 곳은?

☑ **다음 글을 읽고 물음에 답하시오.** (22)

This technology might be thought of as a classic time-shifting device, as it enables mothers to exercise more control over the timing of feeding.

We tend to overrate the impact of new technologies in part because older technologies have become absorbed into the furniture of our lives, so as to be almost invisible.(①) Take the baby bottle.(②) Here is a simple implement that has transformed a fundamental human experience for vast numbers of infants and mothers.(③) Yet it finds no place in our histories of technology.(④) It can also function to save time, as bottle feeding allows for someone else to substitute for the mother's time.(⑤) Potentially, therefore, it has huge implications for the management of time in everyday life, yet it is entirely overlooked in discussions of high-speed society.

5. 5)글의 흐름으로 보아, 주어진 문장이 들어가기에 가장 적절한 곳은?

☑ **다음 글을 읽고 물음에 답하시오.** (23)

In other words, an "empathic" company understands the needs and wants of its customers and seeks to fulfill those needs and wants.

Empathy is frequently listed as one of the most desired skills in an employer or employee, although without specifying exactly what is meant by empathy.(①) Some businesses stress cognitive empathy, emphasizing the need for leaders to understand the perspective of employees and customers when negotiating deals and making decisions.(②) Others stress affective empathy and empathic concern.(③) They emphasize the ability of leaders to gain trust from employees and customers by treating them with real concern and compassion.(④) When some consultants argue that successful companies foster empathy, what that translates to is that companies should conduct good market research.(⑤) When some people speak of design with empathy, what that translates to is that companies should take into account the specific needs of different populations — the blind, the deaf, the elderly, non-English speakers, the color-blind, and so on — when designing products.

6. 6)글의 흐름으로 보아, 주어진 문장이 들어가기에 가장 적절한 곳은?

☑ **다음 글을 읽고 물음에 답하시오.** (24)

Now it's easy for your child to think, "This person doesn't want to be my friend anymore"! So he texts again, and again, and again — "blowing up their phone". This can be stress-inducing and even read as aggressive.

The most prevalent problem kids report is that they feel like they need to be accessible at all times.(①) Because technology allows for it, they feel an obligation.(②) It's easy for most of us to relate — you probably feel the same pressure in your own life! It is really challenging to deal with the fact that we're human and can't always respond instantly.(③) For a teen or tween who's still learning the ins and outs of social interactions, it's even worse.(④) Here's how this behavior plays out sometimes: Your child texts one of his friends, and the friend doesn't text back right away.(⑤) But you can see how easily this could happen.

7. 7)글의 흐름으로 보아, 주어진 문장이 들어가기에 가장 적절한 곳은?

☑ **다음 글을 읽고 물음에 답하시오.** (26)

In the 1920s, he began traveling as a lecturer and consultant to industry.

Theodore von Kármán, a Hungarian-American engineer, was one of the greatest minds of the twentieth century.(①) He was born in Hungary and at an early age, he showed a talent for math and science.(②) In 1908, he received a doctoral degree in engineering at the University of Göttingen in Germany.(③) He was invited to the United States to advise engineers on the design of a wind tunnel at California Institute of Technology (Caltech).(④) He became the director of the Guggenheim Aeronautical Laboratory at Caltech in 1930.(⑤) Later, he was awarded the National Medal of Science for his leadership in science and engineering.

8. 8)글의 흐름으로 보아, 주어진 문장이 들어가기에 가장 적절한 곳은?

☑ **다음 글을 읽고 물음에 답하시오.** (29)

Although this technique alone will not produce changes, when used alongside other behavior modification tactics and coping strategies, behavioral changes have proved effective for some people.

For years, many psychologists have held strongly to the belief that the key to addressing negative health habits is to change behavior.(①) This, more than values and attitudes, is the part of personality that is easiest to change. Ingestive habits such as smoking, drinking and various eating behaviors are the most common health concerns targeted for behavioral changes.(②) Process-addiction behaviors (workaholism, shopaholism, and the like) fall into this category as well.(③) Mental imagery combined with power of suggestion was taken up as the premise of behavioral medicine to help people change negative health behaviors into positive ones.(④) What mental imagery does is reinforce a new desired behavior.(⑤) Repeated use of images reinforces the desired behavior more strongly over time.

9. 9)글의 흐름으로 보아, 주어진 문장이 들어가기에 <u>가장 적절한</u> 곳은?

☑ **다음 글을 읽고 물음에 답하시오.** (30)

Whereas direct soothing and directive guidance of what to do are beneficial for younger children, they may intrude on adolescents' autonomy striving.

Emotion socialization — learning from other people about emotions and how to deal with them — starts early in life and plays a foundational role for emotion regulation development.(①) Although extra-familial influences, such as peers or media, gain in importance during adolescence, parents remain the primary socialization agents.(②) For example, their own responses to emotional situations serve as a role model for emotion regulation, increasing the likelihood that their children will show similar reactions in comparable situations.(③) Parental practices at times when their children are faced with emotional challenges also impact emotion regulation development.(④) In consequence, adolescents might pull away from, rather than turn toward, their parents in times of emotional crisis, unless parental practices are adjusted.(⑤) More suitable in adolescence is indirect support of autonomous emotion regulation, such as through interest in, as well as awareness and nonjudgmental acceptance of, adolescents' emotional experiences, and being available when the adolescent wants to talk.

10. 10)글의 흐름으로 보아, 주어진 문장이 들어가기에 <u>가장 적절한</u> 곳은?

☑ **다음 글을 읽고 물음에 답하시오.** (31)

But a short-footed dancer may have no trouble! Another dancer may be struggling to complete a half-turn in the air.

Dancers often push themselves to the limits of their physical capabilities.(①) But that push is misguided if it is directed toward accomplishing something physically impossible.(②) For instance, a tall dancer with long feet may wish to perform repetitive vertical jumps to fast music, pointing his feet while in the air and lowering his heels to the floor between jumps.(③) That may be impossible no matter how strong the dancer is.(④) Understanding the connection between a rapid turn rate and the alignment of the body close to the rotation axis tells her how to accomplish her turn successfully.(⑤) In both of these cases, understanding and working within the constraints imposed by nature and described by physical laws allows dancers to work efficiently, minimizing potential risk of injury.

11. 11)글의 흐름으로 보아, 주어진 문장이 들어가기에 <u>가장 적절한</u> 곳은?

☑ 다음 글을 읽고 물음에 답하시오. (32)

This phenomenon corresponds with a broader, international embrace of what is seemingly children's culture among audiences of diverse ages.

We must explore the relationship between children's film production and consumption habits.(①) The term "children's film" implies ownership by children —their cinema.(②) But films supposedly made for children have always been consumed by audiences of all ages, particularly in commercial cinemas.(③) The considerable crossover in audience composition for children's films can be shown. The fact that, in 2007, eleven Danish children's and youth films attracted 59 percent of theatrical admissions, and in 2014, German children's films comprised seven out of the top twenty films at the national box office is the evidence. (④) The old prejudice that children's film is some other realm, separate from (and forever subordinate to) a more legitimate cinema for adults is not supported by the realities of consumption.(⑤) Children's film is at the heart of contemporary popular culture.

12. 12)글의 흐름으로 보아, 주어진 문장이 들어가기에 가장 적절한 곳은?

☑ 다음 글을 읽고 물음에 답하시오. (33)

In the case of Beethoven, computer modeling focused on the thirty-two piano sonatas written after age thirteen revealed that the musical patterns found in all of Beethoven's music decreased in later sonatas, while novel patterns, including patterns that were unique to a particular sonata, increased.

Beethoven's drive to create something novel is a reflection of his state of curiosity.(①) Our brains experience a sense of reward when we create something new in the process of exploring something uncertain, such as a musical phrase that we've never played or heard before.(②) When our curiosity leads to something novel, the resulting reward brings us a sense of pleasure.(③) A number of investigators have

modeled how curiosity influences musical composition.(④) In other words, Beethoven's music became less predictable over time as his curiosity drove the exploration of new musical ideas.(⑤) Curiosity is a powerful driver of human creativity.

13. 13)글의 흐름으로 보아, 주어진 문장이 들어가기에 가장 적절한 곳은?

☑ 다음 글을 읽고 물음에 답하시오. (34)

But simple metrics can take us further away from the important goals we really care about, which may require complicated metrics or be extremely difficult, or perhaps impossible, to reduce to any measure.

Technologists are always on the lookout for quantifiable metrics.(①) Measurable inputs to a model are their lifeblood, and like a social scientist, a technologist needs to identify concrete measures, or "proxies", for assessing progress.(②) This need for quantifiable proxies produces a bias toward measuring things that are easy to quantify.(③) And when we have imperfect or bad proxies, we can easily fall under the illusion that we are solving for a good end without actually making genuine progress toward a worthy solution.(④) The problem of proxies results in technologists frequently substituting what is measurable for what is meaningful.(⑤) As the saying goes, "Not everything that counts can be counted, and not everything that can be counted counts".

14. 14)글의 흐름으로 보아, 주어진 문장이 들어가기에 가장 적절한 곳은?

☑ **다음 글을 읽고 물음에 답하시오.** (35)

In contrast, the most lightly spiced cuisines — those of Scandinavia and northern Europe — are from cooler climates.

We are the only species that seasons its food, deliberately altering it with the highly flavored plant parts we call herbs and spices.(①) It's quite possible that our taste for spices has an evolutionary root.(②) Many spices have antibacterial properties — in fact, common seasonings such as garlic, onion, and oregano inhibit the growth of almost every bacterium tested.(③) And think of the garlic and black pepper of Thai food, the ginger and coriander of India, the chili peppers of Mexico.(④) The cultures that make those heaviest use of spices come from warmer climates, where bacterial spoilage is a bigger issue.(⑤) Our uniquely human attention to flavor, in this case the flavor of spices, turns out to have arisen as a matter of life and death.

15. 15)글의 흐름으로 보아, 주어진 문장이 들어가기에 가장 적절한 곳은?

☑ **다음 글을 읽고 물음에 답하시오.** (36)

This process is much like sculpting.

Development of the human body from a single cell provides many examples of the structural richness that is possible when the repeated production of random variation is combined with nonrandom selection. All phases of body development from embryo to adult exhibit random activities at the cellular level, and body formation depends on the new possibilities generated by these activities coupled with selection of those outcomes that satisfy previously builtin criteria.(①) Always new structure is based on old structure, and at every stage selection favors some cells and eliminates others.(②) The survivors serve to produce new cells that undergo further rounds of selection.(③) Except in the immune system, cells and extensions of cells are not genetically selected during development, but rather, are positionally selected.(④) Those in the right place that make the right connections are stimulated, and those that don't are eliminated.(⑤) A natural

consequence of the strategy is great variability from individual to individual at the cell and molecular levels, even though large-scale structures are quite similar.

16. 16)글의 흐름으로 보아, 주어진 문장이 들어가기에 가장 적절한 곳은?

☑ **다음 글을 읽고 물음에 답하시오.** (37)

This, in the view of managers, has contributed to the resolution of the problem.

In order to bring the ever-increasing costs of home care for elderly and needy persons under control, managers of home care providers have introduced management systems.(①) These systems specify tasks of home care workers and the time and budget available to perform these tasks.(②) Electronic reporting systems require home care workers to report on their activities and the time spent, thus making the distribution of time and money visible and, in the perception of managers, controllable.(③) The home care workers, on the other hand, may perceive their work not as a set of separate tasks to be performed as efficiently as possible, but as a service to be provided to a client with whom they may have developed a relationship.(④) This includes having conversations with clients and enquiring about the person's wellbeing.(⑤) Restricted time and the requirement to report may be perceived as obstacles that make it impossible to deliver the service that is needed. If the management systems are too rigid, this may result in home care workers becoming overloaded and demotivated.

17. 17)글의 흐름으로 보아, 주어진 문장이 들어가기에 가장 적절한 곳은?

☑ **다음 글을 읽고 물음에 답하시오.** (38)

> However, there are many lines of evidence to suggest that vagrancy can, on rare occasions, dramatically alter the fate of populations, species or even whole ecosystems.

It is a common assumption that most vagrant birds are ultimately doomed, aside from the rare cases where individuals are able to reorientate and return to their normal ranges.(①)   In turn, it is also commonly assumed that vagrancy itself is a relatively unimportant biological phenomenon.(②)   This is undoubtedly true for the majority of cases. (③)   The most likely outcome of any given vagrancy event is that the individual will fail to find enough resources, and/or be exposed to inhospitable environmental conditions, and perish.(④)   Despite being infrequent, these events can be extremely important when viewed at the timescales over which ecological and evolutionary processes unfold. The most profound consequences of vagrancy relate to the establishment of new breeding sites, new migration routes and wintering locations.(⑤)   Each of these can occur through different mechanisms, and at different frequencies, and they each have their own unique importance.

18. 18)글의 흐름으로 보아, 주어진 문장이 들어가기에 <u>가장 적절한</u> 곳은?

☑ **다음 글을 읽고 물음에 답하시오.** (39)

> Yet most people are not experts, though they often think they are.

Intuition can be great, but it ought to be hard-earned.(①)   Experts, for example, are able to think on their feet because they've invested thousands of hours in learning and practice: their intuition has become data-driven.(②)   Only then are they able to act quickly in accordance with their internalized expertise and evidence-based experience.(③)   Most of us, especially when we interact with others on social media, act with expert-like speed and conviction, offering a wide range of opinions on global crises, without the substance of knowledge that supports it.(④)   And thanks to AI, which ensures that our messages are delivered to an audience more inclined to believing it, our delusions of expertise can be reinforced by our personal filter bubble.(⑤)   We have an interesting tendency to find people more open-minded, rational, and sensible when they think just like us.

19. 19)글의 흐름으로 보아, 주어진 문장이 들어가기에 <u>가장 적절한</u> 곳은?

☑ **다음 글을 읽고 물음에 답하시오.** (40)

> However, this procedure is likely to cause biases and errors and is extremely costly and time consuming.

The fast-growing, tremendous amount of data, collected and stored in large and numerous data repositories, has far exceeded our human ability for understanding without powerful tools.(①)   As a result, data collected in large data repositories become "data tombs".(②)   That is, data archives that are hardly visited.(③)   Important decisions are often made based not on the information–rich data stored in data repositories but rather on a decision maker's instinct, simply because the decision maker does not have the tools to extract the valuable knowledge hidden in the vast amounts of data.(④)   Efforts have been made to develop expert system and knowledge-based technologies, which typically rely on users or domain experts to manually input knowledge into knowledge bases.(⑤)   The widening gap between data and information calls for the systematic development of tools that can turn data tombs into "golden nuggets" of knowledge.

20. 20)글의 흐름으로 보아, 주어진 문장이 들어가기에 <u>가장 적절한</u> 곳은?

☑ **다음 글을 읽고 물음에 답하시오.** (41 ~ 42)

> But if two tasks are performed at once, one of them has to be familiar. Our brains perform a familiar task on "automatic pilot" while really paying attention to the other one.

It's untrue that teens can focus on two things at once — what they're doing is shifting their attention from one task to another. In this digital age, teens wire their brains to make these shifts very quickly, but they are still, like everyone else, paying attention to one thing at a time, sequentially.(①)　Common sense tells us multitasking should increase brain activity, but Carnegie Mellon University scientists using the latest brain imaging technology find it doesn't. As a matter of fact, they discovered that multitasking actually decreases brain activity.(②)　Neither task is done as well as if each were performed individually.(③)　Fractions of a second are lost every time we make a switch, and a person's interrupted task can take 50 percent longer to finish, with 50 percent more errors.(④)　Turns out the latest brain research supports the old advice "one thing at a time". It's not that kids can't do some tasks simultaneously.(⑤)　That's why insurance companies consider talking on a cell phone and driving to be as dangerous as driving while drunk — it's the driving that goes on "automatic pilot" while the conversation really holds our attention. Our kids may be living in the Information Age but our brains have not been redesigned yet.

21. 21)글의 흐름으로 보아, 주어진 문장이 들어가기에 **가장 적절한** 곳은?

☑ **다음 글을 읽고 물음에 답하시오.** (43 ~ 45)

> Finally, it was Leo's turn to see the vet. Christine watched as the vet gently examined him. The vet said, "I think Leo has a minor infection". "Infection? Will he be okay"? asked Christine.

Christine was a cat owner who loved her furry companion, Leo. One morning, she noticed that Leo was not feeling well. Concerned for her beloved cat, Christine decided to take him to the animal hospital. As she always brought Leo to this hospital, she was certain that the vet knew well about Leo.(①)　She desperately hoped Leo got the necessary care as soon as possible. The waiting room was filled with other pet owners.(②)　"We need to do some tests to see if he is infected. But for the tests, it's best for Leo to stay here", replied the vet. It was heartbreaking for Christine to leave Leo at the animal hospital, but she had to accept it was for the best. "I'll call you with updates as soon as we know anything", said the vet.(③)　Throughout the day, Christine anxiously awaited news about Leo. Later that day, the phone rang and it was the vet.(④)　"The tests revealed a minor infection. Leo needs some medication and rest, but he'll be back to his playful self soon". Relieved to hear the news, Christine rushed back to the animal hospital to pick up Leo.(⑤)　The vet provided detailed instructions on how to administer the medication and shared tips for a speedy recovery. Back at home, Christine created a comfortable space for Leo to rest and heal. She patted him with love and attention, ensuring that he would recover in no time. As the days passed, Leo gradually regained his strength and playful spirit.

22. 22)글의 흐름으로 보아, 주어진 문장이 들어가기에 **가장 적절한** 곳은?

1. 23) 18

Dear Art Crafts People of Greenville,

(A) For the annual Crafts Fair on May 25 from 1 p.m. to 6 p.m., the Greenville Community Center is providing booth spaces to rent as in previous years. To reserve your space, please visit our website and complete a registration form by April 20.

(B) We expect all available spaces to be fully booked soon, so don't get left out.

(C) We hope to see you at the fair.

(D) The rental fee is $50. All the money we receive from rental fees goes to support upcoming activities throughout the year.

2. 24) 19

Sarah, a young artist with a love for painting, entered a local art contest.

(A) We loved the uniqueness of your work." Sarah was overcome with joy, and she couldn't stop smiling. This experience meant more than just winning; it confirmed her identity as an artist.

(B) It wasn't until the end that she heard her name. The head of the judges said, "Congratulations, Sarah Parker! You won first prize.

(C) As she looked at the amazing artworks made by others, her confidence dropped. She quietly thought, 'I might not win an award'. The moment of judgment arrived, and the judges began announcing winners one by one.

3. 25) 20

Too many times people, especially in today's generation, expect things to just happen overnight.

(A) Great things take time to build.

(B) When we have these false expectations, it tends to discourage us from continuing to move forward. Because this is a high tech society, everything we want has to be within the parameters of our comfort and convenience.

(C) Success is not a matter of mere desire; you should develop patience in order to achieve it.

(D) If it doesn't happen fast enough, we're tempted to lose interest. So many people don't want to take the time it requires to be successful.

(E) Have you fallen prey to impatience?

4. 26) 21

If you had wanted to create a "self-driving" car in the 1950s, your best option might have been to strap a brick to the accelerator.

(A) Two decades ago, we were still taping bricks to accelerators. Today, we are approaching the point where we can begin to bring some appropriate technology to bear in ways that advance our understanding of patients as unique individuals. In fact, many patients are already wearing devices that monitor their conditions in real time, which allows doctors to talk to their patients in a specific, refined, and feedback-driven way that was not even possible a decade ago.

(B) Yes, the vehicle would have been able to move forward on its own, but it could not slow down, stop, or turn to avoid barriers. Obviously not ideal. But does that mean the entire concept of the self-driving car is not worth pursuing?

(C) No, it only means that at the time we did not yet have the tools we now possess to help enable vehicles to operate both autonomously and safely. This once-distant dream now seems within our reach. It is much the same story in medicine.

5. 27) 22

We tend to overrate the impact of new technologies in part because older technologies have become absorbed into the furniture of our lives, so as to be almost invisible.

(A) This technology might be thought of as a classic time-shifting device, as it enables mothers to exercise more control over the timing of feeding. It can also function to save time, as bottle feeding allows for someone else to substitute for the mother's time.

(B) Take the baby bottle. Here is a simple implement that has transformed a fundamental human experience for vast numbers of infants and mothers, yet it finds no place in our histories of technology.

(C) Potentially, therefore, it has huge implications for the management of time in everyday life, yet it is entirely overlooked in discussions of high-speed society.

6. 28) 23

Empathy is frequently listed as one of the most desired skills in an employer or employee, although without specifying exactly what is meant by empathy.

(A) When some people speak of design with empathy, what that translates to is that companies should take into account the specific needs of different populations — the blind, the deaf, the elderly, non-English speakers, the color-blind, and so on — when designing products.

(B) Some businesses stress cognitive empathy, emphasizing the need for leaders to understand the perspective of employees and customers when negotiating deals and making decisions. Others stress affective empathy and empathic concern, emphasizing the ability of leaders to gain trust from employees and customers by treating them with real concern and compassion.

(C) When some consultants argue that successful companies foster empathy, what that translates to is that companies should conduct good market research.

(D) In other words, an "empathic" company understands the needs and wants of its customers and seeks to fulfill those needs and wants.

7. 29) 24

The most prevalent problem kids report is that they feel like they need to be accessible at all times.

(A) Because technology allows for it, they feel an obligation. It's easy for most of us to relate — you probably feel the same pressure in your own life! It is really challenging to deal with the fact that we're human and can't always respond instantly.

(B) This can be stress-inducing and even read as aggressive. But you can see how easily this could happen.

(C) For a teen or tween who's still learning the ins and outs of social interactions, it's even worse. Here's how this behavior plays out sometimes: Your child texts one of his friends, and the friend doesn't text back right away.

(D) Now it's easy for your child to think, "This person doesn't want to be my friend anymore!" So he texts again, and again, and again — "blowing up their phone."

8. 30) 25

The graph above shows the animal protein consumption measured as the average daily supply per person in three different countries in 2020.

(A) Fish and Seafood, which was the least consumed animal protein consumption source in the U.S. and Brazil, ranked the highest in Japan.

(B) Japan had less than 50g of the total animal protein consumption per person, which was the smallest among the three countries.

(C) Unlike the U.S., Brazil consumed the most animal protein from Meat, with Eggs and Dairy being the second most.

(D) The U.S. showed the largest amount of total animal protein consumption per person among the three countries. Eggs and Dairy was the top animal protein consumption source among four categories in the U.S., followed by Meat and Poultry at 22.4g and 20.6g, respectively.

9. 31) 26

Theodore von Kármán, a Hungarian-American engineer, was one of the greatest minds of the twentieth century.

(A) He was born in Hungary and at an early age, he showed a talent for math and science. In 1908, he received a doctoral degree in engineering at the University of Göttingen in Germany.

(B) Later, he was awarded the National Medal of Science for his leadership in science and engineering.

(C) He was invited to the United States to advise engineers on the design of a wind tunnel at California Institute of Technology (Caltech).

(D) In the 1920s, he began traveling as a lecturer and consultant to industry.

(E) He became the director of the Guggenheim Aeronautical Laboratory at Caltech in 1930.

10. 32) 29

For years, many psychologists have held strongly to the belief that the key to addressing negative health habits is to change behavior.

(A) Although this technique alone will not produce changes, when used alongside other behavior modification tactics and coping strategies, behavioral changes have proved effective for some people.

(B) What mental imagery does is reinforce a new desired behavior.

(C) This, more than values and attitudes, is the part of personality that is easiest to change. Ingestive habits such as smoking, drinking and various eating behaviors are the most common health concerns targeted for behavioral changes.

(D) Process-addiction behaviors (workaholism, shopaholism, and the like) fall into this category as well. Mental imagery combined with power of suggestion was taken up as the premise of behavioral medicine to help people change negative health behaviors into positive ones.

(E) Repeated use of images reinforces the desired behavior more strongly over time.

11. 33) 30

Emotion socialization — learning from other people about emotions and how to deal with them — starts early in life and plays a foundational role for emotion regulation development.

(A) Parental practices at times when their children are faced with emotional challenges also impact emotion regulation development. Whereas direct soothing and directive guidance of what to do are beneficial for younger children, they may intrude on adolescents' autonomy striving.

(B) In consequence, adolescents might pull away from, rather than turn toward, their parents in times of emotional crisis, unless parental practices are adjusted. More suitable in adolescence is indirect support of autonomous emotion regulation, such as through interest in, as well as awareness and nonjudgmental acceptance of, adolescents' emotional experiences, and being available when the adolescent wants to talk.

(C) Although extra-familial influences, such as peers or media, gain in importance during adolescence, parents remain the primary socialization agents. For example, their own responses to emotional situations

serve as a role model for emotion regulation, increasing the likelihood that their children will show similar reactions in comparable situations.

12. 34) 31

Dancers often push themselves to the limits of their physical capabilities.

(A) But a short-footed dancer may have no trouble! Another dancer may be struggling to complete a half-turn in the air.

(B) Understanding the connection between a rapid turn rate and the alignment of the body close to the rotation axis tells her how to accomplish her turn successfully. In both of these cases, understanding and working within the constraints imposed by nature and described by physical laws allows dancers to work efficiently, minimizing potential risk of injury.

(C) But that push is misguided if it is directed toward accomplishing something physically impossible. For instance, a tall dancer with long feet may wish to perform repetitive vertical jumps to fast music, pointing his feet while in the air and lowering his heels to the floor between jumps. That may be impossible no matter how strong the dancer is.

13. 35) 32

We must explore the relationship between children's film production and consumption habits.

(A) The considerable crossover in audience composition for children's films can be shown by the fact that, in 2007, eleven Danish children's and youth films attracted 59 percent of theatrical admissions, and in 2014, German children's films comprised seven out of the top twenty films at the national box office.

(B) The term "children's film" implies ownership by children —their cinema — but films supposedly made for children have always been consumed by audiences of all ages, particularly in commercial cinemas.

(C) This phenomenon corresponds with a broader, international embrace of what is seemingly children's culture among audiences of diverse ages.

(D) The old prejudice that children's film is some other realm, separate from (and forever subordinate to) a more legitimate cinema for adults is not supported by the realities of consumption: children's film is at the heart of contemporary popular culture.

14. 36) 33

Beethoven's drive to create something novel is a reflection of his state of curiosity.

(A) Our brains experience a sense of reward when we create something new in the process of exploring something uncertain, such as a musical phrase that we've never played or heard before. When our curiosity leads to something novel, the resulting reward brings us a sense of pleasure.

(B) In other words, Beethoven's music became less predictable over time as his curiosity drove the exploration of new musical ideas. Curiosity is a powerful driver of human creativity.

(C) A number of investigators have modeled how curiosity influences musical composition. In the case of Beethoven, computer modeling focused on the thirty-two piano sonatas written after age thirteen revealed that the musical patterns found in all of Beethoven's music decreased in later sonatas, while novel patterns, including patterns that were unique to a particular sonata, increased.

15. 37) 34

Technologists are always on the lookout for quantifiable metrics.

(A) Measurable inputs to a model are their lifeblood, and like a social scientist, a technologist needs to identify concrete measures, or "proxies," for assessing progress. This need for quantifiable proxies produces a bias toward measuring things that are easy to quantify.

(B) And when we have imperfect or bad proxies, we can easily fall under the illusion that we are solving for a good end without actually making genuine progress toward a worthy solution.

(C) But simple metrics can take us further away from the important goals we really care about, which may require complicated metrics or be extremely difficult, or perhaps impossible, to reduce to any measure.

(D) The problem of proxies results in technologists frequently substituting what is measurable for what is meaningful.

(E) As the saying goes, "Not everything that counts can be counted, and not everything that can be counted counts."

16. 38) 35

We are the only species that seasons its food, deliberately altering it with the highly flavored plant parts we call herbs and spices.

(A) It's quite possible that our taste for spices has an evolutionary root. Many spices have antibacterial properties — in fact, common seasonings such as garlic, onion, and oregano inhibit the growth of almost every bacterium tested.

(B) Our uniquely human attention to flavor, in this case the flavor of spices, turns out to have arisen as a matter of life and death.

(C) And the cultures that make the heaviest use of spices — think of the garlic and black pepper of Thai food, the ginger and coriander of India, the chili peppers of Mexico — come from warmer climates, where bacterial spoilage is a bigger issue. In contrast, the most lightly spiced cuisines — those of Scandinavia and northern Europe — are from cooler climates.

17. 39) 36

Development of the human body from a single cell provides many examples of the structural richness that is possible when the repeated production of random variation is combined with nonrandom selection.

(A) All phases of body development from embryo to adult exhibit random activities at the cellular level, and body formation depends on the new possibilities generated by these activities coupled with selection of those outcomes that satisfy previously builtin criteria. Always new structure is based on old structure, and at every stage selection favors some cells and eliminates others. The survivors serve to produce new cells that undergo further rounds of selection.

(B) Except in the immune system, cells and extensions of cells are not genetically selected during development, but rather, are positionally selected. Those in the right place that make the right connections are stimulated, and those that don't are eliminated.

(C) This process is much like sculpting. A natural consequence of the strategy is great variability from individual to individual at the cell and molecular levels, even though large-scale structures are quite similar.

18. 40) 37

In order to bring the ever-increasing costs of home care for elderly and needy persons under control, managers of home care providers have introduced management systems.

(A) These systems specify tasks of home care workers and the time and budget available to perform these tasks. Electronic reporting systems require home care workers to report on their activities and the time spent, thus making the distribution of time and money visible and, in the perception of managers, controllable. This, in the view of managers, has contributed to the resolution of the problem.

(B) The home care workers, on the other hand, may perceive their work not as a set of separate tasks to be performed as efficiently as possible, but as a service to be provided to a client with whom they may have developed a relationship. This includes having conversations with clients and enquiring about the person's wellbeing.

(C) Restricted time and the requirement to report may be perceived as obstacles that make it impossible to deliver the service that is needed. If the management systems are too rigid, this may result in home care workers becoming overloaded and demotivated.

19. 41) 38

It is a common assumption that most vagrant birds are ultimately doomed, aside from the rare cases where individuals are able to reorientate and return to their normal ranges.

(A) The most profound consequences of vagrancy relate to the establishment of new breeding sites, new migration routes and wintering locations.

(B) Each of these can occur through different mechanisms, and at different frequencies, and they each have their own unique importance.

(C) However, there are many lines of evidence to suggest that vagrancy can, on rare occasions, dramatically alter the fate of populations, species or even whole ecosystems. Despite being infrequent, these events can be extremely important when viewed at the timescales over which ecological and evolutionary processes unfold.

(D) In turn, it is also commonly assumed that vagrancy itself is a relatively unimportant biological phenomenon. This is undoubtedly true for the majority of cases, as the most likely outcome of any given vagrancy event is that the individual will fail to find enough resources, and/or be exposed to inhospitable environmental conditions, and perish.

20. 42) 39

Intuition can be great, but it ought to be hard-earned.

(A) And thanks to AI, which ensures that our messages are delivered to an audience more inclined to believing it, our delusions of expertise can be reinforced by our personal filter bubble. We have an interesting tendency to find people more open-minded, rational, and sensible when they think just like us.

(B) Experts, for example, are able to think on their feet because they've invested thousands of hours in learning and practice: their intuition has become data-driven. Only then are they able to act quickly in accordance with their internalized expertise and evidence-based experience.

(C) Yet most people are not experts, though they often think they are. Most of us, especially when we interact with others on social media, act with expert-like speed and conviction, offering a wide range of opinions on global crises, without the substance of knowledge that supports it.

21. 43) 40

The fast-growing, tremendous amount of data, collected and stored in large and numerous data repositories, has far exceeded our human ability for understanding without powerful tools.

(A) As a result, data collected in large data repositories become "data tombs" — data archives that are hardly visited.

(B) The widening gap between data and information calls for the systematic development of tools that can turn data tombs into "golden nuggets" of knowledge.

(C) Efforts have been made to develop expert system and knowledge-based technologies, which typically rely on users or domain experts to manually input knowledge into knowledge bases.

(D) However, this procedure is likely to cause biases and errors and is extremely costly and time consuming.

(E) Important decisions are often made based not on the information–rich data stored in data repositories but rather on a decision maker's instinct, simply because the decision maker does not have the tools to extract the valuable knowledge hidden in the vast amounts of data.

22. 44) [41 ~ 42]

It's untrue that teens can focus on two things at once — what they're doing is shifting their attention from one task to another.

(A) It's not that kids can't do some tasks simultaneously. But if two tasks are performed at once, one of them has to be familiar. Our brains perform a familiar task on "automatic pilot" while really paying attention to the other one.

(B) In this digital age, teens wire their brains to make these shifts very quickly, but they are still, like everyone else, paying attention to one thing at a time, sequentially. Common sense tells us multitasking should increase brain activity, but Carnegie Mellon University scientists using the latest brain imaging technology find it doesn't. As a matter of fact, they discovered that multitasking actually decreases brain activity.

(C) Neither task is done as well as if each were performed individually. Fractions of a second are lost every time we make a switch, and a person's interrupted task can take 50 percent longer to finish, with 50 percent more errors. Turns out the latest brain research supports the old advice "one thing at a time."

(D) That's why insurance companies consider talking on a cell phone and driving to be as dangerous as driving while drunk — it's the driving that goes on "automatic pilot" while the conversation really holds our attention. Our kids may be living in the Information Age but our brains have not been redesigned yet.

23. 45) [43 ~ 45]

Christine was a cat owner who loved her furry companion, Leo.

(A) Finally, it was Leo's turn to see the vet. Christine watched as the vet gently examined him. The vet said, "I think Leo has a minor infection." "Infection? Will he be okay?" asked Christine.

(B) Later that day, the phone rang and it was the vet. "The tests revealed a minor infection. Leo needs some medication and rest, but he'll be back to his playful self soon." Relieved to hear the news, Christine rushed back to the animal hospital to pick up Leo.

(C) One morning, she noticed that Leo was not feeling well. Concerned for her beloved cat, Christine decided to take him to the animal hospital. As she always brought Leo to this hospital, she was certain that the vet knew well about Leo. She desperately hoped Leo got the necessary care as soon as possible. The waiting room was filled with other pet owners.

(D) "We need to do some tests to see if he is infected. But for the tests, it's best for Leo to stay here," replied the vet. It was heartbreaking for Christine to leave Leo at the animal hospital, but she had to accept it was for the best. "I'll call you with updates as soon as we know anything," said the vet. Throughout the day, Christine anxiously awaited news about Leo.

(E) The vet provided detailed instructions on how to administer the medication and shared tips for a speedy recovery. Back at home, Christine created a comfortable space for Leo to rest and heal. She patted him with love and attention, ensuring that he would recover in no time. As the days passed, Leo gradually regained his strength and playful spirit.

2024 고2 3월 모의고사

❶ voca   ❷ text   ❸ [/]   ❹ _____   ❺ quiz 1   ❻ quiz 2   ❼ quiz 3   ❽ quiz 4   ❾ quiz 5

1. 1)밑줄 친 부분 중, 어법, 혹은 문맥상 어색한 곳을 고르시오. 18.

For the annual Crafts Fair ① **on** May 25 from 1 p.m. to 6 p.m., the Greenville Community Center ② **is providing** booth spaces to rent as in previous years. To ③ **reserve** your space, please visit our website and complete a registration form by April 20. The rental fee is $50. All the money we receive from rental fees ④ **going** to support upcoming activities throughout the year. We expect all available spaces to be fully booked soon, so don't get ⑤ **left** out. We hope to see you at the fair.

2. 2)밑줄 친 부분 중, 어법, 혹은 문맥상 어색한 곳을 고르시오. 19.

Sarah, a young artist with a love for painting, ① **entered into** a local art contest. As she looked at the ② **amazing** artworks made by others, her confidence dropped. She quietly thought, 'I might not ③ **win** an award'. The moment of judgment arrived, and the judges began announcing winners one by one. It wasn't until the end that she heard her name. The head of the judges said, "Congratulations, Sarah Parker! You won first prize. We loved the uniqueness of your work". Sarah ④ **was overcome** with joy, and she couldn't stop smiling. This experience meant more than just winning; it ⑤ **confirmed** her identity as an artist.

3. 3)밑줄 친 부분 중, 어법, 혹은 문맥상 어색한 곳을 고르시오. 20.

Too many times people, especially in today's generation, expect things to just happen overnight. When we have these false expectations, it tends to discourage us from continuing to move forward. Because this is a high tech society, everything we want ① **has** to be within the parameters of our comfort and convenience. If it ② **isn't** happen fast enough, we're ③ **tempted** to lose interest. So many people don't want to take the time it requires ④ **to be** successful. Success is not a matter of mere desire; you should develop patience in order to achieve it. Have you fallen ⑤ **prey** to impatience? Great things take time to build.

4. 4)밑줄 친 부분 중, 어법, 혹은 문맥상 어색한 곳을 고르시오. 21.

If you ① **had wanted** to create a "self-driving" car in the 1950s, your best option might ② **be** to strap a brick to the accelerator. Yes, the vehicle would have been able to move forward on its own, but it could not slow down, stop, or turn to avoid barriers. Obviously not ideal. But does that mean the entire concept of the self-driving car is not worth ③ **pursuing**? No, it only means that at the time we did not yet have the tools we now possess to help enable vehicles ④ **to operate** both autonomously and safely. This once-distant dream now seems within our reach. It is much the same story in medicine. Two decades ago, we were still taping bricks to accelerators. Today, we are approaching the point where we can begin to bring some appropriate technology to bear in ways ⑤ **that** advance our understanding of patients as unique individuals. In fact, many patients are already wearing devices that monitor their conditions in real time, which allows doctors to talk to their patients in a specific, refined, and feedback-driven way that was not even possible a decade ago.

5. 5)밑줄 친 부분 중, 어법, 혹은 문맥상 어색한 곳을 고르시오. 22.

We tend to overrate the impact of new technologies in part because older technologies have become absorbed into the furniture of our lives, so as to be almost invisible. Take the baby bottle. Here is a simple ① **implementaion** that has transformed a fundamental human experience for vast numbers of infants and mothers, yet it finds no place in our histories of technology. This technology might ② **be thought** of as a classic time-shifting device, as it enables mothers to exercise more control over the timing of ③ **feeding**. It can also function to save time, as bottle feeding allows for someone else to ④ **substitute** for the mother's time. Potentially, therefore, it has huge implications for the management of time in everyday life, yet ⑤ **it** is entirely overlooked in discussions of high-speed society.

6. ⁶⁾**밑줄 친 부분 중, 어법, 혹은 문맥상 어색한 곳을 고르시오.** 23.

Empathy is frequently listed as one of the most desired skills in an employer or employee, ① **although** without specifying exactly what is meant by empathy. Some businesses stress cognitive empathy, emphasizing the need for leaders to understand the perspective of employees and customers when negotiating deals and making decisions. Others stress ② **affective** empathy and empathic concern, emphasizing the ability of leaders to gain trust from employees and customers by treating them with real concern and compassion. When some consultants argue that successful companies foster empathy, what that translates ③ **to** is that companies should conduct good market research. In other words, an "empathic" company understands the needs and wants of its customers and seeks to fulfill those needs and wants. When some people speak of design with empathy, what that translates ④ **to** is that companies should take into account the specific needs of different populations — the blind, the deaf, the elderly, non-English speakers, the color-blind, and so on — when ⑤ **designed** products.

7. ⁷⁾**밑줄 친 부분 중, 어법, 혹은 문맥상 어색한 곳을 고르시오.** 24.

The most ① **prevalent** problem kids report is that they feel like they need to be ② **accessible** at all times. Because technology allows for it, they feel an obligation. It's easy for most of us to relate — you probably feel the same pressure in your own life! It is really challenging to deal with the fact that we're human and can't always ③ **respond** instantly. For a teen or tween who's still learning the ins and outs of social interactions, it's even worse. Here's how this behavior plays out sometimes: Your child texts one of his friends, and the friend doesn't text back right away. Now ④ **it** is easy for your child to think, "This person doesn't want to be my friend anymore"! So he texts again, and again, and again — "blowing up their phone". This can be stress-inducing and even read as ⑤ **progressive**. But you can see how easily this could happen.

8. ⁸⁾**밑줄 친 부분 중, 어법, 혹은 문맥상 어색한 곳을 고르시오.** 26.

Theodore von Kármán, a Hungarian-American engineer, ① **being** one of the greatest minds of the twentieth century. He was born in Hungary and at an early age, he showed a talent for math and science. ② **In** 1908, he received a doctoral degree in engineering at the University of Göttingen in Germany. ③ **In** the 1920s, he began traveling as a lecturer and consultant to industry. He ④ **was invited** to the United States to advise engineers on the design of a wind tunnel at California Institute of Technology (Caltech). He became the director of the Guggenheim Aeronautical Laboratory at Caltech in 1930. Later, he ⑤ **was awarded** the National Medal of Science for his leadership in science and engineering.

9. ⁹⁾**밑줄 친 부분 중, 어법, 혹은 문맥상 어색한 곳을 고르시오.** 29.

For years, many psychologists have held strongly to the belief that the key to addressing negative health habits is to change behavior. This, more than values and attitudes, is the part of personality that is easiest to change. ① **Ingestive** habits such as smoking, drinking and various eating behaviors are the most common health concerns ② **targeted** for behavioral changes. Process-addiction behaviors (workaholism, shopaholism, and the like) fall into this category as well. Mental ③ **imaginary** combined with power of suggestion was taken up as the premise of behavioral medicine to help people change negative health behaviors into positive ones. Although this technique alone will not produce changes, when ④ **using** alongside other behavior modification tactics and coping strategies, behavioral changes have proved effective for some people. What mental ⑤ **imagery** does is reinforce a new desired behavior. Repeated use of images reinforces the desired behavior more strongly over time.

10. ¹⁰⁾**밑줄 친 부분 중, 어법, 혹은 문맥상 어색한 곳을 고르시오.** ^{30.}

Emotion socialization — learning from other people about emotions and how to deal with ① **them** — starts early in life and plays a foundational role for emotion regulation development. Although extra-familial influences, such as peers or media, gain in importance during adolescence, parents remain the primary socialization agents. For example, their own responses to emotional situations serve as a role model for emotion regulation, increasing the likelihood that their children will show similar reactions in comparable situations. Parental practices at times when their children ② **are faced** with emotional challenges also impact emotion regulation development. Whereas direct soothing and directive guidance of what to do ③ **are** beneficial for younger children, they may intrude on adolescents' autonomy striving. In consequence, adolescents might pull away from, rather than ④ **turning** toward, their parents in times of emotional crisis, unless parental practices are adjusted. More suitable in adolescence is indirect support of ⑤ **autonomous** emotion regulation, such as through interest in, as well as awareness and nonjudgmental acceptance of, adolescents' emotional experiences, and being available when the adolescent wants to talk.

11. ¹¹⁾**밑줄 친 부분 중, 어법, 혹은 문맥상 어색한 곳을 고르시오.** ^{31.}

Dancers often push themselves to the limits of their physical capabilities. But that push ① **is misguided** if it is directed toward ② **accomplish** something physically impossible. For instance, a tall dancer with long feet may wish to perform repetitive vertical jumps to fast music, pointing his feet while in the air and lowering his heels to the floor between jumps. That may be impossible no matter ③ **how** strong the dancer is. But a short-footed dancer may have no trouble! Another dancer may be struggling to complete a half-turn in the air. Understanding the connection between a rapid turn rate and the ④ **alignment** of the body close to the rotation axis tells her how to accomplish her turn successfully. In both of these cases, understanding and working within the constraints imposed by nature and described by physical laws ⑤ **allows** dancers to work efficiently, minimizing potential risk of injury.

12. ¹²⁾**밑줄 친 부분 중, 어법, 혹은 문맥상 어색한 곳을 고르시오.** ^{32.}

We must explore the relationship between children's film ① **productivity** and consumption habits. The term "children's film" implies ownership by children —their cinema — but films supposedly ② **made** for children have always been consumed by audiences of all ages, particularly in commercial cinemas. The considerable crossover in audience composition for children's films can be shown by the fact that, in 2007, eleven Danish children's and youth films attracted 59 percent of theatrical admissions, and in 2014, German children's films comprised seven out of the top twenty films at the national box office. This phenomenon ③ **corresponds** with a broader, international embrace of what is seemingly children's culture among audiences of diverse ages. The old prejudice that children's film is some other realm, separate from (and forever ④ **subordinate** to) a more legitimate cinema for adults ⑤ **is** not supported by the realities of consumption: children's film is at the heart of contemporary popular culture.

13. ¹³⁾**밑줄 친 부분 중, 어법, 혹은 문맥상 어색한 곳을 고르시오.** ^{33.}

Beethoven's drive to create something ① **novel** is a reflection of his state of curiosity. Our brains experience a sense of reward when we create something new in the process of exploring something uncertain, such as a musical phrase that we've never played or heard before. When our curiosity leads to something novel, the resulting reward brings us a sense of pleasure. ② **A** number of investigators have modeled how curiosity influences musical composition. In the case of Beethoven, computer modeling focused on the thirty-two piano sonatas written after age thirteen ③ **revealed** that the musical patterns found in all of Beethoven's music decreased in later sonatas, while ④ **novel** patterns, including patterns that were unique to a particular sonata, increased. In other words, Beethoven's music became ⑤ **more** predictable over time as his curiosity drove the exploration of new musical ideas. Curiosity is a powerful driver of human creativity.

14. 14)밑줄 친 부분 중, 어법, 혹은 문맥상 어색한 곳을 고르시오. 34.

Technologists are always on the lookout for quantifiable metrics. Measurable inputs to a model ① **are** their lifeblood, and like a social scientist, a technologist needs to identify concrete measures, or "proxies", for assessing progress. This need for quantifiable proxies ② **produce** a bias toward measuring things that are easy to quantify. But simple metrics can take us further away from the important goals we really care about, ③ **which** may require ④ **complicated** metrics or be extremely difficult, or perhaps impossible, to reduce to any measure. And when we have imperfect or bad proxies, we can easily fall under the illusion that we are solving for a good end without actually making genuine progress toward a worthy solution. The problem of proxies ⑤ **results** in technologists frequently substituting what is measurable for what is meaningful. As the saying goes, "Not everything that counts can be counted, and not everything that can be counted counts".

15. 15)밑줄 친 부분 중, 어법, 혹은 문맥상 어색한 곳을 고르시오. 35.

We are the only species that seasons its food, ① **deliberately** altering it with the ② **highly** flavored plant parts we call herbs and spices. It's quite possible that our taste for spices has an evolutionary root. Many spices have antibacterial properties — in fact, common seasonings such as garlic, onion, and oregano inhibit the growth of almost every bacterium tested. And the cultures that make the heaviest use of spices — think of the garlic and black pepper of Thai food, the ginger and coriander of India, the chili peppers of Mexico — come from warmer climates, where bacterial spoilage is a ③ **bigger** issue. In contrast, the most lightly spiced cuisines — those of Scandinavia and northern Europe — ④ **are** from cooler climates. Our uniquely human attention to flavor, in this case the flavor of spices, ⑤ **turning** out to have arisen as a matter of life and death.

16. 16)밑줄 친 부분 중, 어법, 혹은 문맥상 어색한 곳을 고르시오. 36.

Development of the human body from a single cell provides many examples of the structural richness that is possible when the ① **repeated** production of random variation is combined with nonrandom selection. All phases of body development from embryo to adult ② **exhibit** random activities at the cellular level, and body formation ③ **depends** on the new possibilities generated by these activities ④ **coupled** with selection of those outcomes that satisfy previously builtin criteria. Always new structure is based on old structure, and at every stage selection favors some cells and eliminates others. The survivors serve to produce new cells that undergo further rounds of selection. Except in the immune system, cells and extensions of cells are not genetically selected during development, but rather, are positionally selected. Those in the right place that make the right connections are stimulated, and those that don't are ⑤ **illuminated**. This process is much like sculpting. A natural consequence of the strategy is great variability from individual to individual at the cell and molecular levels, even though large-scale structures are quite similar.

17. 17)밑줄 친 부분 중, 어법, 혹은 문맥상 어색한 곳을 고르시오. 37.

In order to bring the ever-increasing costs of home care for elderly and needy persons under control, managers of home care providers have introduced management systems. These systems specify tasks of home care workers and the time and budget available to perform these tasks. Electronic reporting systems require home care workers to report on their activities and the time spent, thus ① **making** the distribution of time and money visible and, in the perception of managers, controllable. This, in the view of managers, ② **has** ③ **contributed** to the resolution of the problem. The home care workers, on the other hand, may perceive their work not as a set of separate tasks to be performed as efficiently as possible, but as a service to be provided to a client with whom they may have developed a relationship. This includes having conversations with clients and enquiring about the person's well-being. ④ **Restricted** time and the requirement to report may be perceived as obstacles that make ⑤ **them** impossible to deliver the service that is needed. If the management systems are too rigid, this may result in home care workers becoming overloaded and demotivated.

18. 18)밑줄 친 부분 중, 어법, 혹은 문맥상 어색한 곳을 고르시오. 38.

It is a common assumption that most ① **vagrant** birds are ultimately doomed, aside from the rare cases where individuals are able to reorientate and return to their normal ranges. In turn, it is also commonly assumed that vagrancy itself is a relatively unimportant biological phenomenon. This is undoubtedly true for the majority of cases, as the most likely outcome of any given vagrancy event is that the individual will fail to find enough resources, and/or be exposed to ② **inhospitable** environmental conditions, and perish. However, there are many lines of evidence to suggest that vagrancy can, on rare occasions, dramatically ③ **alter** the fate of populations, species or even whole ecosystems. Despite being infrequent, these events can be extremely important when ④ **viewed** at the timescales over ⑤ **what** ecological and evolutionary processes unfold. The most profound consequences of vagrancy relate to the establishment of new breeding sites, new migration routes and wintering locations. Each of these can occur through different mechanisms, and at different frequencies, and they each have their own unique importance.

19. 19)밑줄 친 부분 중, 어법, 혹은 문맥상 어색한 곳을 고르시오. 39.

Intuition can be great, but it ought to be hard-earned. Experts, for example, are able to think on their feet because they've invested thousands of hours in learning and practice: their intuition has become data-driven. Only then are they able to act quickly in accordance with their ① **internalized** expertise and evidence-based experience. Yet most people are not experts, though they often think they ② **are**. Most of us, especially when we interact with others on social media, act with expert-like speed and conviction, ③ **offering** a wide range of opinions on global crises, without the substance of knowledge that supports it. And thanks to AI, which ensures that our messages are delivered to an audience more inclined to believing it, our ④ **illusions** of expertise can be reinforced by our personal filter bubble. We have an interesting tendency to find people more open-minded, rational, and ⑤ **sensible** when they think just like us.

20. 20)밑줄 친 부분 중, 어법, 혹은 문맥상 어색한 곳을 고르시오. 40.

The fast-growing, tremendous amount of data, ① **x** collected and stored in large and numerous data repositories, has far exceeded our human ability for understanding without powerful tools. As a result, data ② **collected** in large data repositories become "data tombs" — data archives that are hardly visited. Important decisions are often made based not on the information–rich data stored in data repositories but rather on a decision maker's instinct, simply because the decision maker does not have the tools to ③ **subtract** the valuable knowledge hidden in the vast amounts of data. Efforts have been made to develop expert system and knowledge-based technologies, ④ **which** typically rely on users or domain experts to manually input knowledge into knowledge bases. However, this procedure is likely to cause biases and errors and is extremely ⑤ **costly** and time consuming. The widening gap between data and information calls for the systematic development of tools that can turn data tombs into "golden nuggets" of knowledge.

21. 21)**밑줄 친 부분 중, 어법, 혹은 문맥상 어색한 곳을 고르시오.** 41~42.

It's untrue that teens can focus on two things at once — what they're doing is shifting their attention from one task to another. In this digital age, teens wire their brains to make these shifts very ① **quick**, but they are still, like everyone else, ② **paying** attention to one thing at a time, sequentially. Common sense tells us multitasking should ③ **increase** brain activity, but Carnegie Mellon University scientists using the latest brain imaging technology find it doesn't. As a matter of fact, they discovered ④ **that** multitasking actually decreases brain activity. Neither task is done as well as if each were performed individually. Fractions of a second are lost every time we make a switch, and a person's ⑤ **interrupted** task can take 50 percent longer to finish, with 50 percent more errors. Turns out the latest brain research supports the old advice "one thing at a time". It's not that kids can't do some tasks simultaneously. But if two tasks are performed at once, one of them has to be familiar. Our brains perform a familiar task on "automatic pilot" while really paying attention to the other one. That's why insurance companies consider talking on a cell phone and driving to be as dangerous as driving while drunk — it's the driving that goes on "automatic pilot" while the conversation really holds our attention. Our kids may be living in the Information Age but our brains have not been redesigned yet.

22. 22)**밑줄 친 부분 중, 어법, 혹은 문맥상 어색한 곳을 고르시오.** 43~45.

Christine was a cat owner who loved her furry companion, Leo. One morning, she noticed that Leo was not feeling well. Concerned for her beloved cat, Christine decided to take him to the animal hospital. As she always brought Leo to this hospital, she was ① **certain** that the vet knew well about Leo. She desperately hoped Leo got the necessary care as soon as possible. The waiting room was filled with other pet owners. Finally, it was Leo's turn to see the vet. Christine watched as the vet gently examined him. The vet said, "I think Leo has a minor infection". "Infection? Will he be okay"? asked Christine. "We need to do some tests to see ② **if** he is infected. But for the tests, it's best for Leo to stay here", replied the vet. ③ **It** was ④ **heartbroken** for Christine to leave Leo at the animal hospital, but she had to accept it was for the best. "I'll call you with updates as soon as we know anything", said the vet. Throughout the day, Christine anxiously awaited news about Leo. Later that day, the phone rang and it was the vet. "The tests revealed a minor infection. Leo needs some medication and rest, but he'll be back to his playful self soon". Relieved to hear the news, Christine rushed back to the animal hospital to pick up Leo. The vet provided detailed instructions on ⑤ **how** to administer the medication and shared tips for a speedy recovery. Back at home, Christine created a comfortable space for Leo to rest and heal. She patted him with love and attention, ensuring that he would recover in no time. As the days passed, Leo gradually regained his strength and playful spirit.

2024 고2 3월 모의고사

❶ voca　　❷ text　　❸ [/]　　❹ ____　　❺ quiz 1　　❻ quiz 2　　❼ quiz 3　　❽ quiz 4　　❾ quiz 5

1. 1)밑줄 친 ⓐ~ⓕ 중 어법, 혹은 문맥상 어휘의 사용이 어색한 것끼리 짝지어진 것을 고르시오. 18.

For the annual Crafts Fair ⓐ **on** May 25 from 1 p.m. to 6 p.m., the Greenville Community Center ⓑ **providing** booth spaces to rent as in previous years. To ⓒ **conserve** your space, please visit our website and complete a registration form by April 20. The rental fee is $50. All the money we receive from rental fees ⓓ **goes** to support upcoming activities throughout the year. We expect all available spaces to be fully ⓔ **booked** soon, so don't get ⓕ **left** out. We hope to see you at the fair.

① ⓐ, ⓑ　　　② ⓑ, ⓒ　　　③ ⓒ, ⓔ
④ ⓒ, ⓓ, ⓔ　　⑤ ⓒ, ⓔ, ⓕ

2. 2)밑줄 친 ⓐ~ⓘ 중 어법, 혹은 문맥상 어휘의 사용이 어색한 것끼리 짝지어진 것을 고르시오. 19.

Sarah, a young artist with a love for painting, ⓐ **entered** a local art contest. As she looked at the ⓑ **amazing** artworks ⓒ **were made** by others, her confidence dropped. She quietly thought, 'I might not ⓓ **win** an award'. The moment of judgment ⓔ **arrived**, and the judges began announcing winners one by one. It wasn't until the end that she heard her name. The head of the judges said, "Congratulations, Sarah Parker! You ⓕ **won** first prize. We loved the uniqueness of your work". Sarah ⓖ **overcame** with joy, and she couldn't stop ⓗ **smiling**. This experience meant more than just winning; it ⓘ **conformed** her identity as an artist.

① ⓐ, ⓕ　　　② ⓐ, ⓔ, ⓕ　　③ ⓑ, ⓖ, ⓘ
④ ⓒ, ⓔ, ⓗ　　⑤ ⓒ, ⓖ, ⓘ

3. 3)밑줄 친 ⓐ~ⓖ 중 어법, 혹은 문맥상 어휘의 사용이 어색한 것끼리 짝지어진 것을 고르시오. 20.

Too many times people, especially in today's generation, ⓐ **expect** things to just happen overnight. When we have these false expectations, it tends to ⓑ **encourage** us from continuing to move forward. Because this is a high tech society, everything we want ⓒ **have** to be within the parameters of our comfort and convenience. If it ⓓ **doesn't** happen fast enough, we're ⓔ **tempted** to lose interest. So many people don't want to take the time it requires ⓕ **being** successful. Success is not a matter of mere desire; you should develop patience in order to achieve it. Have you fallen ⓖ **pray** to impatience? Great things take time to build.

① ⓐ, ⓒ　　　② ⓐ, ⓕ　　　③ ⓐ, ⓓ, ⓔ
④ ⓑ, ⓒ, ⓔ, ⓕ　　⑤ ⓑ, ⓒ, ⓕ, ⓖ

4. 4)밑줄 친 ⓐ~ⓚ 중 어법, 혹은 문맥상 어휘의 사용이 어색한 것끼리 짝지어진 것을 고르시오. 21.

If you ⓐ **had wanted** to create a "self-driving" car in the 1950s, your best option might ⓑ **be** to strap a brick to the accelerator. Yes, the vehicle would have been able to move forward on its own, but it could not slow down, stop, or turn to avoid barriers. Obviously not ideal. But does that mean the entire concept of the self-driving car is not worth ⓒ **pursuing**? No, it only means ⓓ **that** at the time we did not yet have the tools we now possess to help enable vehicles ⓔ **to operate** both ⓕ **autonomously** and safely. This once-distant dream now seems within our reach. It is much the same story in medicine. Two decades ago, we were still taping bricks to accelerators. Today, we are ⓖ **approaching to** the point where we can begin to bring some appropriate technology to bear in ways ⓗ **that** advance our understanding of patients as unique individuals. In fact, many patients are already wearing devices that monitor their conditions in real time, ⓘ **that** allows doctors ⓙ **to talk** to their patients in a specific, ⓚ **refined**, and feedback-driven way that was not even possible a decade ago.

① ⓐ, ⓖ　　　② ⓑ, ⓔ, ⓘ　　③ ⓑ, ⓖ, ⓘ
④ ⓒ, ⓖ, ⓘ　　⑤ ⓒ, ⓓ, ⓖ, ⓗ

5. 5)밑줄 친 ⓐ~ⓗ 중 어법, 혹은 문맥상 어휘의 사용이 어색한 것끼리 짝지어진 것을 고르시오. 22.

We tend to overrate the impact of new technologies in part because older technologies have ⓐ **absorbed** into the furniture of our lives, so as to be almost ⓑ **invisible**. Take the baby bottle. Here is a simple ⓒ **implement** that has ⓓ **transformed** a fundamental human experience for vast numbers of infants and mothers, yet it finds no place in our histories of technology. This technology might ⓔ **think** of as a classic time-shifting device, as it enables mothers to exercise more control over the timing of ⓕ **feeding on**. It can also function to save time, as bottle feeding allows for someone else to ⓖ **substitute** for the mother's time. Potentially, therefore, it has huge implications for the management of time in everyday life, yet ⓗ **it** is entirely overlooked in discussions of high-speed society.

① ⓐ, ⓒ   ② ⓓ, ⓔ   ③ ⓐ, ⓔ, ⓕ
④ ⓐ, ⓑ, ⓒ, ⓔ   ⑤ ⓐ, ⓑ, ⓒ, ⓕ

6. 6)밑줄 친 ⓐ~ⓚ 중 어법, 혹은 문맥상 어휘의 사용이 어색한 것끼리 짝지어진 것을 고르시오. 23.

Empathy is frequently listed as one of the most ⓐ **desired** skills in an employer or employee, ⓑ **although** without specifying exactly what is meant by empathy. Some businesses stress cognitive empathy, ⓒ **emphasized** the need for leaders to understand the perspective of employees and customers when ⓓ **negotiating** deals and ⓔ **make** decisions. Others stress ⓕ **affective** empathy and empathic concern, emphasizing the ability of leaders to gain trust from employees and customers by treating ⓖ **them** with real concern and compassion. When some consultants argue that successful companies foster empathy, what that translates ⓗ **to** is that companies should conduct good market research. In other words, an "empathic" company understands the needs and wants of its customers and seeks to fulfill those needs and wants. When some people speak of design with empathy, what that translates ⓘ **to** is ⓙ **which** companies should take into account the specific needs of different populations — the blind, the deaf, the elderly, non-English speakers, the color-blind, and so on — when ⓚ **designed** products.

① ⓖ, ⓙ   ② ⓐ, ⓔ, ⓗ   ③ ⓐ, ⓖ, ⓗ
④ ⓓ, ⓕ, ⓖ   ⑤ ⓒ, ⓔ, ⓙ, ⓚ

7. 7)밑줄 친 ⓐ~ⓗ 중 어법, 혹은 문맥상 어휘의 사용이 어색한 것끼리 짝지어진 것을 고르시오. 24.

The most ⓐ **prevalent** problem kids report is that they feel like they need to be ⓑ **accessible** at all times. Because technology allows for it, they feel an obligation. It's easy for most of us to relate — you probably feel the same pressure in your own life! It is really ⓒ **challenging** to deal with the fact that we're human and can't always ⓓ **respond** instantly. For a teen or tween who's still learning the ins and outs of social interactions, it's even worse. Here's how this behavior plays out sometimes: Your child texts one of his friends, and the friend doesn't text back right away. Now ⓔ **it** is easy for your child to think, "This person doesn't want to be my friend anymore"! So he texts again, and again, and again — "blowing up their phone". This can be ⓕ **stress-inducing** and even read as ⓖ **progressive**. But you can see how easily this could ⓗ **be happened**.

① ⓐ, ⓖ   ② ⓐ, ⓗ   ③ ⓒ, ⓗ
④ ⓖ, ⓗ   ⑤ ⓒ, ⓓ, ⓔ

8. 8)밑줄 친 ⓐ~ⓔ 중 어법, 혹은 문맥상 어휘의 사용이 어색한 것끼리 짝지어진 것을 고르시오. 26.

Theodore von Kármán, a Hungarian-American engineer, ⓐ **being** one of the greatest minds of the twentieth century. He was born in Hungary and at an early age, he showed a talent for math and science. ⓑ **On** 1908, he received a doctoral degree in engineering at the University of Göttingen in Germany. ⓒ **In** the 1920s, he began traveling as a lecturer and consultant to industry. He ⓓ **invited** to the United States to advise engineers on the design of a wind tunnel at California Institute of Technology (Caltech). He became the director of the Guggenheim Aeronautical Laboratory at Caltech in 1930. Later, he ⓔ **was awarded** the National Medal of Science for his leadership in science and engineering.

① ⓒ, ⓓ   ② ⓐ, ⓑ, ⓒ   ③ ⓐ, ⓑ, ⓓ
④ ⓐ, ⓒ, ⓔ   ⑤ ⓑ, ⓒ, ⓓ

9. 9)밑줄 친 ⓐ~ⓝ 중 어법, 혹은 문맥상 어휘의 사용이 어색한 것끼리 짝지어진 것을 고르시오. 29.

For years, many psychologists have held strongly to the belief that the key to ⓐ **address** negative health habits ⓑ **is** to change behavior. This, more than values and attitudes, ⓒ **is** the part of personality that is easiest to change. ⓓ **Ingestive** habits such as smoking, drinking and various eating behaviors are the most common health concerns ⓔ **targeting** for behavioral changes. Process-addiction behaviors (workaholism, shopaholism, and the like) fall into this category as well. Mental ⓕ **imagery** combined with power of suggestion ⓖ **was taken** up as the premise of behavioral medicine to help people ⓗ **change** negative health behaviors into positive ones. Although this technique alone will not produce changes, when ⓘ **using** alongside other behavior modification tactics and coping strategies, behavioral changes have ⓙ **proved** effective for some people. What mental ⓚ **imagery** does is ⓛ **reinforcing** a new desired behavior. ⓜ **Repeated** use of images ⓝ **reinforce** the desired behavior more strongly over time.

① ⓘ, ⓙ, ⓛ   ② ⓐ, ⓔ, ⓖ, ⓝ   ③ ⓐ, ⓔ, ⓛ, ⓝ
④ ⓓ, ⓕ, ⓙ, ⓝ   ⑤ ⓔ, ⓙ, ⓜ, ⓝ

10. 10)밑줄 친 ⓐ~ⓙ 중 어법, 혹은 문맥상 어휘의 사용이 어색한 것끼리 짝지어진 것을 고르시오. 30.

Emotion socialization — learning from other people about emotions and how to deal with ⓐ **them** — ⓑ **starting** early in life and plays a foundational role for emotion regulation development. ⓒ **Although** extra-familial influences, such as peers or media, gain in importance during adolescence, parents ⓓ **are remained** the primary socialization agents. For example, their own responses to emotional situations serve as a role model for emotion regulation, increasing the likelihood that their children will show similar reactions in comparable situations. Parental practices at times when their children ⓔ **are faced** with emotional challenges also impact emotion regulation development. Whereas direct soothing and directive guidance of what to do ⓕ **is**

beneficial for younger children, they may intrude on adolescents' autonomy striving. In consequence, adolescents might pull away from, rather than ⓖ **turn** toward, their parents in times of emotional crisis, unless parental practices are adjusted. More suitable in adolescence is ⓗ **direct** support of ⓘ **autonomous** emotion regulation, such as through interest in, as well as awareness and nonjudgmental acceptance ⓙ **of**, adolescents' emotional experiences, and being available when the adolescent wants to talk.

① ⓐ, ⓕ, ⓘ   ② ⓐ, ⓑ, ⓒ, ⓓ   ③ ⓑ, ⓓ, ⓕ, ⓗ
④ ⓑ, ⓓ, ⓖ, ⓗ   ⑤ ⓒ, ⓔ, ⓖ, ⓘ

11. 11)밑줄 친 ⓐ~ⓖ 중 어법, 혹은 문맥상 어휘의 사용이 어색한 것끼리 짝지어진 것을 고르시오. 31.

Dancers often push themselves to the limits of their physical capabilities. But that push ⓐ **misguides** if it is directed toward ⓑ **accomplishing** something physically impossible. For instance, a tall dancer with long feet may wish to perform repetitive vertical jumps to fast music, pointing his feet while in the air and lowering his heels to the floor between jumps. That may be impossible no matter ⓒ **what** strong the dancer is. But a short-footed dancer may have no trouble! Another dancer may be struggling to complete a half-turn in the air. Understanding the connection between a rapid turn rate and the ⓓ **alignment** of the body close to the rotation axis ⓔ **tells** her how to accomplish her turn successfully. In both of these cases, understanding and working within the constraints ⓕ **composed** by nature and described by physical laws ⓖ **allows** dancers to work efficiently, minimizing potential risk of injury.

① ⓒ, ⓔ   ② ⓐ, ⓒ, ⓔ   ③ ⓐ, ⓒ, ⓕ
④ ⓑ, ⓓ, ⓔ, ⓖ   ⑤ ⓓ, ⓔ, ⓕ, ⓖ

12. 12)밑줄 친 ⓐ~ⓙ 중 어법, 혹은 문맥상 어휘의 사용이 어색한 것끼리 짝지어진 것을 고르시오. 32.

We must explore the relationship between children's film ⓐ **productivity** and consumption habits. The term "children's film" ⓑ **implies** ownership by children —their cinema — but films supposedly ⓒ **made** for children have always ⓓ **consumed** by audiences of all ages, particularly in commercial cinemas. The ⓔ **considerable** crossover in audience composition for children's films can be shown by the fact that, in 2007, eleven Danish children's and youth films attracted 59 percent of theatrical admissions, and in 2014, German children's films ⓕ **comprised** seven out of the top twenty films at the national box office. This phenomenon ⓖ **corresponds** with a broader, international embrace of what is seemingly children's culture among audiences of diverse ages. The old prejudice that children's film is some other realm, ⓗ **separate** from (and forever ⓘ **substitute** to) a more legitimate cinema for adults ⓙ **is** not supported by the realities of consumption: children's film is at the heart of contemporary popular culture.

① ⓐ, ⓒ   ② ⓐ, ⓒ, ⓖ   ③ ⓐ, ⓓ, ⓘ
④ ⓑ, ⓔ, ⓘ   ⑤ ⓔ, ⓕ, ⓗ, ⓙ

13. 13)밑줄 친 ⓐ~ⓙ 중 어법, 혹은 문맥상 어휘의 사용이 어색한 것끼리 짝지어진 것을 고르시오. 33.

Beethoven's drive to create something ⓐ **novel** is a reflection of his state of curiosity. Our brains experience a sense of reward when we create something new in the process of ⓑ **exploring** something uncertain, such as a musical phrase that we've never played or heard before. When our curiosity leads to something ⓒ **novel**, the ⓓ **resulting** reward brings us a sense of pleasure. ⓔ **The** number of investigators have ⓕ **modeled** how curiosity influences musical composition. In the case of Beethoven, computer modeling focused on the thirty-two piano sonatas written after age thirteen ⓖ **revealed** that the musical patterns ⓗ **found** in all of Beethoven's music decreased in later sonatas, while ⓘ **noble** patterns, including patterns that were unique to a particular sonata, increased. In other words, Beethoven's music became ⓙ **less** predictable over time as his curiosity drove the exploration of new musical ideas. Curiosity is a powerful driver of human creativity.

① ⓐ, ⓔ   ② ⓒ, ⓔ   ③ ⓒ, ⓘ
④ ⓔ, ⓖ   ⑤ ⓔ, ⓘ

14. 14)밑줄 친 ⓐ~ⓙ 중 어법, 혹은 문맥상 어휘의 사용이 어색한 것끼리 짝지어진 것을 고르시오. 34.

Technologists are always on the lookout for ⓐ **quantifiable** metrics. Measurable inputs to a model ⓑ **are** their lifeblood, and like a social scientist, a technologist needs to identify concrete measures, or "proxies", for assessing progress. This need for quantifiable proxies ⓒ **produces** a bias toward ⓓ **measuring** things that are easy to quantify. But simple metrics can take us further away from the important goals we really care ⓔ **x**, ⓕ **which** may require ⓖ **complicated** metrics or be extremely difficult, or perhaps impossible, to reduce to any measure. And when we have imperfect or bad proxies, we can easily fall under the illusion that we are solving for a good end without actually making genuine progress toward a worthy solution. The problem of proxies ⓗ **result** ⓘ **in** technologists frequently ⓙ **substituting** what is measurable for what is meaningful. As the saying goes, "Not everything that counts can be counted, and not everything that can be counted counts".

① ⓐ, ⓓ   ② ⓔ, ⓗ   ③ ⓕ, ⓗ
④ ⓖ, ⓙ   ⑤ ⓑ, ⓒ, ⓕ

15. 15)밑줄 친 ⓐ~ⓖ 중 어법, 혹은 문맥상 어휘의 사용이 어색한 것끼리 짝지어진 것을 고르시오. 35.

We are the only species that seasons its food, ⓐ **deliberately** altering it with the ⓑ **high** flavored plant parts we call herbs and spices. It's quite possible that our taste for spices has an evolutionary root. Many spices have antibacterial properties — in fact, common seasonings such as garlic, onion, and oregano ⓒ **inhabit** the growth of almost every bacterium tested. And the cultures that make the heaviest use of spices — think of the garlic and black pepper of Thai food, the ginger and coriander of India, the chili peppers of Mexico — ⓓ **coming** from warmer climates, where bacterial spoilage is a ⓔ **bigger** issue. In contrast, the most lightly spiced cuisines — those of Scandinavia and northern Europe — ⓕ **are** from cooler climates. Our uniquely human attention to flavor, in this case the flavor of spices, ⓖ **turns** out to have arisen as a matter of life and death.

① ⓐ, ⓒ, ⓕ   ② ⓑ, ⓒ, ⓓ   ③ ⓑ, ⓓ, ⓔ
④ ⓒ, ⓓ, ⓖ   ⑤ ⓐ, ⓔ, ⓕ, ⓖ

16. 16)**밑줄 친 ⓐ~ⓕ 중 어법, 혹은 문맥상 어휘의 사용이 어색한 것끼리 짝지어진 것을 고르시오.** 36.

Development of the human body from a single cell provides many examples of the structural richness that is possible when the ⓐ **repeating** production of random variation is combined with nonrandom selection. All phases of body development from embryo to adult ⓑ **exhibit** random activities at the cellular level, and body formation ⓒ **depending** on the new possibilities generated by these activities ⓓ **coupled** with selection of those outcomes that satisfy previously builtin criteria. Always new structure is based on old structure, and at every stage selection favors some cells and eliminates others. The survivors serve to produce new cells that undergo further rounds of selection. Except in the immune system, cells and extensions of cells are not genetically selected ⓔ **while** development, but rather, are positionally selected. Those in the right place that make the right connections are stimulated, and those that don't are ⓕ **eliminated**. This process is much like sculpting. A natural consequence of the strategy is great variability from individual to individual at the cell and molecular levels, even though large-scale structures are quite similar.

① ⓐ, ⓑ, ⓔ   ② ⓐ, ⓒ, ⓔ   ③ ⓐ, ⓓ, ⓕ
④ ⓐ, ⓒ, ⓓ, ⓕ   ⑤ ⓑ, ⓓ, ⓔ, ⓕ

17. 17)**밑줄 친 ⓐ~ⓜ 중 어법, 혹은 문맥상 어휘의 사용이 어색한 것끼리 짝지어진 것을 고르시오.** 37.

In order to bring the ever-increasing costs of home care for elderly and needy persons under control, managers of home care providers have ⓐ **introduced** management systems. These systems specify tasks of home care workers and the time and budget available to perform these tasks. Electronic reporting systems require home care workers to report on their activities and the time spent, thus ⓑ **making** the ⓒ **distribution** of time and money visible and, in the perception of managers, controllable. This, in the view of managers, ⓓ **has** ⓔ **contributed** to the resolution of the problem. The home care workers, on the other hand, may perceive

their work not as a set of separate tasks to ⓕ **performing** as ⓖ **efficiently** as possible, but as a service to be provided to a client with ⓗ **that** they may have developed a relationship. This includes ⓘ **to have** conversations with clients and enquiring about the person's well-being. ⓙ **Restricted** time and the requirement to report may be perceived as obstacles that make ⓚ **it** impossible to deliver the service that is needed. If the management systems are too rigid, ⓛ **this** may result ⓜ **in** home care workers becoming overloaded and demotivated.

① ⓔ, ⓕ   ② ⓕ, ⓗ, ⓘ   ③ ⓕ, ⓙ, ⓚ
④ ⓗ, ⓘ, ⓚ   ⑤ ⓔ, ⓕ, ⓛ, ⓜ

18. 18)**밑줄 친 ⓐ~ⓘ 중 어법, 혹은 문맥상 어휘의 사용이 어색한 것끼리 짝지어진 것을 고르시오.** 38.

It is a common ⓐ **consumption** that most ⓑ **vagrant** birds are ultimately doomed, aside from the rare cases where individuals are able to reorientate and return to their normal ranges. In turn, it is also commonly assumed that ⓒ **vagrancy** itself is a relatively unimportant biological phenomenon. This is undoubtedly true for the majority of cases, as the most likely outcome of any given vagrancy event is that the individual will fail to find enough resources, and/or be exposed to ⓓ **inhospitable** environmental conditions, and perish. However, there are many lines of evidence to suggest that vagrancy can, on rare occasions, dramatically ⓔ **alter** the fate of populations, species or even whole ecosystems. ⓕ **Despite** being infrequent, these events can be extremely important when ⓖ **viewed** at the timescales over ⓗ **what** ecological and evolutionary processes unfold. The most profound consequences of vagrancy relate to the establishment of new breeding sites, new migration routes and wintering locations. Each of these can ⓘ **occur** through different mechanisms, and at different frequencies, and they each have their own unique importance.

① ⓐ, ⓕ   ② ⓐ, ⓗ   ③ ⓐ, ⓘ
④ ⓒ, ⓖ   ⑤ ⓖ, ⓗ

19. ¹⁹⁾밑줄 친 ⓐ~ⓗ 중 어법, 혹은 문맥상 어휘의 사용이 어색한 것끼리 짝지어진 것을 고르시오. ^{39.}

Intuition can be great, but it ought to be hard-ⓐ **earned**. Experts, for example, are able to think on their feet because they've invested thousands of hours in learning and practice: their intuition has become data-driven. Only then ⓑ **are they** able to act quickly in accordance with their ⓒ **internalized** expertise and evidence-based experience. Yet most people are not experts, though they often think they ⓓ **are**. Most of us, especially when we interact with others on social media, act with expert-like speed and conviction, ⓔ **offering** a wide range of opinions on global crises, without the substance of knowledge that supports it. And thanks to AI, which ⓕ **ensures** that our messages are delivered to an audience more inclined to believing it, our ⓖ **illusions** of expertise can be reinforced by our personal filter bubble. We have an interesting tendency to find people more open-minded, rational, and ⓗ **sensitive** when they think just like us.

① ⓐ, ⓑ   ② ⓒ, ⓖ   ③ ⓓ, ⓖ
④ ⓕ, ⓗ   ⑤ ⓖ, ⓗ

20. ²⁰⁾밑줄 친 ⓐ~ⓕ 중 어법, 혹은 문맥상 어휘의 사용이 어색한 것끼리 짝지어진 것을 고르시오. ^{40.}

The fast-growing, tremendous amount of data, ⓐ **x** collected and stored in large and numerous data repositories, has far exceeded our human ability for understanding without powerful tools. As a result, data ⓑ **collected** in large data repositories become "data tombs" — data archives that are ⓒ **hard** visited. Important decisions are often made based not on the information–rich data stored in data repositories but rather on a decision maker's instinct, simply because the decision maker does not have the tools to ⓓ **subtract** the valuable knowledge hidden in the vast amounts of data. Efforts have been made to develop expert system and knowledge-based technologies, ⓔ **that** typically rely on users or domain experts to manually input knowledge into knowledge bases. However, this procedure is likely to cause biases and errors and is extremely ⓕ **costly** and time consuming. The widening gap between data and information calls for the systematic development of tools that can turn data tombs into "golden nuggets" of knowledge.

① ⓐ, ⓑ, ⓓ   ② ⓐ, ⓒ, ⓕ   ③ ⓑ, ⓒ, ⓔ
④ ⓑ, ⓒ, ⓕ   ⑤ ⓒ, ⓓ, ⓔ

21. 21)밑줄 친 ⓐ~ⓠ 중 어법, 혹은 문맥상 어휘의 사용이 어색한 것끼리 짝지어진 것을 고르시오. 41~42.

It's untrue that teens can focus on two things at once — what they're doing is ⓐ **shifting** their attention from one task to another. In this digital age, teens wire their brains to make these shifts very ⓑ **quickly**, but they are still, like everyone else, ⓒ **paying** attention to one thing at a time, sequentially. Common sense tells us multitasking should ⓓ **decrease** brain activity, but Carnegie Mellon University scientists using the ⓔ **latest** brain imaging technology find it doesn't. As a matter of fact, they discovered ⓕ **that** multitasking actually decreases brain activity. ⓖ **Neither** task is done as well as if each were performed individually. ⓗ **Frictions** of a second are lost every time we make a switch, and a person's ⓘ **interrupted** task can take 50 percent longer to finish, with 50 percent more errors. Turns out the latest brain research supports the old advice "one thing at a time". It's not that kids can't do some tasks ⓙ **simultaneously**. But if two tasks are performed at once, one of them has to be familiar. Our brains perform a ⓚ **familiar** task on "ⓛ **automatic** pilot" while really ⓜ **paying** attention to the other one. That's ⓝ **why** insurance companies consider ⓞ **talking** on a cell phone and driving to be as dangerous as driving while ⓟ **drinking** — it's the driving that goes on "automatic pilot" while the conversation really holds our attention. Our kids may be living in the Information Age but our brains have not ⓠ **been redesigned** yet.

① ⓐ, ⓞ   ② ⓔ, ⓛ   ③ ⓐ, ⓓ, ⓛ
④ ⓓ, ⓗ, ⓟ   ⑤ ⓕ, ⓗ, ⓝ

22. 22)밑줄 친 ⓐ~ⓖ 중 어법, 혹은 문맥상 어휘의 사용이 어색한 것끼리 짝지어진 것을 고르시오. 43~45.

Christine was a cat owner who loved her furry companion, Leo. One morning, she noticed that Leo was not feeling well. ⓐ **Concerned** for her beloved cat, Christine decided to take him to the animal hospital. As she always brought Leo to this hospital, she was ⓑ **certain** that the vet knew well about Leo. She desperately hoped Leo got the necessary care as soon as possible. The waiting room was filled with other pet owners. Finally, it was Leo's turn to see the vet. Christine watched as the vet gently examined him. The vet said, "I think Leo has a minor infection". "Infection? Will he be okay"? asked Christine. "We need to do some tests to see ⓒ **if** he is infected. But for the tests, it's best for Leo to stay here", replied the vet. ⓓ **It** was ⓔ **heartbroken** for Christine to leave Leo at the animal hospital, but she had to accept it was for the best. "I'll call you with updates as soon as we know anything", said the vet. Throughout the day, Christine anxiously awaited news about Leo. Later that day, the phone rang and it was the vet. "The tests revealed a minor infection. Leo needs some medication and rest, but he'll be back to his playful self soon". Relieved to hear the news, Christine rushed back to the animal hospital to pick up Leo. The vet provided detailed instructions on ⓕ **how** to administer the medication and shared tips for a speedy recovery. Back at home, Christine created a comfortable space for Leo to rest and heal. She patted him with love and attention, ⓖ **ensured** that he would recover in no time. As the days passed, Leo gradually regained his strength and playful spirit.

① ⓑ, ⓕ   ② ⓒ, ⓔ   ③ ⓒ, ⓖ
④ ⓔ, ⓖ   ⑤ ⓐ, ⓑ, ⓕ

2024 고2 3월 모의고사

❶ voca ❷ text ❸ [/] ❹ _____ ❺ quiz 1 ❻ quiz 2 ❼ quiz 3 ⑧ quiz 4 ❾ quiz 5

---

1. 1)**밑줄 부분 중 어법, 혹은 문맥상 어휘의 쓰임이 어색한 것을 올바르게 고쳐 쓰시오. (6개)** 18.

For the annual Crafts Fair ① **in** May 25 from 1 p.m. to 6 p.m., the Greenville Community Center ② **providing** booth spaces to rent as in previous years. To ③ **conserve** your space, please visit our website and complete a registration form by April 20. The rental fee is $50. All the money we receive from rental fees ④ **going** to support upcoming activities throughout the year. We expect all available spaces to be fully ⑤ **booking** soon, so don't get ⑥ **to leave** out. We hope to see you at the fair.

기호	어색한 표현	올바른 표현
( )	_____	⇨ _____
( )	_____	⇨ _____
( )	_____	⇨ _____
( )	_____	⇨ _____
( )	_____	⇨ _____
( )	_____	⇨ _____

---

2. 2)**밑줄 부분 중 어법, 혹은 문맥상 어휘의 쓰임이 어색한 것을 올바르게 고쳐 쓰시오. (4개)** 19.

Sarah, a young artist with a love for painting, ① **entered into** a local art contest. As she looked at the ② **amazing** artworks ③ **made** by others, her confidence dropped. She quietly thought, 'I might not ④ **win at** an award'. The moment of judgment ⑤ **was arrived**, and the judges began announcing winners one by one. It wasn't until the end that she heard her name. The head of the judges said, "Congratulations, Sarah Parker! You ⑥ **won** first prize. We loved the uniqueness of your work". Sarah ⑦ **overcame** with joy, and she couldn't stop ⑧ **smiling**. This experience meant more than just winning; it ⑨ **confirmed** her identity as an artist.

기호	어색한 표현	올바른 표현
( )	_____	⇨ _____
( )	_____	⇨ _____
( )	_____	⇨ _____
( )	_____	⇨ _____

3. 3)**밑줄 부분 중 어법, 혹은 문맥상 어휘의 쓰임이 어색한 것을 올바르게 고쳐 쓰시오. (1개)** 20.

Too many times people, especially in today's generation, ① **expect** things to just happen overnight. When we have these false expectations, it tends to ② **discourage** us from continuing to move forward. Because this is a high tech society, everything we want ③ **has** to be within the parameters of our comfort and convenience. If it ④ **doesn't** happen fast enough, we're ⑤ **tempted** to lose interest. So many people don't want to take the time it requires ⑥ **being** successful. Success is not a matter of mere desire; you should develop patience in order to achieve it. Have you fallen ⑦ **prey** to impatience? Great things take time to build.

기호   어색한 표현   올바른 표현

(   ) _____ ⇨ _____

4. 4)**밑줄 부분 중 어법, 혹은 문맥상 어휘의 쓰임이 어색한 것을 올바르게 고쳐 쓰시오. (9개)** 21.

If you ① **had wanted** to create a "self-driving" car in the 1950s, your best option might ② **be** to strap a brick to the accelerator. Yes, the vehicle would have been able to move forward on its own, but it could not slow down, stop, or turn to avoid barriers. Obviously not ideal. But does that mean the entire concept of the self-driving car is not worth ③ **of pursuing**? No, it only means ④ **what** at the time we did not yet have the tools we now possess to help enable vehicles ⑤ **operating** both ⑥ **automatically** and safely. This once-distant dream now seems within our reach. It is much the same story in medicine. Two decades ago, we were still taping bricks to accelerators. Today, we are ⑦ **approaching to** the point where we can begin to bring some appropriate technology to bear in ways ⑧ **in which** advance our understanding of patients as unique individuals. In fact, many patients are already wearing devices that monitor their conditions in real time, ⑨ **that** allows doctors ⑩ **talking** to their patients in a specific, ⑪ **refined**, and feedback-driven way that was not even possible a decade ago.

기호   어색한 표현   올바른 표현

(   ) _____ ⇨ _____
(   ) _____ ⇨ _____
(   ) _____ ⇨ _____
(   ) _____ ⇨ _____
(   ) _____ ⇨ _____
(   ) _____ ⇨ _____
(   ) _____ ⇨ _____
(   ) _____ ⇨ _____
(   ) _____ ⇨ _____

www.englishmygod.com

5. 5)밑줄 부분 중 어법, 혹은 문맥상 어휘의 쓰임이 어색한 것을 올바르게 고쳐 쓰시오. (4개) 22.

We tend to overrate the impact of new technologies in part because older technologies have ① **become absorbed** into the furniture of our lives, so as to be almost ② **invisible**. Take the baby bottle. Here is a simple ③ **implementaion** that has ④ **been transformed** a fundamental human experience for vast numbers of infants and mothers, yet it finds no place in our histories of technology. This technology might ⑤ **be thought** of as a classic time-shifting device, as it enables mothers to exercise more control over the timing of ⑥ **feeding on**. It can also function to save time, as bottle feeding allows for someone else to ⑦ **subordinate** for the mother's time. Potentially, therefore, it has huge implications for the management of time in everyday life, yet ⑧ **it** is entirely overlooked in discussions of high-speed society.

기호	어색한 표현		올바른 표현
( )	_____	⇨	_____
( )	_____	⇨	_____
( )	_____	⇨	_____
( )	_____	⇨	_____

6. 6)밑줄 부분 중 어법, 혹은 문맥상 어휘의 쓰임이 어색한 것을 올바르게 고쳐 쓰시오. (7개) 23.

Empathy is frequently listed as one of the most ① **desired** skills in an employer or employee, ② **despite** without specifying exactly what is meant by empathy. Some businesses stress cognitive empathy, ③ **emphasized** the need for leaders to understand the perspective of employees and customers when ④ **to negotiate** deals and ⑤ **making** decisions. Others stress ⑥ **effective** empathy and empathic concern, emphasizing the ability of leaders to gain trust from employees and customers by treating ⑦ **themselves** with real concern and compassion. When some consultants argue that successful companies foster empathy, what that translates ⑧ **x** is that companies should conduct good market research. In other words, an "empathic" company understands the needs and wants of its customers and seeks to fulfill those needs and wants. When some people speak of design with empathy, what that translates ⑨ **to** is ⑩ **that** companies should take into account the specific needs of different populations — the blind, the deaf, the elderly, non-English speakers, the color-blind, and so on — when ⑪ **designed** products.

기호	어색한 표현		올바른 표현
( )	_____	⇨	_____
( )	_____	⇨	_____
( )	_____	⇨	_____
( )	_____	⇨	_____
( )	_____	⇨	_____
( )	_____	⇨	_____
( )	_____	⇨	_____

7. 7)밑줄 부분 중 어법, 혹은 문맥상 어휘의 쓰임이 어색한 것을 올바르게 고쳐 쓰시오. (5개) 24.

The most ① **previous** problem kids report is that they feel like they need to be ② **accessible** at all times. Because technology allows for it, they feel an obligation. It's easy for most of us to relate — you probably feel the same pressure in your own life! It is really ③ **challengeable** to deal with the fact that we're human and can't always ④ **respond** instantly. For a teen or tween who's still learning the ins and outs of social interactions, it's even worse. Here's how this behavior plays out sometimes: Your child texts one of his friends, and the friend doesn't text back right away. Now ⑤ **it** is easy for your child to think, "This person doesn't want to be my friend anymore"! So he texts again, and again, and again — "blowing up their phone". This can be ⑥ **stress-induced** and even read as ⑦ **progressive**. But you can see how easily this could ⑧ **be happened**.

기호	어색한 표현		올바른 표현
( )	_____	⇨	_____
( )	_____	⇨	_____
( )	_____	⇨	_____
( )	_____	⇨	_____
( )	_____	⇨	_____

8. 8)밑줄 부분 중 어법, 혹은 문맥상 어휘의 쓰임이 어색한 것을 올바르게 고쳐 쓰시오. (2개) 26.

Theodore von Kármán, a Hungarian-American engineer, ① **was** one of the greatest minds of the twentieth century. He was born in Hungary and at an early age, he showed a talent for math and science. ② **On** 1908, he received a doctoral degree in engineering at the University of Göttingen in Germany. ③ **In** the 1920s, he began traveling as a lecturer and consultant to industry. He ④ **invited** to the United States to advise engineers on the design of a wind tunnel at California Institute of Technology (Caltech). He became the director of the Guggenheim Aeronautical Laboratory at Caltech in 1930. Later, he ⑤ **was awarded** the National Medal of Science for his leadership in science and engineering.

기호	어색한 표현		올바른 표현
( )	_____	⇨	_____
( )	_____	⇨	_____

9. 9)**밑줄 부분 중 어법, 혹은 문맥상 어휘의 쓰임이 어색한 것을 올바르게 고쳐 쓰시오. (1개)** 29.

For years, many psychologists have held strongly to the belief that the key to ① **addressing** negative health habits ② **is** to change behavior. This, more than values and attitudes, ③ **is** the part of personality that is easiest to change. ④ **Ingestive** habits such as smoking, drinking and various eating behaviors are the most common health concerns ⑤ **targeting** for behavioral changes. Process-addiction behaviors (workaholism, shopaholism, and the like) fall into this category as well. Mental ⑥ **imagery** combined with power of suggestion ⑦ **was taken** up as the premise of behavioral medicine to help people ⑧ **change** negative health behaviors into positive ones. Although this technique alone will not produce changes, when ⑨ **using** alongside other behavior modification tactics and coping strategies, behavioral changes have ⑩ **proved** effective for some people. What mental ⑪ **imagery** does is ⑫ **reinforce** a new desired behavior. ⑬ **Repeated** use of images ⑭ **reinforces** the desired behavior more strongly over time.

기호   어색한 표현   올바른 표현

(   ) _____ ⇨ _____

10. 10)**밑줄 부분 중 어법, 혹은 문맥상 어휘의 쓰임이 어색한 것을 올바르게 고쳐 쓰시오. (4개)** 30.

Emotion socialization — learning from other people about emotions and how to deal with ① **it** — ② **starts** early in life and plays a foundational role for emotion regulation development. ③ **Although** extra-familial influences, such as peers or media, gain in importance during adolescence, parents ④ **are remained** the primary socialization agents. For example, their own responses to emotional situations serve as a role model for emotion regulation, increasing the likelihood that their children will show similar reactions in comparable situations. Parental practices at times when their children ⑤ **are faced** with emotional challenges also impact emotion regulation development. Whereas direct soothing and directive guidance of what to do ⑥ **are** beneficial for younger children, they may intrude on adolescents' autonomy striving. In consequence, adolescents might pull away from, rather than ⑦ **turning** toward, their parents in times of emotional crisis, unless parental practices are adjusted. More suitable in adolescence is ⑧ **indirect** support of ⑨ **autonomous** emotion regulation, such as through interest in, as well as awareness and nonjudgmental acceptance ⑩ **x**, adolescents' emotional experiences, and being available when the adolescent wants to talk.

기호   어색한 표현   올바른 표현

(   ) _____ ⇨ _____

(   ) _____ ⇨ _____

(   ) _____ ⇨ _____

(   ) _____ ⇨ _____

11. 11)밑줄 부분 중 <u>어법, 혹은 문맥상 어휘</u>의 쓰임이 어색한 것을 올바르게 고쳐 쓰시오. (7개) 31.

Dancers often push themselves to the limits of their physical capabilities. But that push ① **misguides** if it is directed toward ② **accomplish** something physically impossible. For instance, a tall dancer with long feet may wish to perform repetitive vertical jumps to fast music, pointing his feet while in the air and lowering his heels to the floor between jumps. That may be impossible no matter ③ **what** strong the dancer is. But a short-footed dancer may have no trouble! Another dancer may be struggling to complete a half-turn in the air. Understanding the connection between a rapid turn rate and the ④ **allotment** of the body close to the rotation axis ⑤ **telling** her how to accomplish her turn successfully. In both of these cases, understanding and working within the constraints ⑥ **composed** by nature and described by physical laws ⑦ **allow** dancers to work efficiently, minimizing potential risk of injury.

기호	어색한 표현		올바른 표현
( )	_____	⇨	_____
( )	_____	⇨	_____
( )	_____	⇨	_____
( )	_____	⇨	_____
( )	_____	⇨	_____
( )	_____	⇨	_____
( )	_____	⇨	_____

12. 12)밑줄 부분 중 <u>어법, 혹은 문맥상 어휘</u>의 쓰임이 어색한 것을 올바르게 고쳐 쓰시오. (7개) 32.

We must explore the relationship between children's film ① **productivity** and consumption habits. The term "children's film" ② **implies** ownership by children —their cinema — but films supposedly ③ **are made** for children have always ④ **consumed** by audiences of all ages, particularly in commercial cinemas. The ⑤ **considerate** crossover in audience composition for children's films can be shown by the fact that, in 2007, eleven Danish children's and youth films attracted 59 percent of theatrical admissions, and in 2014, German children's films ⑥ **comprised** seven out of the top twenty films at the national box office. This phenomenon ⑦ **corresponds** with a broader, international embrace of what is seemingly children's culture among audiences of diverse ages. The old prejudice that children's film is some other realm, ⑧ **separately** from (and forever ⑨ **substitute** to) a more legitimate cinema for adults ⑩ **are** not supported by the realities of consumption: children's film is at the heart of contemporary popular culture.

기호	어색한 표현		올바른 표현
( )	_____	⇨	_____
( )	_____	⇨	_____
( )	_____	⇨	_____
( )	_____	⇨	_____
( )	_____	⇨	_____
( )	_____	⇨	_____
( )	_____	⇨	_____

13. 13)밑줄 부분 중 어법, 혹은 문맥상 어휘의 쓰임이 어색한 것을 올바르게 고쳐 쓰시오. (1개) 33.

Beethoven's drive to create something ① **novel** is a reflection of his state of curiosity. Our brains experience a sense of reward when we create something new in the process of ② **exploring** something uncertain, such as a musical phrase that we've never played or heard before. When our curiosity leads to something ③ **novel**, the ④ **resulting** reward brings us a sense of pleasure. ⑤ **A** number of investigators have ⑥ **been modeled** how curiosity influences musical composition. In the case of Beethoven, computer modeling focused on the thirty-two piano sonatas written after age thirteen ⑦ **revealed** that the musical patterns ⑧ **found** in all of Beethoven's music decreased in later sonatas, while ⑨ **novel** patterns, including patterns that were unique to a particular sonata, increased. In other words, Beethoven's music became ⑩ **less** predictable over time as his curiosity drove the exploration of new musical ideas. Curiosity is a powerful driver of human creativity.

기호	어색한 표현	올바른 표현
( )	_____ ⇨	_____

14. 14)밑줄 부분 중 어법, 혹은 문맥상 어휘의 쓰임이 어색한 것을 올바르게 고쳐 쓰시오. (9개) 34.

Technologists are always on the lookout for ① **qualifiable** metrics. Measurable inputs to a model ② **is** their lifeblood, and like a social scientist, a technologist needs to identify concrete measures, or "proxies", for assessing progress. This need for quantifiable proxies ③ **produce** a bias toward ④ **to measure** things that are easy to quantify. But simple metrics can take us further away from the important goals we really care ⑤ **x**, ⑥ **which** may require ⑦ **complicating** metrics or be extremely difficult, or perhaps impossible, to reduce to any measure. And when we have imperfect or bad proxies, we can easily fall under the illusion that we are solving for a good end without actually making genuine progress toward a worthy solution. The problem of proxies ⑧ **result** ⑨ **from** technologists frequently ⑩ **substituted** what is measurable for what is meaningful. As the saying goes, "Not everything that counts can be counted, and not everything that can be counted counts".

기호	어색한 표현	올바른 표현
( )	_____ ⇨	_____
( )	_____ ⇨	_____
( )	_____ ⇨	_____
( )	_____ ⇨	_____
( )	_____ ⇨	_____
( )	_____ ⇨	_____
( )	_____ ⇨	_____
( )	_____ ⇨	_____
( )	_____ ⇨	_____

15. 15)**밑줄 부분 중 어법, 혹은 문맥상 어휘의 쓰임이 어색한 것을 올바르게 고쳐 쓰시오. (6개)** 35.

We are the only species that seasons its food, ① **decorately** altering it with the ② **high** flavored plant parts we call herbs and spices. It's quite possible that our taste for spices has an evolutionary root. Many spices have antibacterial properties — in fact, common seasonings such as garlic, onion, and oregano ③ **inhabit** the growth of almost every bacterium tested. And the cultures that make the heaviest use of spices — think of the garlic and black pepper of Thai food, the ginger and coriander of India, the chili peppers of Mexico — ④ **coming** from warmer climates, where bacterial spoilage is a ⑤ **bigger** issue. In contrast, the most lightly spiced cuisines — those of Scandinavia and northern Europe — ⑥ **is** from cooler climates. Our uniquely human attention to flavor, in this case the flavor of spices, ⑦ **turning** out to have arisen as a matter of life and death.

기호	어색한 표현		올바른 표현
( )	_____	⇨	_____
( )	_____	⇨	_____
( )	_____	⇨	_____
( )	_____	⇨	_____
( )	_____	⇨	_____
( )	_____	⇨	_____

16. 16)**밑줄 부분 중 어법, 혹은 문맥상 어휘의 쓰임이 어색한 것을 올바르게 고쳐 쓰시오. (6개)** 36.

Development of the human body from a single cell provides many examples of the structural richness that is possible when the ① **repeating** production of random variation is combined with nonrandom selection. All phases of body development from embryo to adult ② **inhibit** random activities at the cellular level, and body formation ③ **depending** on the new possibilities generated by these activities ④ **are coupled** with selection of those outcomes that satisfy previously builtin criteria. Always new structure is based on old structure, and at every stage selection favors some cells and eliminates others. The survivors serve to produce new cells that undergo further rounds of selection. Except in the immune system, cells and extensions of cells are not genetically selected ⑤ **while** development, but rather, are positionally selected. Those in the right place that make the right connections are stimulated, and those that don't are ⑥ **illuminated**. This process is much like sculpting. A natural consequence of the strategy is great variability from individual to individual at the cell and molecular levels, even though large-scale structures are quite similar.

기호	어색한 표현		올바른 표현
( )	_____	⇨	_____
( )	_____	⇨	_____
( )	_____	⇨	_____
( )	_____	⇨	_____
( )	_____	⇨	_____
( )	_____	⇨	_____

17. ¹⁷⁾**밑줄 부분 중 어법, 혹은 문맥상 어휘의 쓰임이 어색한 것을 올바르게 고쳐 쓰시오. (8개)** ³⁷·

In order to bring the ever-increasing costs of home care for elderly and needy persons under control, managers of home care providers have ① **been introduced** management systems. These systems specify tasks of home care workers and the time and budget available to perform these tasks. Electronic reporting systems require home care workers to report on their activities and the time spent, thus ② **making** the ③ **distribution** of time and money visible and, in the perception of managers, controllable. This, in the view of managers, ④ **have** ⑤ **contributed** to the resolution of the problem. The home care workers, on the other hand, may perceive their work not as a set of separate tasks to ⑥ **performing** as ⑦ **efficient** as possible, but as a service to be provided to a client with ⑧ **that** they may have developed a relationship. This includes ⑨ **having** conversations with clients and enquiring about the person's well-being. ⑩ **Restrict** time and the requirement to report may be perceived as obstacles that make ⑪ **it** impossible to deliver the service that is needed. If the management systems are too rigid, ⑫ **which** may result ⑬ **from** home care workers becoming overloaded and demotivated.

기호	어색한 표현		올바른 표현
( )	_____	⇨	_____
( )	_____	⇨	_____
( )	_____	⇨	_____
( )	_____	⇨	_____
( )	_____	⇨	_____
( )	_____	⇨	_____
( )	_____	⇨	_____
( )	_____	⇨	_____

18. ¹⁸⁾**밑줄 부분 중 어법, 혹은 문맥상 어휘의 쓰임이 어색한 것을 올바르게 고쳐 쓰시오. (1개)** ³⁸·

It is a common ① **assumption** that most ② **vagrant** birds are ultimately doomed, aside from the rare cases where individuals are able to reorientate and return to their normal ranges. In turn, it is also commonly assumed that ③ **vagrancy** itself is a relatively unimportant biological phenomenon. This is undoubtedly true for the majority of cases, as the most likely outcome of any given vagrancy event is that the individual will fail to find enough resources, and/or be exposed to ④ **inhospitable** environmental conditions, and perish. However, there are many lines of evidence to suggest that vagrancy can, on rare occasions, dramatically ⑤ **alter** the fate of populations, species or even whole ecosystems. ⑥ **Despite** being infrequent, these events can be extremely important when ⑦ **viewed** at the timescales over ⑧ **which** ecological and evolutionary processes unfold. The most profound consequences of vagrancy relate to the establishment of new breeding sites, new migration routes and wintering locations. Each of these can ⑨ **be occurred** through different mechanisms, and at different frequencies, and they each have their own unique importance.

기호	어색한 표현		올바른 표현
( )	_____	⇨	_____

19. ¹⁹⁾**밑줄 부분 중 어법, 혹은 문맥상 어휘의 쓰임이 어색한 것을 올바르게 고쳐 쓰시오. (3개)** ³⁹⁾

Intuition can be great, but it ought to be hard-① **earning**. Experts, for example, are able to think on their feet because they've invested thousands of hours in learning and practice: their intuition has become data-driven. Only then ② **they are** able to act quickly in accordance with their ③ **internalized** expertise and evidence-based experience. Yet most people are not experts, though they often think they ④ **are**. Most of us, especially when we interact with others on social media, act with expert-like speed and conviction, ⑤ **offering** a wide range of opinions on global crises, without the substance of knowledge that supports it. And thanks to AI, which ⑥ **ensures** that our messages are delivered to an audience more inclined to believing it, our ⑦ **illusions** of expertise can be reinforced by our personal filter bubble. We have an interesting tendency to find people more open-minded, rational, and ⑧ **sensible** when they think just like us.

기호	어색한 표현		올바른 표현
( )	_____	⇨	_____
( )	_____	⇨	_____
( )	_____	⇨	_____

20. ²⁰⁾**밑줄 부분 중 어법, 혹은 문맥상 어휘의 쓰임이 어색한 것을 올바르게 고쳐 쓰시오. (2개)** ⁴⁰⁾

The fast-growing, tremendous amount of data, ① **x** collected and stored in large and numerous data repositories, has far exceeded our human ability for understanding without powerful tools. As a result, data ② **collected** in large data repositories become "data tombs" — data archives that are ③ **hard** visited. Important decisions are often made based not on the information–rich data stored in data repositories but rather on a decision maker's instinct, simply because the decision maker does not have the tools to ④ **extract** the valuable knowledge hidden in the vast amounts of data. Efforts have been made to develop expert system and knowledge-based technologies, ⑤ **which** typically rely on users or domain experts to manually input knowledge into knowledge bases. However, this procedure is likely to cause biases and errors and is extremely ⑥ **cost** and time consuming. The widening gap between data and information calls for the systematic development of tools that can turn data tombs into "golden nuggets" of knowledge.

기호	어색한 표현		올바른 표현
( )	_____	⇨	_____
( )	_____	⇨	_____

21. ²¹⁾**밑줄 부분 중 어법, 혹은 문맥상 어휘의 쓰임이 어색한 것을 올바르게 고쳐 쓰시오. (5개)** ⁴¹~⁴²⁾

It's untrue that teens can focus on two things at once — what they're doing is ① **shifted** their attention from one task to another. In this digital age, teens wire their brains to make these shifts very ② **quickly**, but they are still, like everyone else, ③ **paid** attention to one thing at a time, sequentially. Common sense tells us multitasking should ④ **increase** brain activity, but Carnegie Mellon University scientists using the ⑤ **latest** brain imaging technology find it doesn't. As a matter of fact, they discovered ⑥ **that** multitasking actually decreases brain activity. ⑦ **Neither** task is done as well as if each were performed individually. ⑧ **Fractions** of a second are lost every time we make a switch, and a person's ⑨ **interrupted** task can take 50 percent longer to finish, with 50 percent more errors. Turns out the latest brain research supports the old advice "one thing at a time". It's not that kids can't do some tasks ⑩ **simultaneously**. But if two tasks are performed at once, one of them has to be familiar. Our brains perform a ⑪ **similar** task on "⑫ **automatic** pilot" while really ⑬ **pay** attention to the other one. That's ⑭ **why** insurance companies consider ⑮ **to take** on a cell phone and driving to be as dangerous as driving while ⑯ **drunk** — it's the driving that goes on "automatic pilot" while the conversation really holds our attention. Our kids may be living in the Information Age but our brains have not ⑰ **been redesigned** yet.

기호	어색한 표현		올바른 표현
( )	_____	⇨	_____
( )	_____	⇨	_____
( )	_____	⇨	_____
( )	_____	⇨	_____
( )	_____	⇨	_____

22. 22)밑줄 부분 중 어법, 혹은 문맥상 어휘의 쓰임이 어색한 것을 올바르게 고쳐 쓰시오. (2개) ⁴³~⁴⁵·

Christine was a cat owner who loved her furry companion, Leo. One morning, she noticed that Leo was not feeling well. ① **Concerning** for her beloved cat, Christine decided to take him to the animal hospital. As she always brought Leo to this hospital, she was ② **certain** that the vet knew well about Leo. She desperately hoped Leo got the necessary care as soon as possible. The waiting room was filled with other pet owners. Finally, it was Leo's turn to see the vet. Christine watched as the vet gently examined him. The vet said, "I think Leo has a minor infection". "Infection? Will he be okay"? asked Christine. "We need to do some tests to see ③ **that** he is infected. But for the tests, it's best for Leo to stay here", replied the vet. ④ **It** was ⑤ **heartbreaking** for Christine to leave Leo at the animal hospital, but she had to accept it was for the best. "I'll call you with updates as soon as we know anything", said the vet. Throughout the day, Christine anxiously awaited news about Leo. Later that day, the phone rang and it was the vet. "The tests revealed a minor infection. Leo needs some medication and rest, but he'll be back to his playful self soon". Relieved to hear the news, Christine rushed back to the animal hospital to pick up Leo. The vet provided detailed instructions on ⑥ **how** to administer the medication and shared tips for a speedy recovery. Back at home, Christine created a comfortable space for Leo to rest and heal. She patted him with love and attention, ⑦ **ensuring** that he would recover in no time. As the days passed, Leo gradually regained his strength and playful spirit.

기호	어색한 표현		올바른 표현
( )	_____	⇨	_____
( )	_____	⇨	_____

2024 고2 3월 모의고사

❶ voca   **❷** text   **❸** [/]   **❹** _____   **❺** quiz 1   **❻** quiz 2   **❼** quiz 3   **❽** quiz 4   **❾** quiz 5

☑ **다음 글을 읽고 물음에 답하시오.** (18)

Dear Art Crafts People of Greenville, For the annual Crafts Fair on May 25 from 1 p.m. to 6 p.m., the Greenville Community Center is providing booth spaces to rent as in ^{이전의}_____ years. To ^{예약하다}_____ your space, please visit our website and complete a registration form by April 20. The rental fee is $50. All the money we receive from rental fees goes to support upcoming activities throughout the year. (가) <u>모든 이용할 수 있는 공간이 곧 모두 예약될 것으로 예상되니 놓치지 마세요.</u> We hope to see you at the fair.

1. ¹⁾힌트를 참고하여 각 빈칸에 알맞은 단어를 쓰시오.

2. ²⁾위 글에 주어진 (가)의 한글과 같은 의미를 가지도록, 각각의 주어진 단어들을 알맞게 배열하시오.

(가) booked / We / soon, / expect / available / spaces / don't / be / fully / get / all / left / to / out. / so

☑ **다음 글을 읽고 물음에 답하시오.** (19)

Sarah, a young artist with a love for painting, entered a local art contest. As she looked at the amazing artworks made by others, her ^{자신감}_____ dropped. She quietly thought, 'I might not win an award'. The moment of judgment arrived, and the judges began announcing winners one by one. It wasn't until the end that she heard her name. The head of the judges said, "Congratulations, Sarah Parker! You won first prize. We loved the ^{독창성}_____ of your work". Sarah was overcome with joy, and she couldn't stop smiling. This experience meant more than just winning; it ^{확인하다}_____ her ^{정체성}_____ as an artist.

3. ³⁾힌트를 참고하여 각 빈칸에 알맞은 단어를 쓰시오.

☑ **다음 글을 읽고 물음에 답하시오.** (20)

Too many times people, especially in today's ^{세대}_____, expect things to just happen overnight. ⓐ <u>When we have these false expectations, it tends to encourage us from continuing to move forward. Because this is a high tech society, everything we want has to be within the parameters of our comfort and convenience. If it doesn't happen enough fast, we're tempted to lose interest. So many people want to take the time it requires to be successful. Success is not a matter of mere desire; you should develop patience in order to achieve it. Have you fallen pray to patience? Great things take time to build.</u>

4. ⁴⁾힌트를 참고하여 각 빈칸에 알맞은 단어를 쓰시오.

5. ⁵⁾밑줄 친 ⓐ에서, 어법 혹은 문맥상 어색한 부분을 찾아 올바르게 고쳐 쓰시오.

    ⓐ   잘못된 표현   바른 표현

    (   ) ⇨ (   )

    (   ) ⇨ (   )

    (   ) ⇨ (   )

    (   ) ⇨ (   )

    (   ) ⇨ (   )

☑ 다음 글을 읽고 물음에 답하시오. ⁽²¹⁾

If you had wanted to create a "self-driving" car in the 1950s, your best option might have been to strap a brick to the accelerator. Yes, the vehicle would have been able to move forward on its own, but it could not slow down, stop, or turn to avoid ᵈ장애물 _____. Obviously not ideal. But does that mean the entire concept of the self-driving car is not worth ᵖᵘʳˢᵘᵉ의 바른 형태 _____? No, (가) <u>그것은 단지 우리가 지금은 갖고 있는, 자동차를 자율적이고도 안전하게 작동할 수 있도록 해 주는 도구를, 그 당시에는 우리가 아직 갖고 있지 않았다는 것을 의미할 뿐이다.</u> This once-distant dream now seems within our reach. It is much the same story in medicine. Two decades ago, we were still taping bricks to accelerators. Today, (나) <u>우리는 환자를 고유한 개인으로서 이해하는 것을 증진하는 방식에 맞는 적절한 기술을 도입하기 시작하는 지점에 접근하고 있다.</u> In fact, many patients are already wearing devices that monitor their conditions in real time, which allows doctors to talk to their patients in a specific, ᵈ정제된 _____, and feedback-driven way that was not even possible a decade ago.

6. ⁶⁾힌트를 참고하여 각 빈칸에 알맞은 단어를 쓰시오.

7. ⁷⁾위 글에 주어진 (가) ~ (나)의 한글과 같은 의미를 가지도록, 각각의 주어진 단어들을 알맞게 배열하시오.

(가) have / to / and / help / both / the time / operate / autonomously / to / at / did / safely. / that / only / we / it / possess / means / now / vehicles / yet / we / the tools / enable / not

(나) bear / to / appropriate / we / as / can / technology / patients / the point / ways / approaching / that / to / we / where / our / bring / individuals. / in / of / advance / unique / understanding / some / begin / are

☑ **다음 글을 읽고 물음에 답하시오.** (22)

We tend to ^{과대평가하다} _____ the impact of new technologies in part because older technologies have become absorbed into the furniture of our lives, so as to be almost invisible. ⓐ <u>Taking the baby bottle. Here is a simple implement that has been transformed by a fundamental human experience for vast numbers of infants and mothers, yet it finds no place in our histories of technology. This technology might be thinking of as a classic time-shifting device, as it enables mothers to exercise less control over the timing of feeding.</u> It can also function to save time, as bottle feeding allows for someone else to substitute for the mother's time. ^{잠재적으로} _____, therefore, it has huge implications for the management of time in everyday life, yet it is entirely ^{간과하다} _____ in discussions of high-speed society.

8. 8)힌트를 참고하여 각 빈칸에 알맞은 단어를 쓰시오.

9. 9)밑줄 친 ⓐ에서, 어법 혹은 문맥상 어색한 부분을 찾아 올바르게 고쳐 쓰시오.

　ⓐ　　　잘못된 표현　　　　　　바른 표현

　　(　　　　　　　) ⇨ (　　　　　　　　)

　　(　　　　　　　) ⇨ (　　　　　　　　)

　　(　　　　　　　) ⇨ (　　　　　　　　)

　　(　　　　　　　) ⇨ (　　　　　　　　)

☑ **다음 글을 읽고 물음에 답하시오.** (23)

ⓐ <u>Empathy is frequently listed as one of the most desriing skills in an employer or employee, although with specifying exactly that is meant by empathy.</u> Some businesses stress cognitive empathy, emphasize the need for leaders to understand the perspective of employees and customers when negotiating deals and making decisions. Others stress affective empathy and empathic concern, emphasizing the ability of leaders to gain trust from employees and customers by treating them with real concern and compassion. When some consultants argue that successful companies ^{기르다} _____ empathy, what that translates to is that companies should conduct good market research. In other words, an "empathic" company understands the needs and wants of its customers and seeks to fulfill those needs and wants. When some people speak of design with empathy, (가) <u>그것이 의미하는 바는 회사가 제품을 디자인할 때 다양한 사람들의 구체적인 필요 사항을 고려해야 한다는 것이다.</u> — the blind, the deaf, the elderly, non-English speakers, the color-blind, and so on — when designing products.

10. 10)힌트를 참고하여 각 빈칸에 알맞은 단어를 쓰시오.

11. 11)밑줄 친 ⓐ에서, 어법 혹은 문맥상 어색한 부분을 찾아 올바르게 고쳐 쓰시오.

ⓐ　　　　잘못된 표현　　　　　　바른 표현

(　　　　　　　) ⇨ (　　　　　　　)

(　　　　　　　) ⇨ (　　　　　　　)

(　　　　　　　) ⇨ (　　　　　　　)

(　　　　　　　) ⇨ (　　　　　　　)

12. 12)위 글에 주어진 (가)의 한글과 같은 의미를 가지도록, 각각의 주어진 단어들을 알맞게 배열하시오.

(가) is / of / populations / translates / needs / to / should / what / into / that / the / account / that / take / companies / different / specific

☑ **다음 글을 읽고 물음에 답하시오.** (24)

(가) 아이들이 이야기하는 가장 일반적인 문제는 그들이 항상 연락될 수 있어야 한다고 느낀다는 것이다. Because technology allows for it, they feel an 들어갈 단어 ＿＿＿＿＿＿. It's easy for most of us to relate — you probably feel the same pressure in your own life! It is really challenging to deal with the fact that we're human and can't always respond 즉각 ＿＿＿＿＿＿. ⓐ For a teen or tween who's still learning the ins and outs of social interactions, it's even better. Here's that this behavior plays out sometimes: Your child texts one of his friends, and the friend doesn't text back right away. Now it's easy for your child to think, "This person doesn't want to be my friend anymore"! So he texts again, and again, and again — "blowing up their phone". This can be stress-reducing and even read as aggressive. But you can see how easily this could happen.

13. 13)힌트를 참고하여 각 빈칸에 알맞은 단어를 쓰시오.

14. 14)밑줄 친 ⓐ에서, 어법 혹은 문맥상 어색한 부분을 찾아 올바르게 고쳐 쓰시오.

ⓐ　　　　잘못된 표현　　　　　　바른 표현

(　　　　　　　) ⇨ (　　　　　　　)

(　　　　　　　) ⇨ (　　　　　　　)

(　　　　　　　) ⇨ (　　　　　　　)

15. 15)위 글에 주어진 (가)의 한글과 같은 의미를 가지도록, 각각의 주어진 단어들을 알맞게 배열하시오.

(가) be / they / kids / prevalent / accessible / The / at / need / feel / most / problem / like / all / is / report / to / that / times. / they

☑ **다음 글을 읽고 물음에 답하시오.** (25)

The graph above shows the animal protein consumption measured as the average daily ^{공급} _____ per person in three different countries in 2020. The U.S. showed the largest amount of total animal protein consumption per person among the three countries. Eggs and Dairy was the top animal protein consumption source among four categories in the U.S., followed by Meat and Poultry at 22.4g and 20.6g, ^{각각} _____. ^{~와 다르게} _____ the U.S., Brazil consumed the most animal protein from Meat, with Eggs and Dairy being the second most. Japan had less than 50g of the total animal protein consumption per person, which was the smallest among the three countries. Fish and Seafood, which was the least consumed animal protein consumption source in the U.S. and Brazil, ^{순위를 기록하다} _____ the highest in Japan.

16. 16)힌트를 참고하여 각 빈칸에 알맞은 단어를 쓰시오.

☑ **다음 글을 읽고 물음에 답하시오.** (26)

Theodore von Kármán, a Hungarian-American engineer, was one of the greatest minds of the twentieth century. He was born in Hungary and at an early age, he showed a talent for math and science. In 1908, he received a doctoral degree in engineering at the University of Göttingen in Germany. In the 1920s, he began traveling as a lecturer and consultant to industry. ⓐ <u>He invited to the United States to advise engineers on the design of a wind tunnel at California Institute of Technology (Caltech). He became the director of the Guggenheim Aeronautical Laboratory at Caltech in 1930. Later, he was awarded by the National Medal of Science for his leadership in science and engineering.</u>

17. 17)밑줄 친 ⓐ에서, 어법 혹은 문맥상 어색한 부분을 찾아 올바르게 고쳐 쓰시오.

    ⓐ   잘못된 표현   바른 표현

    (   ) ⇨ (   )

    (   ) ⇨ (   )

☑ **다음 글을 읽고 물음에 답하시오.** (29)

For years, (가)<u>많은 심리학자들이 부정적인 건강 습관을 해결하기 위한 열쇠는 행동을 바꾸는 것이라는 믿음을 굳게 갖고 있었다.</u> This, more than values and attitudes, is the part of personality that is easiest to change. ^{섭취 습관} _____ such as smoking, drinking and various eating behaviors are the most common health concerns targeted for behavioral changes. Process-addiction behaviors (workaholism, shopaholism, and the like) fall into this category as well. Mental imagery combined with power of suggestion was taken up as the ^{전제} _____ of behavioral medicine to help people change negative health behaviors into positive ones. Although this technique alone will not produce changes, when used alongside other behavior modification tactics and coping strategies, behavioral changes have proved effective for some people. (나)마음 속 이미지가 하는 일은 새로운 바람직한 행동을 강화하는 것이다. Repeated use of images reinforces the desired behavior more strongly over time.

18. ¹⁸⁾힌트를 참고하여 각 빈칸에 알맞은 단어를 쓰시오.

19. ¹⁹⁾위 글에 주어진 (가) ~ (나)의 한글과 같은 의미를 가지도록, 각각의 주어진 단어들을 알맞게 배열하시오.

(가) to / have / the belief / addressing / negative / change / many / health / habits / strongly / to / psychologists / held / to / is / the key / that / behavior.

(나) mental / new / imagery / does / a / behavior. / reinforce / What / is / desired

☑ 다음 글을 읽고 물음에 답하시오. ⁽³⁰⁾

Emotion socialization — learning from other people about emotions and how to deal with them — starts early in life and plays a ᵏⁱ초적인 _____ role for emotion regulation development. Although extra-familial influences, such as peers or media, gain in importance during adolescence, parents remain the primary socialization ²ᵘ체 _____. ⓐ For example, their own responses to emotional situations serve as a role model for emotion regulation, increase the likelihood what their children will show similar reactions in comparable situations. Parental practices at times when their children are faced with emotional challenges also impact emotion regulation development. Whereas direct soothing and directive guidance of what to do is beneficial for younger children, they may intrude on adolescents' autonomy striving. In consequence, adolescents might pull away from, rather than turn toward, their parents in times of emotional crisis, unless parental practices are adjusted. More suitable in adolescence is indirect support of ²ᵘ율적인 _____ emotion regulation, such as through interest in, as well as awareness and ᵐᵘ비판적인 _____ acceptance of, adolescents' emotional experiences, and being available when the adolescent wants to talk.

20. ²⁰⁾힌트를 참고하여 각 빈칸에 알맞은 단어를 쓰시오.

21. ²¹⁾밑줄 친 ⓐ에서, 어법 혹은 문맥상 어색한 부분을 찾아 올바르게 고쳐 쓰시오.

ⓐ	잘못된 표현		바른 표현	
	(	) ⇨ (	)	
	(	) ⇨ (	)	
	(	) ⇨ (	)	

☑ **다음 글을 읽고 물음에 답하시오.** (31)

Dancers often push themselves to the limits of their physical capabilities. But (가)그렇게 밀어붙이는 것이 물리적으로 불가능한 것을 달성하는 쪽으로 향하게 된다면, 잘못 이해한 것이다. For instance, a tall dancer with long feet may wish to perform ᵇᵇⁱⁿ 반복적인 _____ vertical jumps to fast music, pointing his feet while in the air and lowering his heels to the floor between jumps. That may be impossible no matter how strong the dancer is. But a short-footed dancer may have no trouble! Another dancer may be struggling to complete a half-turn in the air. Understanding the connection between a rapid turn rate and the 정렬 _____ of the body close to the rotation axis tells her how to accomplish her turn successfully. In both of these cases, understanding and working within the 제약 _____ imposed by nature and described by physical laws allows dancers to work efficiently, 최소화하다 _____ potential risk of injury.

22. ²²⁾힌트를 참고하여 각 <u>빈칸에 알맞은</u> 단어를 쓰시오.

23. ²³⁾위 글에 주어진 (가)의 한글과 같은 의미를 가지도록, 각각의 주어진 단어들을 알맞게 배열하시오.

(가) is / physically / something / misguided / is / toward / it / directed / accomplishing / that push / impossible. / if

☑ **다음 글을 읽고 물음에 답하시오.** (32)

We must explore the relationship between children's film production and consumption habits. The term "children's film" implies 소유권 _____ by children —their cinema — but films supposedly made for children have always been consumed by audiences of all ages, particularly in commercial cinemas. The 상당한 _____ crossover in audience composition for children's films can be shown by the fact that, in 2007, eleven Danish children's and youth films attracted 59 percent of theatrical admissions, and in 2014, German children's films comprised seven out of the top twenty films at the national box office. This 현상 _____ corresponds with a broader, international embrace of what is seemingly children's culture among audiences of diverse ages. The old 편견 _____ that children's film is some other realm, separate from (and forever subordinate to) a more legitimate cinema for adults is not supported by the realities of consumption: children's film is at the heart of 현대의 _____ popular culture.

24. ²⁴⁾힌트를 참고하여 각 <u>빈칸에 알맞은</u> 단어를 쓰시오.

☑ **다음 글을 읽고 물음에 답하시오.** (33)

Beethoven's drive to create something novel is a 반영 _____ of his state of curiosity. Our brains experience a sense of reward when we create something new in the process of exploring something uncertain, such as a musical phrase that we've never played or heard before. When our curiosity leads to something novel, the resulting reward brings us a sense of pleasure. A ____ number of investigators have modeled how curiosity influences musical composition. In the case of Beethoven, computer modeling ᶠᵒᶜᵘˢᵉᵈ _____ on the thirty-two piano sonatas written after age thirteen revealed that the musical patterns found in all of Beethoven's music ᵈᵉᶜʳᵉᵃˢᵉᵈ _____ in later sonatas, while novel patterns, including patterns that were unique to a particular sonata, ^{increased} _____.] In other words, (가) 베토벤의 호기심이 새로운 음악적 아이디어의 탐구를 이끌게 됨에 따라 그의 음악은 시간이 지날수록 덜 예측 가능하게 되었다 Curiosity is a powerful driver of human creativity.

25. ²⁵⁾힌트를 참고하여 각 <u>빈칸에 알맞은</u> 단어를 쓰시오.

26. ²⁶⁾위 글에 주어진 (가)의 한글과 같은 의미를 가지도록, 각각의 주어진 단어들을 알맞게 배열하시오.

(가) as / over / time / the / new / less / curiosity / drove / became / predictable / exploration / ideas. / Beethoven's / musical / his / of / music

☑ **다음 글을 읽고 물음에 답하시오.** ⁽³⁴⁾

Technologists are always on the lookout for quantifiable metrics. Measurable inputs to a model are their lifeblood, and like a social scientist, a technologist needs to identify concrete measures, or "proxies", for assessing progress. ⓐ <u>This need for quantifiable proxies produces a bias toward measuring things that are easy to qualify. But simple metrics can take us further away from the important goals we really care about, what may require complicated metrics or be extremely difficult, or perhaps impossible, to reduce to any measure. And when we have imperfect or bad proxies, we can easily fall under the ^{착각} _____ that we are solving for a good end without actually making genuine progress toward a worthy solution. (가) 프록시의 문제는 기술자들이 흔히 의미 있는 것을 측정 가능한 것으로 대체하는 결과를 낳는다. As the saying goes, "(나) 중요한 모든 것들이 셀 수 있는 것은 아니고, 셀 수 있는 모든 것들이 중요한 것도 아니다."

27. ²⁷⁾힌트를 참고하여 각 <u>빈칸에 알맞은</u> 단어를 쓰시오.

28. ²⁸⁾밑줄 친 ⓐ에서, 어법 혹은 문맥상 어색한 부분을 찾아 올바르게 고쳐 쓰시오.

ⓐ   잘못된 표현   바른 표현
    (   ) ⇨ (   )
    (   ) ⇨ (   )

29. ²⁹⁾위 글에 주어진 (가) ~ (나)의 한글과 같은 의미를 가지도록, 각각의 주어진 단어들을 알맞게 배열하시오.

(가) frequently / proxies / is / meaningful. / of / what / substituting / results / measurable / what / in / The   problem / for / technologists / is

(나) be / be / not / counted / that / and / that / Not / counts / everything / everything / counted, / counts / can / can

☑ **다음 글을 읽고 물음에 답하시오.** (35)

We are the only species that seasons its food, ^{의도적으로} _____ altering it with the highly flavored plant parts we call herbs and spices. It's quite possible that our taste for spices has an ^{진화적인} _____ root. Many spices have antibacterial ^{특성} _____ — in fact, common seasonings such as garlic, onion, and oregano inhibit the growth of almost every bacterium tested. ⓐ <u>And the cultures that make the heaviest use of spices — think of the garlic and black pepper of Thai food, the ginger and coriander of India, the chili peppers of Mexico — come from cooler climates, where bacterial spoilage is a bigger issue. Similary, the most lightly spiced cuisines — those of Scandinavia and northern Europe — are from warmer climates. Our uniquely human attention to flavor, in this case the flavor of spices, turns out to have arisen as a matter of life and death.</u>

30. 30)힌트를 참고하여 각 <u>빈칸에 알맞은</u> 단어를 쓰시오.

31. 31)밑줄 친 ⓐ에서, 어법 혹은 문맥상 어색한 부분을 찾아 올바르게 고쳐 쓰시오.

   ⓐ   잘못된 표현   바른 표현

   (   ) ⇨ (   )

   (   ) ⇨ (   )

   (   ) ⇨ (   )

☑ **다음 글을 읽고 물음에 답하시오.** (36)

Development of the human body from a single cell provides many examples of the structural ^{풍부함} _____ that is possible when the repeated production of random variation is combined with nonrandom selection. All phases of body development from embryo to adult exhibit random activities at the cellular level, and body formation ^{~에 의존하다} _____ the new possibilities generated by these activities coupled with selection of those outcomes that satisfy previously builtin criteria. ⓐ <u>Always old structure is based on new structure, and at every stage selection favors some cells and eliminates others. The survivors serve to be produced by new cells that undergo further rounds of selection.[Except in the immune system, cells and extensions of cells are not genetically selecting during development, but rather, are positionally selected. Those in the right place that make the right connections are stimulated, and those that don't are stimulated.</u> This process is much like sculpting. A natural ^{결과} _____ of the strategy is great variability from individual to individual at the cell and molecular levels, even though large-scale structures are quite similar.

32. 32)힌트를 참고하여 각 <u>빈칸에 알맞은</u> 단어를 쓰시오.

33. 33)밑줄 친 ⓐ에서, 어법 혹은 문맥상 어색한 부분을 찾아 올바르게 고쳐 쓰시오.

ⓐ	잘못된 표현		바른 표현		잘못된 표현		바른 표현
(	)	⇨ (	)	(	)	⇨ (	)
(	)	⇨ (	)	(	)	⇨ (	)
(	)	⇨ (	)				

☑ **다음 글을 읽고 물음에 답하시오.** (37)

In order to bring the ever-increasing costs of home care for elderly and needy persons under control, managers of home care providers have introduced management systems. ⓐ <u>These systems specify tasks of home care workers and the time and budget unavailble to perform these tasks.</u> Electronic reporting systems require home care workers to report on their activities and the time spending, thus make the distribution of time and money visible and, in the perception of managers, controllable. This, in the view of managers, has contributed to the resolution of the problem. The home care workers, on the one hand, may perceive their work not as a set of separate tasks to be performed as efficiently as possible, but as a service to provide to a client with whom they may have developed a relationship. This includes having conversations with clients and enquiring about the person's wellbeing. (가) <u>제한된 시간과 보고를 해야 한다는 요구 사항은 필요한 서비스를 제공하는 것을 불가능하게 하는 장애물로 여겨질 것이다.</u> If the management systems are too ^{엄격한} _____, this may result in home care workers becoming overloaded and ^{의욕을 잃는} _____.

34. ³⁴⁾힌트를 참고하여 각 빈칸에 알맞은 단어를 쓰시오.

35. ³⁵⁾밑줄 친 ⓐ에서, 어법 혹은 문맥상 어색한 부분을 찾아 올바르게 고쳐 쓰시오.

ⓐ	잘못된 표현		바른 표현
(	)	⇨ (	)
(	)	⇨ (	)
(	)	⇨ (	)
(	)	⇨ (	)
(	)	⇨ (	)

36. ³⁶⁾위 글에 주어진 (가)의 한글과 같은 의미를 가지도록, 각각의 주어진 단어들을 알맞게 배열하시오.

(가) as / to / deliver / obstacles / it / impossible / that / make / be / is / Restricted / and / the _____ requirement / to / that / the service / time / may / perceived / needed. / report

☑ **다음 글을 읽고 물음에 답하시오.** (38)

It is a common assumption that most vagrant birds are ultimately doomed, ^{~를 제외하고} _____ the rare cases where individuals are able to reorientate and return to their normal ranges. In turn, it is also commonly assumed that ^{들어갈 단어} _____ itself is a relatively unimportant biological ^{현상} _____. ⓐ <u>This is doubtly true for the majority of cases, as the most likely outcome of any given vagrancy event is that the individual will fail to find enough resources, and/or be exposed to hospitbale environmental conditions, and perish.</u> However, there are many lines of evidence to suggest that vagrancy can, on rare occasions, dramatically alter the ^{운명} ____ of populations, species or even whole ecosystems. Despite being infrequent, (가) <u>이러한 경우들은 생태학적이고 진화적인 과정이 진행되는 시간의 관점에서 볼 때 매우 중요할 수 있다.</u> The most ^{중대한} _____ consequences of vagrancy relate to the establishment of new breeding sites, new migration routes and wintering locations. Each of these can occur through different mechanisms, and at different frequencies, and they each have their own unique importance

37. ³⁷⁾힌트를 참고하여 각 빈칸에 알맞은 단어를 쓰시오.

38. ³⁸⁾밑줄 친 ⓐ에서, 어법 혹은 문맥상 어색한 부분을 찾아 올바르게 고쳐 쓰시오.

　　ⓐ　　　　잘못된 표현　　　　　　　바른 표현

　　(　　　　　　　) ⇨ (　　　　　　　)
　　(　　　　　　　) ⇨ (　　　　　　　)

39. ³⁹⁾위 글에 주어진 (가)의 한글과 같은 의미를 가지도록, 각각의 주어진 단어들을 알맞게 배열하시오.

(가) these / ecological / be / at / extremely / processes / unfold. / evolutionary / when / timescales / over / events / the / important / viewed / can / which / and

---

☑ **다음 글을 읽고 물음에 답하시오.** ⁽³⁹⁾

Intuition can be great, but it ought to be hard-earned. Experts, for example, are able to think on their feet because they've ⁱⁿᵛᵉˢᵗ(투자하다) _____ thousands of hours in learning and practice: their intuition has become data-driven. (가) <u>그래야만 그들이 내재화된 전문 지식과 증거에 기반한 경험에 따라 빠르게 행동할 수 있다.</u> Yet most people are not experts, though they often think they are. Most of us, especially when we interact with others on social media, act with expert-like speed and ᶜᵒⁿᶠⁱᵈᵉⁿᶜᵉ(확신) _____, offering a wide range of opinions on global crises, without the substance of knowledge that supports it. And ᵗʰᵃⁿᵏˢ ᵗᵒ(~덕분에) _____ AI, which ensures that our messages are delivered to an audience more inclined to believing it, our ⁱˡˡᵘˢⁱᵒⁿ(착각) _____ of expertise can be reinforced by our personal filter bubble. We have an interesting tendency to find people more open-minded, rational, and sensible when they think just like us.

40. ⁴⁰⁾힌트를 참고하여 각 빈칸에 알맞은 단어를 쓰시오.

41. ⁴¹⁾위 글에 주어진 (가)의 한글과 같은 의미를 가지도록, 각각의 주어진 단어들을 알맞게 배열하시오.

(가) they / with / in / accordance / quickly / experience. / are / expertise / able / / then / and / their / internalized / evidence-based / act / Only / to

---

☑ **다음 글을 읽고 물음에 답하시오.** ⁽⁴⁰⁾

The fast-growing, ᵉⁿᵒʳᵐᵒᵘˢ(엄청난) _____ amount of data, collected and stored in large and numerous data repositories, has far exceeded our human ability for understanding without powerful tools. As a result, data collected in large data repositories become "data tombs" — data archives that are hardly visited. Important decisions are often made based not on the information–rich data stored in data repositories but rather on a decision maker's ⁱⁿᵗᵘⁱᵗⁱᵒⁿ(직관) _____, simply because the decision maker does not have the tools to ^{추출하다} _____ the valuable knowledge hidden in the vast amounts of data. (가) 전문가 시스템과 지식 기반 기술을 개발하려는 노력이 있어 왔는데, 이는 일반적으로 사용자나 분야 However, this procedure is likely to cause ^{편견} _____ and errors and is extremely costly and time consuming. The widening gap between data and information calls for the systematic development of tools that can turn data tombs into "golden nuggets" of knowledge.

42. 42)힌트를 참고하여 각 빈칸에 알맞은 단어를 쓰시오.

43. 43)위 글에 주어진 (가)의 한글과 같은 의미를 가지도록, 각각의 주어진 단어들을 알맞게 배열하시오.

(가) ^별 bases. / on / knowledge / made / have / or   domain / knowledge-based / knowledge / expert / rely / system / technologies, / develop / been / typically / to / experts / to / and / Efforts / which / manually / into / users / input

☑ 다음 글을 읽고 물음에 답하시오. (41 ~ 42)

ⓐ It's untrue that teens can focus on two things at once — that they're doing is shifting their attention from one task to another. In this digital age, teens wire their brains to make these shifts very slowly, but they are still, like everyone else, paying attention to one thing at a time, sequentially. Common sense tells us multitasking should decrease brain activity, but Carnegie Mellon University scientists using the latest brain imaging technology find it doesn't. As a matter of fact, they discovered that multitasking actually decreases brain activity. (가) 어느 작업도 각각 개별적으로 수행될 때만큼 잘 되지 못한다. Fractions of a second are lost every time we make a switch, and a person's interrupted task can take 50 percent longer to finish, with 50 percent more errors. Turns out the latest brain research supports the old advice "one thing at a time". It's not that kids can't do some tasks ^{동시에} _____. But if two tasks are performed at once, one of them has to be familiar. Our brains perform a familiar task on "automatic pilot" while really paying attention to the other one. (나) 그것이 보험 회사가 휴대전화로 통화하면서 운전하는 것을 술에 취한 상태에서 운전하는 것만큼 위험한 것으로 간주하는 이유이다 — it's the driving that goes on "automatic pilot" while the conversation really holds our attention. Our kids may be living in the Information Age but our brains have not been redesigned yet.

44. 44)힌트를 참고하여 각 빈칸에 알맞은 단어를 쓰시오.

45. 45)밑줄 친 ⓐ에서, 어법 혹은 문맥상 어색한 부분을 찾아 올바르게 고쳐 쓰시오.

ⓐ   잘못된 표현   바른 표현

(   ) ⇨ (   )

(   ) ⇨ (   )

(   ) ⇨ (   )

46. ⁴⁶⁾위 글에 주어진 (가) ~ (나)의 한글과 같은 의미를 가지도록, 각각의 주어진 단어들을 알맞게 배열하시오.

(가) each / is / as / performed / task / done / if / were / as / Neither / individually. / well

(나) talking / on / dangerous / phone / driving / be / driving / consider / and / cell / as / while / to / That's / why / as / insurance / a / companies / drunk

☑ 다음 글을 읽고 물음에 답하시오. ^(43 ~ 45)

Christine was a cat owner who loved her furry ^{반려동물} _____, Leo. One morning, she noticed that Leo was not feeling well. Concerned for her beloved cat, Christine decided to take him to the animal hospital. As she always brought Leo to this hospital, she was certain that the vet knew well about Leo. She ^{간절히} _____ hoped Leo got the necessary care as soon as possible. The waiting room was filled with other pet owners. Finally, it was Leo's turn to see the vet. Christine watched as the vet gently ^{검사하다} _____ him. The vet said, "I think Leo has a minor infection". "Infection? Will he be okay"? asked Christine. "We need to do some tests to see if he is infected. But for the tests, it's best for Leo to stay here", replied the vet. It was heartbreaking for Christine to leave Leo at the animal hospital, but she had to accept it was for the best. "I'll call you with updates as soon as we know anything", said the vet. Throughout the day, Christine anxiously awaited news about Leo. Later that day, the phone rang and it was the vet. "The tests revealed a minor ^{감염} _____. Leo needs some medication and rest, but he'll be back to his playful self soon". Relieved to hear the news, Christine rushed back to the animal hospital to pick up Leo. The vet provided detailed instructions on how to administer the medication and shared tips for a speedy recovery. Back at home, Christine created a comfortable space for Leo to rest and heal. She patted him with love and attention, ensuring that he would ^{회복하다} _____ in no time. As the days passed, Leo gradually regained his strength and ^{장난기 넘치는} _____ spirit.

47. ⁴⁷⁾힌트를 참고하여 각 <u>빈칸에 알맞은</u> 단어를 쓰시오.

보듬영어

정답

WORK BOOK

2024년 고2 3월 모의고사 내신대비용 WorkBook & 변형문제

Answer Keys

Answers

1) annual
2) previous
3) complete
4) goes
5) fully
6) left
7) entered
8) others
9) confidence
10) that
11) overcome
12) smiling
13) confirmed
14) expect
15) continuing
16) Because
17) has
18) convenience
19) successful
20) mere
21) to
22) had
23) ideal
24) pursuing
25) that
26) possess
27) autonomously
28) safely.
29) much
30) where
31) advance
32) monitor
33) which
34) overrate
35) because
36) invisible
37) that
38) fundamental
39) more
40) allows
41) overlooked
42) skills
43) specifying
44) emphasizing
45) making
46) Others
47) from
48) them
49) successful
50) translates
51) its
52) seeks
53) what
54) specific
55) different
56) that
57) Because
58) that
59) instantly
60) worse
61) texts
62) blowing
63) inducing
64) aggressive
65) easily
66) measured
67) supply
68) followed
69) respectively
70) which
71) least
72) ranked
73) minds

74) at
75) for
76) received
77) on
78) awarded
79) for
80) have
81) strongly
82) addressing
83) is
84) targeted
85) Mental
86) change
87) other
88) effective
89) reinforce
90) reinforces
91) strongly
92) other
93) gain
94) serve
95) increasing
96) comparable
97) impact
98) what
99) intrude
100) autonomy
101) unless
102) indirect
103) themselves
104) misguided
105) physically
106) vertical
107) while
108) lowering
109) how
110) Another
111) complete
112) tells
113) both
114) allows
115) minimizing
116) explore
117) supposedly
118) considerable
119) attracted
120) what
121) diverse
122) separate
123) is
124) contemporary
125) novel
126) something new
127) uncertain
128) reward
129) A
130) focused
131) revealed
132) decreased
133) while
134) less
135) exploration
136) quantifiable
137) are
138) identify
139) assessing
140) produces
141) easy
142) which
143) complicated
144) that
145) progress
146) in
147) what
148) seasons
149) highly
150) inhibit

151) come
152) bigger
153) spiced
154) those
155) uniquely
156) have
157) that
158) to
159) depends
160) satisfy
161) favors
162) further
163) selected
164) that
165) like
166) similar
167) needy
168) budget
169) on
170) distribution
171) visible
172) separate
173) efficiently
174) be provided
175) conversations
176) Restricted
177) make
178) in
179) becoming
180) that
181) relatively
182) most
183) inhospitable
184) alter
185) infrequent
186) viewed
187) relate
188) different
189) because
190) internalized
191) are
192) on
193) offering
194) it
195) are delivered
196) believing
197) find
198) exceeded
199) become
200) hardly
201) rather
202) extract
203) manually
204) widening
205) untrue
206) latest
207) Neither
208) individually
209) simultaneously
210) while
211) why
212) dangerous
213) been redesigned
214) that
215) other
216) replied
217) heartbreaking
218) revealed
219) medication
220) ensuring

Prac 1 **Answers**

1) annual
2) previous
3) complete
4) goes
5) fully
6) left
7) entered
8) others
9) confidence
10) that
11) overcome
12) smiling
13) confirmed
14) expect
15) continuing
16) Because
17) has
18) convenience
19) successful
20) mere
21) to
22) had
23) ideal
24) pursuing
25) that
26) possess
27) autonomously
28) safely.
29) much
30) where
31) advance
32) monitor
33) which
34) overrate
35) because
36) invisible
37) that
38) fundamental
39) more
40) allows
41) overlooked
42) skills
43) specifying
44) emphasizing
45) making
46) Others
47) from
48) them
49) successful
50) translates
51) its
52) seeks
53) what
54) specific
55) different
56) that
57) Because
58) that
59) instantly
60) worse
61) texts
62) blowing
63) inducing
64) aggressive
65) easily
66) measured
67) supply
68) followed
69) respectively
70) which
71) least
72) ranked
73) minds

74) at
75) for
76) received
77) on
78) awarded
79) for
80) have
81) strongly
82) addressing
83) is
84) targeted
85) Mental
86) change
87) other
88) effective
89) reinforce
90) reinforces
91) strongly
92) other
93) gain
94) serve
95) increasing
96) comparable
97) impact
98) what
99) intrude
100) autonomy
101) unless
102) indirect
103) themselves
104) misguided
105) physically
106) vertical
107) while
108) lowering
109) how
110) Another
111) complete
112) tells
113) both
114) allows
115) minimizing
116) explore
117) supposedly
118) considerable
119) attracted
120) what
121) diverse
122) separate
123) is
124) contemporary
125) novel
126) something new
127) uncertain
128) reward
129) A
130) focused
131) revealed
132) decreased
133) while
134) less
135) exploration
136) quantifiable
137) are
138) identify
139) assessing
140) produces
141) easy
142) which
143) complicated
144) that
145) progress
146) in
147) what
148) seasons
149) highly
150) inhibit

151) come
152) bigger
153) spiced
154) those
155) uniquely
156) have
157) that
158) to
159) depends
160) satisfy
161) favors
162) further
163) selected
164) that
165) like
166) similar
167) needy
168) budget
169) on
170) distribution
171) visible
172) separate
173) efficiently
174) be provided
175) conversations
176) Restricted
177) make
178) in
179) becoming
180) that
181) relatively
182) most
183) inhospitable
184) alter
185) infrequent
186) viewed
187) relate
188) different
189) because
190) internalized
191) are
192) on
193) offering
194) it
195) are delivered
196) believing
197) find
198) exceeded
199) become
200) hardly
201) rather
202) extract
203) manually
204) widening
205) untrue
206) latest
207) Neither
208) individually
209) simultaneously
210) while
211) why
212) dangerous
213) been redesigned
214) that
215) other
216) replied
217) heartbreaking
218) revealed
219) medication
220) ensuring

Answers

1) annual
2) providing
3) reserve
4) registration
5) fees
6) available
7) booked
8) left
9) fair
10) entered
11) confidence
12) quietly
13) award
14) judgment
15) announcing
16) that
17) uniqueness
18) overcome
19) meant
20) confirmed
21) identity
22) generation
23) false
24) discourage
25) continuing
26) parameters
27) comfort
28) convenience
29) tempted
30) requires
31) successful
32) desire
33) patience
34) prey
35) impatience
36) strap
37) brick
38) accelerator
39) vehicle
40) ideal
41) pursuing
42) possess
43) enable
44) autonomously
45) reach
46) taping
47) approaching
48) bear
49) advance
50) unique
51) **which**
52) overrate
53) absorbed
54) furniture
55) invisible
56) implement
57) transformed
58) time-shifting
59) exercise
60) control
61) function
62) save
63) substitute
64) implications
65) management
66) overlooked
67) Empathy
68) desired
69) specifying
70) cognitive
71) perspective
72) negotiating
73) affective
74) concern
75) compassion
76) foster
77) translates
78) company
79) fulfill
80) translates
81) account
82) prevalent
83) accessible
84) obligation
85) relate
86) pressure
87) instantly
88) interactions
89) blowing
90) aggressive
91) easily
92) minds
93) talent
94) doctoral
95) consultant
96) awarded
97) belief
98) addressing
99) habits
100) attitudes
101) personality
102) Ingestive
103) concerns
104) Process-addiction
105) premise
106) medicine
107) alongside
108) modification
109) tactics
110) coping
111) strategies
112) effective
113) does
114) reinforce
115) Repeated
116) reinforces
117) strongly
118) socialization
119) foundational
120) regulation
121) gain
122) primary
123) serve
124) likelihood
125) comparable
126) impact
127) soothing
128) guidance
129) beneficial
130) intrude
131) autonomy
132) striving
133) adjusted
134) suitable
135) indirect
136) nonjudgmental
137) acceptance
138) limits
139) misguided
140) accomplishing
141) vertical
142) lowering
143) connection
144) alignment
145) rotation
146) axis
147) successfully
148) constraints
149) imposed
150) minimizing

151) explore
152) consumption
153) ownership
154) consumed
155) considerable
156) composition
157) attracted
158) comprised
159) corresponds
160) broader
161) embrace
162) diverse
163) prejudice
164) realm
165) separate
166) legitimate
167) contemporary
168) drive
169) novel
170) reflection
171) curiosity
172) uncertain
173) curiosity
174) resulting
175) pleasure
176) modeled
177) composition
178) written
179) decreased
180) novel
181) predictable
182) exploration
183) creativity
184) quantifiable
185) Measurable
186) inputs
187) lifeblood
188) identify
189) concrete
190) measures
191) assessing
192) progress
193) quantifiable
194) bias
195) quantify
196) metrics
197) complicated
198) reduce
199) imperfect
200) illusion
201) genuine
202) results
203) substituting
204) counts
205) counted
206) counted
207) counts
208) seasons
209) deliberately
210) altering
211) flavored
212) evolutionary
213) antibacterial
214) properties
215) inhibit
216) bacterium
217) tested
218) bacterial
219) spoilage
220) cuisines
221) cooler
222) arisen
223) structural
224) richness
225) repeated
226) variation
227) selection

228) phases
229) embryo
230) exhibit
231) random
232) formation
233) generated
234) coupled
235) selection
236) satisfy
237) builtin
238) favors
239) eliminates
240) genetically
241) stimulated
242) don't
243) sculpting
244) variability
245) molecular
246) **similar**
247) elderly
248) needy
249) introduced
250) specify
251) perform
252) **reporting**
253) require
254) distribution
255) visible
256) perception
257) controllable
258) resolution
259) perceive
260) efficiently
261) provided
262) enquiring
263) Restricted
264) obstacles
265) rigid
266) overloaded
267) demotivated
268) vagrant
269) doomed
270) where
271) reorientate
272) vagrancy
273) unimportant
274) biological
275) vagrancy
276) inhospitable
277) perish
278) vagrancy
279) alter
280) unfold
281) vagrancy
282) establishment
283) migration
284) wintering
285) **mechanisms**
286) frequencies
287) importance
288) Intuition
289) hard-earned
290) feet
291) invested
292) they
293) able
294) accordance
295) internalized
296) expertise
297) are
298) interact
299) conviction
300) ensures
301) delusions
302) reinforced
303) sensible
304) repositories

305) exceeded
306) archives
307) hardly
308) instinct
309) extract
310) hidden
311) input
312) procedure
313) biases
314) costly
315) widening
316) knowledge
317) shifting
318) wire
319) sequentially
320) multitasking
321) latest
322) doesn't
323) decreases
324) Neither
325) were
326) lost
327) interrupted
328) latest
329) simultaneously
330) familiar
331) automatic
332) insurance
333) drunk
334) redesigned
335) well
336) Concerned
337) beloved
338) vet
339) desperately
340) filled
341) examined
342) infection
343) awaited
344) revealed
345) medication
346) Relieved
347) instructions
348) administer
349) patted
350) ensuring

Prac 2 **Answers**

1) annual
2) providing
3) reserve
4) registration
5) fees
6) available
7) booked
8) left
9) fair
10) entered
11) confidence
12) quietly
13) award
14) judgment
15) announcing
16) that
17) uniqueness
18) overcome
19) meant
20) confirmed
21) identity
22) generation
23) false
24) discourage
25) continuing
26) parameters
27) comfort
28) convenience
29) tempted
30) requires
31) successful
32) desire
33) patience
34) prey
35) impatience
36) strap
37) brick
38) accelerator
39) vehicle
40) ideal
41) pursuing
42) possess
43) enable
44) autonomously
45) reach
46) taping
47) approaching
48) bear
49) advance
50) unique
51) **which**
52) overrate
53) absorbed
54) furniture
55) invisible
56) implement
57) transformed
58) time-shifting
59) exercise
60) control
61) function
62) save
63) substitute
64) implications
65) management
66) overlooked
67) Empathy
68) desired
69) specifying
70) cognitive
71) perspective
72) negotiating
73) affective

74) concern
75) compassion
76) foster
77) translates
78) company
79) fulfill
80) translates
81) account
82) prevalent
83) accessible
84) obligation
85) relate
86) pressure
87) instantly
88) interactions
89) blowing
90) aggressive
91) easily
92) minds
93) talent
94) doctoral
95) consultant
96) awarded
97) belief
98) addressing
99) habits
100) attitudes
101) personality
102) Ingestive
103) concerns
104) Process-addiction
105) premise
106) medicine
107) alongside
108) modification
109) tactics
110) coping
111) strategies
112) effective
113) does
114) reinforce
115) Repeated
116) reinforces
117) strongly
118) socialization
119) foundational
120) regulation
121) gain
122) primary
123) serve
124) likelihood
125) comparable
126) impact
127) soothing
128) guidance
129) beneficial
130) intrude
131) autonomy
132) striving
133) adjusted
134) suitable
135) indirect
136) nonjudgmental
137) acceptance
138) limits
139) misguided
140) accomplishing
141) vertical
142) lowering
143) connection
144) alignment
145) rotation
146) axis
147) successfully
148) constraints
149) imposed
150) minimizing

151) explore
152) consumption
153) ownership
154) consumed
155) considerable
156) composition
157) attracted
158) comprised
159) corresponds
160) broader
161) embrace
162) diverse
163) prejudice
164) realm
165) separate
166) legitimate
167) contemporary
168) drive
169) novel
170) reflection
171) curiosity
172) uncertain
173) curiosity
174) resulting
175) pleasure
176) modeled
177) composition
178) written
179) decreased
180) novel
181) predictable
182) exploration
183) creativity
184) quantifiable
185) Measurable
186) inputs
187) lifeblood
188) identify
189) concrete
190) measures
191) assessing
192) progress
193) quantifiable
194) bias
195) quantify
196) metrics
197) complicated
198) reduce
199) imperfect
200) illusion
201) genuine
202) results
203) substituting
204) counts
205) counted
206) counted
207) counts
208) seasons
209) deliberately
210) altering
211) flavored
212) evolutionary
213) antibacterial
214) properties
215) inhibit
216) bacterium
217) tested
218) bacterial
219) spoilage
220) cuisines
221) cooler
222) arisen
223) structural
224) richness
225) repeated
226) variation
227) selection

228) phases
229) embryo
230) exhibit
231) random
232) formation
233) generated
234) coupled
235) selection
236) satisfy
237) builtin
238) favors
239) eliminates
240) genetically
241) stimulated
242) don't
243) sculpting
244) variability
245) molecular
246) **similar**
247) elderly
248) needy
249) introduced
250) specify
251) perform
252) **reporting**
253) require
254) distribution
255) visible
256) perception
257) controllable
258) resolution
259) perceive
260) efficiently
261) provided
262) enquiring
263) Restricted
264) obstacles
265) rigid
266) overloaded
267) demotivated
268) vagrant
269) doomed
270) where
271) reorientate
272) vagrancy
273) unimportant
274) biological
275) vagrancy
276) inhospitable
277) perish
278) vagrancy
279) alter
280) unfold
281) vagrancy
282) establishment
283) migration
284) wintering
285) **mechanisms**
286) frequencies
287) importance
288) Intuition
289) hard-earned
290) feet
291) invested
292) they
293) able
294) accordance
295) internalized
296) expertise
297) are
298) interact
299) conviction
300) ensures
301) delusions
302) reinforced
303) sensible
304) repositories

305) exceeded
306) archives
307) hardly
308) instinct
309) extract
310) hidden
311) input
312) procedure
313) biases
314) costly
315) widening
316) knowledge
317) shifting
318) wire
319) sequentially
320) multitasking
321) latest
322) doesn't
323) decreases
324) Neither
325) were
326) lost
327) interrupted
328) latest
329) simultaneously
330) familiar
331) automatic
332) insurance
333) drunk
334) redesigned
335) well
336) Concerned
337) beloved
338) vet
339) desperately
340) filled
341) examined
342) infection
343) awaited
344) revealed
345) medication
346) Relieved
347) instructions
348) administer
349) patted
350) ensuring

Answer Keys

Quiz 1 Answers

1) ③
2) ③
3) ②
4) ⑥
5) ④
6) ⑤
7) ⑤
8) ③
9) ④
10) ④
11) ④
12) ④
13) ④
14) ③
15) ⑤
16) ⑤
17) ③
18) ④
19) ③
20) ⑤
21) ⑤
22) ②
23) (A)-(D)-(B)-(C)
24) (C)-(B)-(A)
25) (B)-(D)-(C)-(E)-(A)
26) (B)-(C)-(A)
27) (B)-(A)-(C)
28) (B)-(C)-(D)-(A)
29) (A)-(C)-(D)-(B)
30) (D)-(C)-(B)-(A)
31) (A)-(D)-(C)-(E)-(B)
32) (C)-(D)-(A)-(B)-(E)
33) (C)-(A)-(B)
34) (C)-(A)-(B)
35) (B)-(A)-(C)-(D)
36) (A)-(C)-(B)
37) (A)-(C)-(B)-(D)-(E)
38) (A)-(C)-(B)
39) (A)-(B)-(C)
40) (A)-(B)-(C)
41) (D)-(C)-(A)-(B)
42) (B)-(C)-(A)
43) (A)-(E)-(C)-(D)-(B)
44) (B)-(C)-(A)-(D)
45) (C)-(A)-(D)-(B)-(E)

Quiz 2 Answers

1) [정답] ④
[해설] going ⇨ goes

2) [정답] ①
[해설] entered into ⇨ entered

3) [정답] ②
[해설] isn't ⇨ doesn't

4) [정답] ②
[해설] be ⇨ have been

5) [정답] ①
[해설] implementaion ⇨ implement

6) [정답] ⑤
[해설] designed ⇨ designing

7) [정답] ⑤
[해설] progressive ⇨ aggressive

8) [정답] ①
[해설] being ⇨ was

9) [정답] ③

[해설] imaginary ⇨ imagery

10) [정답] ④
[해설] turning ⇨ turn

11) [정답] ②
[해설] accomplish ⇨ accomplishing

12) [정답] ①
[해설] productivity ⇨ production

13) [정답] ⑤
[해설] more ⇨ less

14) [정답] ②
[해설] produce ⇨ produces

15) [정답] ⑤
[해설] turning ⇨ turns

16) [정답] ⑤
[해설] illuminated ⇨ eliminated

17) [정답] ⑤
[해설] them ⇨ it

18) [정답] ⑤
[해설] what ⇨ which

19) [정답] ④
[해설] illusions ⇨ delusions

20) [정답] ③
[해설] subtract ⇨ extract

21) [정답] ①
[해설] quick ⇨ quickly

22) [정답] ④
[해설] heartbroken ⇨ heartbreaking

Quiz 3 Answers

1) [정답] ② ⓑ, ⓒ
[해설]
ⓑ providing ⇨ is providing
ⓒ conserve ⇨ reserve

2) [정답] ⑤ ⓒ, ⓖ, ⓘ
[해설] ⓒ were made ⇨ made
ⓖ overcame ⇨ was overcome
ⓘ conformed ⇨ confirmed

3) [정답] ⑤ ⓑ, ⓒ, ⓕ, ⓖ
[해설] ⓑ encourage ⇨ discourage
ⓒ have ⇨ has
ⓕ being ⇨ to be
ⓖ pray ⇨ prey

4) [정답] ③ ⓑ, ⓖ, ⓘ
[해설] ⓑ be ⇨ have been
ⓖ approaching to ⇨ approaching
ⓘ that ⇨ which

5) [정답] ③ ⓐ, ⓔ, ⓕ
[해설] ⓐ absorbed ⇨ become absorbed
ⓔ think ⇨ be thought

ⓕ feeding on ⇨ feeding

6) [정답] ⑤ ⓒ, ⓔ, ⓙ, ⓚ
[해설] ⓒ emphasized ⇨ emphasizing
ⓔ make ⇨ making
ⓙ which ⇨ that
ⓚ designed ⇨ designing

7) [정답] ④ ⓖ, ⓗ
[해설] ⓖ progressive ⇨ aggressive
ⓗ be happened ⇨ happen

8) [정답] ③ ⓐ, ⓑ, ⓓ
[해설] ⓐ being ⇨ was
ⓑ On ⇨ In
ⓓ invited ⇨ was invited

9) [정답] ③ ⓐ, ⓔ, ⓛ, ⓝ
[해설] ⓐ address ⇨ addressing
ⓔ targeting ⇨ targeted
ⓛ reinforcing ⇨ reinforce
ⓝ reinforce ⇨ reinforces

10) [정답] ③ ⓑ, ⓓ, ⓕ, ⓗ
[해설] ⓑ starting ⇨ starts
ⓓ are remained ⇨ remain
ⓕ is ⇨ are
ⓗ direct ⇨ indirect

11) [정답] ③ ⓐ, ⓒ, ⓕ
[해설] ⓐ misguides ⇨ is misguided
ⓒ what ⇨ how
ⓕ composed ⇨ imposed

12) [정답] ③ ⓐ, ⓓ, ⓛ
[해설] ⓐ productivity ⇨ production
ⓓ consumed ⇨ been consumed
ⓛ substitute ⇨ subordinate

13) [정답] ⑤ ⓔ, ⓛ
[해설] ⓔ The ⇨ A
ⓛ noble ⇨ novel

14) [정답] ② ⓔ, ⓗ
[해설] ⓔ x ⇨ about
ⓗ result ⇨ results

15) [정답] ② ⓑ, ⓒ, ⓓ
[해설] ⓑ high ⇨ highly
ⓒ inhabit ⇨ inhibit
ⓓ coming ⇨ come

16) [정답] ② ⓐ, ⓒ, ⓔ
[해설] ⓐ repeating ⇨ repeated
ⓒ depending ⇨ depends
ⓔ while ⇨ during

17) [정답] ② ⓕ, ⓗ, ⓘ
[해설] ⓕ performing ⇨ be performed
ⓗ that ⇨ whom
ⓘ to have ⇨ having

18) [정답] ② ⓐ, ⓗ
[해설] ⓐ consumption ⇨ assumption
ⓗ what ⇨ which

19) [정답] ⑤ ⓖ, ⓗ

[해설] ⓖ illusions ⇨ delusions
ⓗ sensitive ⇨ sensible

20) [정답] ⑤ ⓒ, ⓓ, ⓔ
[해설] ⓒ hard ⇨ hardly
ⓓ subtract ⇨ extract
ⓔ that ⇨ which

21) [정답] ④ ⓓ, ⓗ, ⓟ
[해설] ⓓ decrease ⇨ increase
ⓗ Frictions ⇨ Fractions
ⓟ drinking ⇨ drunk

22) [정답] ④ ⓔ, ⓖ
[해설] ⓔ heartbroken ⇨ heartbreaking
ⓖ ensured ⇨ ensuring

Quiz 4 **Answers**

1) [정답]
① in ⇨ on
② providing ⇨ is providing
③ conserve ⇨ reserve
④ going ⇨ goes
⑤ booking ⇨ booked
⑥ to leave ⇨ left

2) [정답]
① entered into ⇨ entered
④ win at ⇨ win
⑤ was arrived ⇨ arrived
⑦ overcame ⇨ was overcome

3) [정답]
⑥ being ⇨ to be

4) [정답]
② be ⇨ have been
③ of pursuing ⇨ pursuing
④ what ⇨ that
⑤ operating ⇨ to operate
⑥ automatically ⇨ autonomously
⑦ approaching to ⇨ approaching
⑧ in which ⇨ that
⑨ that ⇨ which
⑩ talking ⇨ to talk

5) [정답]
③ implementaion ⇨ implement
④ been transformed ⇨ transformed
⑥ feeding on ⇨ feeding
⑦ subordinate ⇨ substitute

6) [정답]
② despite ⇨ although
③ emphasized ⇨ emphasizing
④ to negotiate ⇨ negotiating
⑥ effective ⇨ affective
⑦ themselves ⇨ them
⑧ x ⇨ to
⑪ designed ⇨ designing

7) [정답]
① previous ⇨ prevalent

③ challengeable ⇨ challenging
⑥ stress-induced ⇨ stress-inducing
⑦ progressive ⇨ aggressive
⑧ be happened ⇨ happen

8) [정답]
② On ⇨ In
④ invited ⇨ was invited

9) [정답]
⑤ targeting ⇨ targeted

10) [정답]
① it ⇨ them
④ are remained ⇨ remain
⑦ turning ⇨ turn
⑩ x ⇨ of

11) [정답]
① misguides ⇨ is misguided
② accomplish ⇨ accomplishing
③ what ⇨ how
④ allotment ⇨ alignment
⑤ telling ⇨ tells
⑥ composed ⇨ imposed
⑦ allow ⇨ allows

12) [정답]
① productivity ⇨ production
③ are made ⇨ made
④ consumed ⇨ been consumed
⑤ considerate ⇨ considerable
⑧ separately ⇨ separate
⑨ substitute ⇨ subordinate
⑩ are ⇨ is

13) [정답]
⑥ been modeled ⇨ modeled

14) [정답]
① qualifiable ⇨ quantifiable
② is ⇨ are
③ produce ⇨ produces
④ to measure ⇨ measuring
⑤ x ⇨ about
⑦ complicating ⇨ complicated
⑧ result ⇨ results
⑨ from ⇨ in
⑩ substituted ⇨ substituting

15) [정답]
① decorately ⇨ deliberately
② high ⇨ highly
③ inhabit ⇨ inhibit
④ coming ⇨ come
⑥ is ⇨ are
⑦ turning ⇨ turns

16) [정답]
① repeating ⇨ repeated
② inhibit ⇨ exhibit
③ depending ⇨ depends
④ are coupled ⇨ coupled
⑤ while ⇨ during
⑥ illuminated ⇨ eliminated

17) [정답]
① been introduced ⇨ introduced
④ have ⇨ has
⑥ performing ⇨ be performed
⑦ efficient ⇨ efficiently
⑧ that ⇨ whom
⑩ Restrict ⇨ Restricted
⑫ which ⇨ this
⑬ from ⇨ in

18) [정답]
⑨ be occurred ⇨ occur

19) [정답]
① earning ⇨ earned
② they are ⇨ are they
⑦ illusions ⇨ delusions

20) [정답]
③ hard ⇨ hardly
⑥ cost ⇨ costly

21) [정답]
① shifted ⇨ shifting
③ paid ⇨ paying
⑪ similar ⇨ familiar
⑬ pay ⇨ paying
⑮ to take ⇨ talking

22) [정답]
① Concerning ⇨ Concerned
③ that ⇨ if

Quiz 5 Answers

1) 이전의 - previous // 예약하다 - reserve
2) (가) We expect all available spaces to be fully booked soon, so don't get left out.
3) 자신감 - confidence // 독창성 - uniqueness // 확인하다 - confirmed // 정체성 - identity
4) 세대 - generation
5) ⓐencourage ⇨ discourage
   enough fast ⇨ fast enough
   want ⇨ don't want
   pray ⇨ prey
   patience ⇨ impatience
6) 장애물 - barriers // pursue의 바른 형태 - pursuing // 정제된 - refined
7) (가) it only means that at the time we did not yet have the tools we now possess to help enable vehicles to operate both autonomously and safely.
   (나) we are approaching the point where we can begin to bring some appropriate technology to bear in ways that advance our understanding of patients as unique individuals.
8) 과대평가하다 - overrate // 잠재적으로 - Potentially // 간과하다 - overlooked
9) ⓐ Taking ⇨ Take
   been transformed by ⇨ transformed
   thinking ⇨ thought
   less ⇨ more
10) 기르다 - foster
11) ⓐ desriing ⇨ desired
   with ⇨ without
   that ⇨ what
   emphasize ⇨ emphasizing
12) (가) what that translates to is that companies should take into account the specific needs of different populations

13) 들어갈 단어 - obligation // 즉각 - instantly

14)

ⓐ

better ⇨ worse

that ⇨ how

stress-reducing ⇨ stress-inducing

15) (가) The most prevalent problem kids report is that they feel like they need to be accessible at all times.

16) 공급 - supply // 각각 - respectively // ~와 다르게 - Unlike // 순위를 기록하다 - ranked

17)

ⓐ

invited ⇨ was invited

was awarded by ⇨ was awarded

18) 섭취 습관 - Ingestive habits // 전제 - premise

19) (가) many psychologists have held strongly to the belief that the key to addressing negative health habits is to change behavior.

(나) What mental imagery does is reinforce a new desired behavior.

20) 기초적인 - foundational // 주체 - agents // 자율적인 - autonomous // 무비판적인 - nonjudgmental

21)

ⓐ

increase ⇨ increasing

what ⇨ that

is ⇨ are

22) 반복적인 - repetitive // 정렬 - alignment // 제약 - constraints // 최소화하다 - minimizing

23) (가) that push is misguided if it is directed toward accomplishing something physically impossible.

24) 소유권 - ownership // 상당한 - considerable // 현상 - phenomenon // 편견 - prejudice // 현대의 - contemporary

25) 반영 - reflection // A - The // focused - focusing // decreased - increased // increased - decreased

26) (가) Beethoven's music became less predictable over time as his curiosity drove the exploration of new musical ideas.

27) 착각 - illusion

28)

ⓐ

qualify ⇨ quantify

what ⇨ which

29) (가) The problem of proxies results in technologists frequently substituting what is measurable for what is meaningful.

(나) Not everything that counts can be counted, and not everything that can be counted counts

30) 의도적으로 - deliberately // 진화적인 - evolutionary // 특성 - properties

31)

ⓐ

cooler ⇨ warmer

Similary ⇨ In contrast

warmer ⇨ cooler

32) 풍부함 - richness // -에 의존하다 - depends on // 결과 - consequence

33)

ⓐ

old ⇨ new

new ⇨ old

be produced by ⇨ produce

selecting ⇨ selected

stimulated ⇨ eliminated

34) 엄격한 - rigid // 의욕을 잃는 - demotivated

35)

ⓐ

unavailble ⇨ available

spending ⇨ spent

make ⇨ making

one ⇨ other

provide ⇨ be provided

36) (가) Restricted time and the requirement to report may be perceived as obstacles that make it impossible to deliver the service that is needed.

37) ~를 제외하고 - aside from // 들어갈 단어 - vagrancy // 현상 - phenomenon // 운명 - fate // 중대한 - profound

38) ⓐ

doubtly ⇨ undoubtedly

hospitbale ⇨ inhospitable

39) (가) these events can be extremely important when viewed at the timescales over which ecological and evolutionary processes unfold.

40) 투자하다 - invested // 확신 - conviction // ~덕분에 - thanks to // 착각 - delusions

41) (가) Only then are they able to act quickly in accordance with their internalized expertise and evidence-based experience.

42) 엄청난 - tremendous // 직관 - instinct // 추출하다 - extract // 편견 - biases

43) (가) Efforts have been made to develop expert system and knowledge-based technologies, which typically rely on users or domain experts to manually input knowledge into knowledge bases.

44) 동시에 - simultaneously

45)

ⓐ

that ⇨ what

slowly ⇨ quickly

decrease ⇨ increase

46) (가) Neither task is done as well as if each were performed individually.

(나) That's why insurance companies consider talking on a cell phone and driving to be as dangerous as driving while drunk

47) 반려동물 - companion // 간절히 - desperately // 검사하다 - examined // 감염 - infection // 회복하다 - recover // 장난기 넘치는 - playful